A COMPREHENSIVE SPANISH COURSE

for first examinations

BY

P. W. PACKER Ph.D.

HEAD OF THE MODERN LANGUAGES DEPARTMENT
MINCHENDEN SCHOOL

AND

E. L. DEAN B.A.

HEAD OF THE MODERN LANGUAGES DEPARTMENT
DOWNER GRAMMAR SCHOOL, MIDDLESEX

SECOND EDITION REVISED

D1146546

HARRAP LONDON

First published in Great Britain 1952
by GEORGE G. HARRAP & CO. LTD
182 High Holborn, London WC1V 7AX

Reprinted: 1954; 1957; 1959; 1960

Second edition, revised and reset, 1962

Reprinted: 1963; 1966; 1968; 1970; 1972; 1974;
1977; 1979

This edition © *P. W. Packer and E. L. Dean* 1962

ISBN 0 245 53129 7

REPRODUCED AND PRINTED BY PHOTOLITHOGRAPHY AND BOUND IN
GREAT BRITAIN AT THE PITMAN PRESS, BATH

NOTE TO THE NEW EDITION

In response to various suggestions and criticisms from users of the book, the present edition has undergone extensive revision. Four new modern Spanish passages have been substituted for two that had proved unsatisfactory in practice; the passages for translation into Spanish have been revised and additional notes provided; the grammar section has been brought into line with modern Spanish usage; and the grammar exercises have been substantially modified. The authors hope that in its new form the book will have gained considerably in usefulness both to teacher and student.

P. W. P.
E. L. D.

PREFACE

As practising teachers of Spanish we have long felt the need of a text-book which would provide suitable material for candidates preparing for the General Certificate of Education (Ordinary Level) and for all other examinations of this standard, such as the examination for Clerical Classes of the Civil Service, the Scottish Leaving Certificate, the Royal Society of Arts examinations, etc.

Our aim, quite straightforwardly, has been to compile the same type of comprehensive course for this stage as is available for French. We believe that it will be useful not only in grammar schools, but also in polytechnics, evening institutes, and to the private student.

The book consists of a series of passages for translation from Spanish, some original, but most of them adapted from modern Spanish authors, with questions on the subject-matter; care has been taken to cover a wide range of subjects and a variety of styles. Corresponding to each of these passages, there is one for translation into Spanish; these have been treated in various ways, some being a continuation of the story, others a rehandling of the subject-matter, others having only a general similarity in theme. The length of both Spanish and English passages has been carefully regulated to conform with the average length of equivalent questions set by the various examining bodies, so as to give experience in timing. Finally, three essay subjects are provided with each pair of translations to afford practice in using the vocabulary and constructions as they occur.

The grammar section adequately covers all the basic grammar required at this stage, and is accompanied by a series of exercises consisting of English sentences for translation into Spanish. The vocabulary of these sentences has been deliberately kept simple, so as not to detract from the main purpose.

Complete Spanish–English and English–Spanish vocabularies have been provided.

In an appendix we have given a selection of types of questions set by the various examining bodies at this level. As there is no vocabulary provided for these they can be used with advantage for testing purposes.

The authors make no apology for not including verse passages for translation into English. For one thing the proportion of candidates who attempt the verse question at this stage in public examinations is infinitesimal; for another, it is felt that the translation of poetry is beset with so many difficulties that it is much better left to the advanced student.

We should like to acknowledge our great debt of gratitude to Sr D. Manuel García Comas of Madrid for his great kindness in writing some of the passages and in revising others.

P. W. P.
E. L. D.

ACKNOWLEDGMENTS

Thanks for permission to reproduce copyright material are due to the following authors, publishers, and authors' representatives:

Don Ramón Pérez de Ayala (14, 23); Don Pío Baroja (7, 18); Doña Albina Cajigal (6, 21); Don W. Fernández Flórez and Librería General, Zaragoza (17); Don Enrique Larreta (2); Señorita Clemencia Miró (30); the family of J. M. de Pereda (3); Editorial Prometeo (15, 27); Don Luis Serrat (10, 22); Don Fernando Sirvent (5, 19, 26); Editorial Sopena Argentina (31, 33); Doña Josefina Blanco V. de Valle-Inclán (13, 20);

and to the following examining bodies: the Oxford and Cambridge Schools Examination Board; the Delegates of the Oxford Local Examinations Syndicate; the University of Cambridge Local Examinations Syndicate; the Senate of the University of London; the Welsh Joint Education Committee. the Northern Universities Joint Board.

CONTENTS

PART I

EACH SECTION CONTAINS:

A. A passage in Spanish, with questions in Spanish appended.

B. A passage in English for translation into Spanish.

C. Subjects for free composition.

The subject-matter and vocabulary of B and C are in each case closely allied to those of A.

CONTENTS

PART II

GRAMMAR SECTION (With Exercises)

PART III

VERB SECTION (With Exercises)

APPENDIX

Questions set in Spanish at the School Certificate Examinations (now the Ordinary Level of the General Certificate of Education).

PART I

1. AN ADVENTURE WITH A DONKEY

A. *Translation into English*

Cuando yo era niño, solía pasar mis vacaciones en el campo en casa de mis abuelos. Me gustaba siempre ir a aquella casa, porque quería mucho a mis abuelos, que me mimaban, por supuesto, pero lo que me deleitaba más era el burro, viejo y manso, que se pasaba la vida comiendo la hierba del prado. Este burro era mi amigo, mi compañero de todos los días; nos paseábamos juntos por todas partes.

Pero un día, al cumplir los cinco años, se me ocurrió montarme en el asno. Dicho y hecho. ¡Ay de mí! El condenado animal echó a correr a toda prisa camino del río. Me agarré desesperadamente a su cuello, dando gritos como un loco. Acudieron mis abuelos, mis padres, los criados, los perros, hasta los gansos del corral, a ver quién me estaba matando. Pero en balde. Al llegar a la ribera, el burro se detuvo de repente. Yo, por mi parte, seguí mi camino por el aire hasta que caí al agua, de donde me pescaron los criados, mojado ~soaked, hasta los huesos. Desde entonces, ya no me gustan los burros. Prefiero la bicicleta.

Questions

1. Explíquese lo que son los abuelos.
2. ¿Por qué mimaban los abuelos al niño?
3. ¿Dónde estaba el burro?
4. ¿Cuándo le acompañaba el niño?
5. ¿Por qué no montó en el burro antes de cumplir los cinco años?
6. ¿Por qué gritó el niño?
7. ¿Quiénes le oyeron?
8. ¿Cuándo cayó al agua?
9. ¿Cómo no se ahogó? to drown
10. ¿Por qué prefiere la bicicleta?

B. *Translation into Spanish*

Tony was walking along the road with his donkey and cart.
The quiet old donkey was his friend and companion, and they
went everywhere together. To-day Tony was smiling; yesterday it had rained cats and dogs[1] and he had been soaked to the
skin, but now the sun was shining, and besides, to-day was his
tenth birthday.[2] Suddenly the cart fell into a pot-hole full of
mud, and the wheels stuck fast.[3] Tony's smile disappeared,
and he began to cry, clinging to the donkey's neck. Just then
the parish priest came up, riding on his donkey, which was big
and strong. On hearing Tony, he stopped to see why the boy
was crying. "Come on,[4] my boy," he said. "Give me that piece
of rope and I'll tie my donkey in front of yours." No sooner
said than done. Both donkeys together gave a great heave
and the cart came out of the mud. Tony's tears disappeared as
if by magic; he smiled at the priest and thanked him, and the
priest, for his part, smiled too, and went on his way.

C. *Composition*

1. The autobiography of a donkey.
2. An incident with a donkey at the seaside.
3. A bicycle accident.

(hermano de leche)

2. A FOSTER-BROTHER ASKS FOR HELP

A. *Translation into English*

De pronto un golpecito seco hizo resonar uno de los vidrios
de la ventana. ¿Qué sería? ¿Un pájaro? ¿Un insecto?
Lucía escuchó. El golpe se repitió; pero esta vez más fuerte,
más enérgico. Levantóse, abrió despacio la ventana y miró
hacia afuera. De pronto, ¡tric! Abajo, al pie de la ventana,
acababa de encenderse un fósforo y, al resplandor de su lumbre
rojiza, apareció en la tiniebla la faz iluminada de Jesús
Benavídez, mirando hacia arriba, con sus grandes ojos salvajes

---

[1] *llover a cántaros.*   Use the verb *cumplir.*   [3] *quedar atascado.*
[4] *¡Anda!*

y dulces. Oyóse el gruñido de un perro. La luz se apagó. ¡Qué temeridad! Se había escapado, seguramente, de la cárcel.

Al rayar el día, Lucía se arrojó de su lecho. Comprendió que Jesús Benavídez deseaba hablar con ella para pedirle consejo y amparo. Cuando terminó de vestirse, tomó de su cómoda todo el dinero que allí tenía y bajó.

Dirigióse primero al corral de las vacas. El aire traía un olor de leche y de tierra labrada. Jesús no andaba por allí. Estaría, tal vez, en el monte. Caminó hacia el sitio en que ellos dos construyeron, siendo muy niños, un ranchito de barro.

ENRIQUE LARRETA, *Zogoibi*

Questions

1. ¿Qué despertó a Lucía?
2. ¿Por qué abrió la ventana?
3. ¿Cómo pudo ver a Jesús Benavídez?
4. ¿Cuándo apagó Benavídez su fósforo?
5. ¿Por qué quería amparo?
6. ¿Con qué motivo tomó Lucía dinero?
7. ¿Dónde vivía Lucía?
8. ¿Dónde pensó encontrar a Jesús?

B. *Translation into Spanish*

She was not mistaken. When she reached the place Jesús was waiting for her, leaning against the trunk of a tree, bare-headed, with his hat in his hands. He was dirty, and he looked tired.

"What has happened, Jesús?"

"I ran away. I couldn't stand it. Just[1] imagine, a fortnight in jail, like a criminal. I'm no thief. And the rogue who tried to ruin me is going to pay for it. I know who he is. I thought at first it was Maldonado. But I was wrong—he came to see me and even brought me cigarettes."

"But who was it, then?"

Omit.

"Don't ask me. You would be sorry if I told[1] you."

"You don't mean it was Federico?"

Jesús hesitated a moment, then shrugged his shoulders. "That's right,"[2] he said. "You don't know him. Good-bye, Lucía." He turned on his heel,[3] and running towards the thickest part[4] of the wood, he disappeared among the trees.

C. *Composition*

1. Finish the story.

2. You are awakened by strange noises at night and get up to investigate.

3. Reconstruct the incident that led up to the imprisonment of Jesús.

3. THE RETURNED EMIGRANT

A. *Translation into English*

Un día fueron Nardo y su mujer a consultarlo con don Damián, indiano[5] muy rico de aquellas inmediaciones. Don Damián había hecho un gran caudal: esto es lo que veía toda la población de la comarca y lo que excitaba más y más en los jóvenes el deseo de emigrar; pero en lo que se fijaban muy pocos era en que don Damián se hizo rico a costa de veinte años de un trabajo constante: que en todo ese tiempo no dejó un solo día de ser hombre de bien,[6] ni de cumplir, por consiguiente, con todos los deberes que se le imponían en las dificilísimas circunstancias por que atravesó. Además, don Damián había ido a América muy bien recomendado y con una educación bastante más esmerada que la que llevan ordinariamente a aquellas regiones los pobres montañeses.[7] Todas estas circunstancias le obligaban a exponérselas a cuantos iban a pedirle cartas de recomendación para La

---

[1] Subjunctive. [2] *el mismo.* [3] *giró sobre sus talones.* [4] Use *lo* + adjective, omitting 'part.' [5] *indiano.* Not 'Indian.' Owing to over-population and poor economic conditions in the north-west of Spain, a large proportion of the inhabitants were driven to emigrate to America, where by dint of many years of hard work they often earned enough money to enable them to retire and return to Spain. These returned emigrants are known as *Indianos.* [6] *hombre de bien,* honest, hard-working man. [7] *montañeses,* inhabitants of the Montaña, the province of Santander.

Habana, y a consultarle sobre la conveniencia[1] de salir a probar fortuna. Cuando semejantes consideraciones no bastaban a desencantar a los ilusos, daba la carta que se le pedía, garantizando el pago del pasaje desde Santander a La Habana.

J. M. DE PEREDA, *Escenas Montañesas*

Questions

1. ¿Quién era don Damián?
2. ¿Por qué tenían los jóvenes deseos de emigrar?
3. ¿Cómo se hizo rico don Damián?
4. ¿Qué ventajas tenía sobre los demás emigrantes?
5. ¿Dónde había adquirido su fortuna?
6. ¿Qué le pedían los montañeses que deseaban emigrar?
7. ¿Por qué era preciso garantizar el pasaje?

B. *Translation into Spanish*

Don Damián was an old man who, when he was young, had set out from Spain for Havana, in order to try his fortune. He had been carefully educated, and in consequence he was able to obtain a good post. Nevertheless, he was obliged to work for many years in order to save enough money to go back to Spain. His capital was not great, but it was enough[2] to buy a large house and an estate. What troubled him most was the tendency of his neighbours to imagine that in order to become rich they also had only to go to America—they did not realize that he had succeeded only at the cost of devoting himself entirely to his work. They often came to him to ask for letters of recommendation, and he always did his duty, as[3] he thought, and explained to them all the difficulties. But they never believed him, so he gave them the letters, and sighed to think how ignorant those people were.[4]

C. *Composition*

1. Imagine the adventures of a young man who goes to America to seek his fortune.

---

[1] N.B. NOT 'convenience.' [2] Use the verb *bastar*. *según.* [4] *lo necia que era aquella gente.*

2. Relate an imaginary interview between don Damián and the parents of a would-be emigrant.

3. An emigrant writes to don Damián to thank him for his help.

4. AN UNTIMELY VISIT

A. *Translation into English*

Serían las nueve de aquella misma noche, cuando el tío[1] Lucas y la señora Frasquita, terminadas todas las haciendas del molino y de la casa, se cenaron una fuente de ensalada, carne guisada con tomates, y algunas uvas, todo ello rociado con un poco de vino; después de lo cual miráronse afablemente los dos esposos, como muy contentos de Dios y de sí mismos, y se dijeron, entre un par de bostezos que revelaban toda la paz y tranquilidad de sus corazones:

— Pues, vamos a acostarnos, y mañana será otro día.

En aquel momento sonaron dos golpes a la puerta del molino. El marido y la mujer se miraron sobresaltados. Era la primera vez que oían llamar a su puerta a semejante hora.

— Voy a ver — dijo la intrépida navarra,[2] encaminándose hacia la plazoleta.

— ¡ Quita ![3] ¡ Eso me toca a mí ![4] — exclamó el tío Lucas con tal dignidad que la señora Frasquita le cedió el paso.

— ¡ Te he dicho que no salgas ! — añadió luego con dureza, viendo que la obstinada molinera[5] quería seguirle. Ésta obedeció.

— ¿ Quién es ? — preguntó el tío Lucas desde la plazoleta.

— ¡ La Justicia ! — contestó una voz al otro lado del portón. — ¡ Abra Vd. al señor alcalde !

P. A. DE ALARCÓN, El Sombrero de Tres Picos

Questions

1. ¿ Qué oficio tenía Lucas ?

---

[1] *tío*, familiar title, best omitted in translation, as with *señora* in the same sentence. [2] *navarra*, native of the province of Navarre. [3] 'Keep out of this.' [4] 'That's my job.' [5] *i.e.*, the miller's wife.

Donkeys are quite a common sight in Spain. Here a patient one waits outside a pottery shop in Toledo. See page 13.

Photo N. S. Peppard

Alcalá de Guadaira, Sevilla. The bright sunshine, low whitewashed houses, and the olive-trees form a typical Southern scene. See page 21.

By kind permission of the Spanish Tourist Office

*A village in the Basque country, scene of Pío Baroja's famous
novel "Zalacaín el Aventurero." See pages 23 and 42.*

Photo R. P. L. Ledésert

A quiet sunny "patio" in Ecija, Sevilla
By kind permission of the Spanish Tourist Office

2. ¿Qué hora era?
3. ¿Cómo se sabe que eran felices los esposos?
4. ¿Qué interrumpió la cena?
5. ¿Por qué se asombraron Lucas y Frasquita?
6. ¿Qué mandó Lucas a su mujer?
7. ¿Por qué le habló con dureza?
8. ¿Qué es un alcalde?

B. *Translation into Spanish*

The miller and his wife were sitting at the table. They had worked hard that day and were very tired. When all the jobs were done, they had for supper meat and salad and some grapes, with a little red wine, and now they were laughing and talking for a while before going to bed. Finally, Lucas yawned, stretched himself, and said to his wife, "Come, Frasquita, I'm sleepy." "Yes, you're right," she answered. "I've a lot to[1] do to-morrow, and I'm going to get up early." They stood up and Lucas was on the point of putting out the lamp when a knocking was heard at the door of the mill. Lucas, startled, remained motionless, staring at his wife. "What can[2] that be?" he asked. "I don't know," said Frasquita, "but I'm going to see." The fearless woman made for the courtyard, but Lucas seized her arm. "Stay here," he said. "*I* will go to the door; remember I have told you not to go out after dark[3]—there is too much danger '

C. *Composition*

1. Continue the story.
2. An adventure in a windmill.
3. Imagine a story related to you by a beggar who knocks at your door asking for money.

5. A MISCHIEVOUS PUPIL

A. *Translation into English*

(The speaker is the Mother Superior of a convent school.)
— Ha sido siempre una criatura traviesa y rebelde. ¡No

---

[1] *que.* [2] Use future of probability. [3] *anochecer.*

puede Vd. figurarse lo que me ha dado que hacer mientras fue educanda![1] ¡Jesús, qué chica! Parecía hecha de rabos de lagartijas. Bastaba ella sola para revolver, no una clase, sino todo el colegio. Los castigos y penitencias nada servían con ella. Al contrario, yo creo que era peor castigarla. Muchas veces estaba de rodillas pidiendo perdón a la comunidad, y se reía a carcajadas, o entraba en las clases a besar el suelo y con sus muecas armaba un belén[2] en todas ellas. ¡Las veces que habrá adelantado el reloj para que llegase primero[3] el momento del recreo! No se podía estar tranquila teniéndola a ella en la clase. Cuando no pellizcaba a las compañeras, les escribía cartitas amorosas poniendo la firma de un hombre, o les mandaba retratos de la hermana que les daba lección, hechos con lápiz. Cuando la dejaba cerrada en la buhardilla, hacía señas y muecas a las oficialas de un taller de modistas que había enfrente. Una vez encendió todos los cirios que teníamos allí en depósito, se prendió fuego a una estera y por poco no ardemos todas.

A. PALACIO VALDÉS, *La Hermana San Sulpicio*

Questions

1. ¿Está todavía la muchacha en la escuela?
2. ¿Por qué se dice que parecía hecha de rabos de lagartijas?
3. ¿Por qué nada servía castigarla?
4. ¿Qué castigos se usan en este colegio? Y ¿en el de Vd.?
5. ¿Cómo alborotaba las otras clases?
6. ¿Cuándo se la encerraba en la buhardilla?
7. ¿Por qué hacía muecas?
8. ¿Dónde estaban los cirios?

B. *Translation into Spanish*

Emily was very fond of boasting about how[4] mischievous she was at school. She had a friend named Jane to whom she used to relate all that she had done during the day, and how her teacher was afraid of her, and dared not punish her for

[1] Pupil in convent school. [2] 'Caused a riot.' [3] Here 'earlier.' [4] *lo.*

fear of what she might do[1] afterwards. One day Emily and Jane caught the bus at half-past four, climbed to the top-deck, found the front seat vacant, and sat down in it for a nice, long chat.[2] At once Emily, in a very loud voice, began her tale of what she had said and done to Miss Brown. After a few minutes she felt[3] someone touch her on the shoulder She turned round, and there was Miss Brown! "I think that's quite enough lies for to-day, Emily," she said. Emily blushed, and said, "Yes, Miss Brown," in a very meek voice. At the next stop she got off in a hurry, and all the other passengers laughed at her.

C. *Composition*

1. A naughty child gets into trouble.
2. Write a letter to your uncle describing your school.
3. The awkward results of a loud conversation on top of a bus. *Or:* say what you think of people who talk loudly in buses and trains.

6. AN ANDALUSIAN FARM

A. *Translation into English*

No hizo caso y salió. Anduvo poco. No le llevaban las piernas lejos de su casa. Cansado, tuvo que sentarse en un altozano, allí cerca. Desde él se dominaba el cortijo, blanco y alegre, con sus ventanas y puertas verdes, con sus azulejos en la fachada y su farolillo. Oía Carmona el rumor de su gente y sus ganados, veía las casitas blancas de los criados. Separó de allí la vista y la tendió por las fértiles tierras que rodeaban el cortijo. Suyo todo aquello, casi hasta el límite del horizonte: los trigales prometedores, verdes y lozanos; los olivos, obscuros; los naranjales, de hojas brillantes, repletos de dorados frutos. Las vacas lecheras, que hacían sonar las campanillas de sus collarones, también suyas; suyas las yuntas con lánguido cuello, la nevada de los perezosos rebaños, el averío que se extendía tragón e insaciable por los corrales y alrededor

---

[1] Subjunctive. [2] *un buen rato de palique.* [3] Insert *que.*

de la casa, vigilado por los gallos, orondos y cantantes; suyo el humo que se elevaba al cielo desde el hogar triste que él soñó tan alegre.

A. PÉREZ LUGÍN, *Currito de la Cruz*

Questions

1. ¿ Por qué tuvo que sentarse Carmona?
2. ¿ Era grande o pequeño el cortijo?
3. ¿ Qué frutas había?
4. ¿ Cómo se distinguían las vacas lecheras?
5. ¿ Qué animales llevan campanillas en Inglaterra?
6. ¿ Qué es una yunta?
7. ¿ Por qué dice "la nevada de los rebaños"?
8. ¿ De qué se compone el averío?
9. Explíquese la palabra "tragón." *greedy*
10. ¿ Qué contraste hay entre el alma de Carmona y el paisaje?

B. *Translation into Spanish*

When I was young I used to spend my holidays on my uncle's farm. Although I have not been there for many years, I can remember it all as if I had seen it yesterday. Everybody got up early, of course—you have to take advantage of every hour of daylight. The first task was to milk the cows. After that, we fed the fowls and the pigs. Meanwhile the farm-servants had gone out to the fields. In summer the hay had to be cut; then it was the turn of the wheat-fields, and later, after the harvest, the yokes of oxen were taken out to the bare fields and the ground was ploughed for the next year's wheat. What I liked best was watching the animals, the mares with their foals, the cows with their calves, and best of all the sheep with their white lambs. I should dearly like to go back there one of these days. *me cansina*

C. *Composition*

1. A holiday on a farm.
2. Hay-making.
3. A boy is caught robbing an orchard.

lo mejor de todo
Best of all

7. A CLEVER TROUT

A. *Translation into English*

Un día, Fernando fue a casa del señor cura de A —. Al entrar en la casa husmeó en la cocina y vio que el ama estaba limpiando dos truchas: una, hermosa, y la otra, pequeñita. Pasó Fernando a ver al señor cura, y éste, según su costumbre, le convidó a comer. Se sentaron a la mesa. Sacaron dos sopas, luego el cocido: después una fuente de berzas con morcilla. Vino el pescado, pero Fernando notó que en vez de poner la trucha grande, la condenada del ama[1] sólo había puesto la pequeña.

— ¡Hombre! — exclamó Fernando. — Le voy a hacer una pregunta a esta trucha.

— ¿Qué le vas a preguntar? — dijo el cura riendo.

— Le voy a preguntar si por los demás peces que ha conocido se ha enterado de cómo están mis parientes allí en América.

— Hombre, sí, pregúntale.

Cogió Fernando la fuente; luego acercó el oído muy serio y escuchó.

— ¿Contesta algo? — dijo burlonamente el ama del cura.

— Sí, ya va contestando.

— ¿Y qué dice? — preguntó el cura.

— Pues dice — contestó Fernando — que es muy pequeña; pero que ahí, en esa despensa, hay una trucha muy grande y que ella debe saber mejores noticias de mis parientes.

PÍO BAROJA, *Zalacaín el Aventurero*

Questions

1. ¿Para qué husmeó Fernando en la cocina?
2. ¿Qué costumbre tenía el cura?
3. ¿Cuántos platos comieron?
4. ¿Qué es una fuente? ¿Conoce Vd. otro sentido?
5. ¿Por qué rio el cura?
6. ¿Qué quería hacer Fernando con la trucha?

[1] *la condenada del ama,* 'the confounded housekeeper.' Note construction carefully.

7. ¿ Por qué no estaba contento Fernando?
8. ¿ Quién sabía noticias de los parientes de Fernando?
9. ¿ Cómo sabe Vd. que este cuento no es verdadero?
10. ¿ Qué es un ama?

B. *Translation into Spanish*   *Siempre que podía*

Pedro was very fond of fishing. Whenever he could he spent the whole afternoon with his friend Miguel trying to catch trout. On returning to the village they would visit the tavern and spend the rest of the evening talking of their exploits. The other customers[1] found them somewhat tiresome. They asked the village carpenter to make[2] them a wooden trout a yard long, and they painted it with great care, so that it should resemble[2] a real one. Then they hung it on the wall of the tavern.

When Pedro and Miguel came in they began to boast as usual of the trout they had caught, and Pedro told them about[3] a big one[4] which had escaped. The inn-keeper pointed to the fish hanging on the wall. "Is that it?" he asked. Pedro stared at the enormous fish. Then Miguel and he looked at each other, looked suspiciously at their glasses, and went out.

C. *Composition*

1. Autobiography of a fish.
2. A fishing story.
3. Imagine another of Fernando's tricks.

8. AN ENCOUNTER WITH A WOLF

A. *Translation into English*

Ávila es tierra de lobos. En el paisaje de Ávila — en cualquier de los cuatro paisajes de Ávila: el del cereal, el del castaño y la pradera, el de los riscos nevados, el del olivo y la vid — el desolado y hondo aullido del lobo sirve de contrapunto al viento. . . .

El caminante ni ve ni escucha al lobo. Va silbando, tan

---

[1] *parroquianos.*   [2] Subjunctive.   [3] Use *hablar de.*   [4] Omit 'one'.

tranquilo, por el sendero. A lo mejor, piensa en el fuego de su cocina, que arde entre dos piedras y no se apaga en toda la noche. Se está a gusto[1] sentado al lado del fuego de la cocina, ya mortecino, pero aún calentador, con el gato al lado y un cuenco de leche tibia esperando. La noche está algo dura, pero el caminante, la boina calada, las manos en los bolsillos, la bufanda de tres vueltas guardándole el aliento,[2] se defiende pisando el suelo.

¿Qué le ha sucedido? De repente tiene miedo. Nota que un tiritón le corre por la espalda. Alerta la vista y aguza el oído. No, el caminante ni ve ni escucha al lobo; pero al caminante la frente le suda frío, las carnes le tiemblan, el cabello se eriza, el corazón parece como desbocársele,[3] le golpea la sangre en las sienes. Se vuelve — y allí está el lobo, con los ojos como carbúnclos, la boca abierta enseñando el colmillo poderoso, la lengua fuera, el pecho fuerte, el espinazo hirsuto. . . .

After: CAMILO JOSÉ CELA, *Judíos, Moros y Cristianos*

Questions

1. ¿Dónde está Ávila?
2. ¿Qué se hace con la vid?
3. ¿Por qué piensa el caminante en su cocina?
4. ¿Para quién será la leche tibia?
5. ¿Qué hace el caminante para resistir al frío?
6. ¿Cómo sabemos que el caminante tiene miedo?
7. ¿Con qué armas ataca el lobo?
8. ¿Por qué tiene miedo la gente de los lobos?
9. ¿En qué otros países de Europa hay lobos todavía?
10. ¿Cuándo son más peligrosos los lobos?

B. *Translation into Spanish*

The wayfarer left the town in the afternoon, and went on his way whistling, thinking of the kitchen fire to which he was returning. The path led him through a desolate landscape

---

[1] 'comfortable.'   [2] *i.e.*, the muffler is wrapped round his neck and face three times.   [3] 'come into his mouth.'

with huge snow-covered crags on each side. Evening was falling; he was very cold, in spite of his muffler and his gloves, and he stamped on the ground to warm his feet. He had been walking[1] since three o'clock, and he still had[2] five kilometres to go. Yes, he would be very comfortable sitting in front of that fire. . . .

Suddenly, behind him, he heard a long, deep howling. His hair stood on end, and he felt a cold sweat on his forehead. He knew only too well[3] what it was. Last week, not very far from this very spot, a soldier returning to his village had been killed by wolves. Perhaps it was his turn[4] now.

C. *Composition*

1. Finish the story.

2. You are a visitor in a house whose owner has a fine wolf-skin on the floor. He tells you how he acquired it. (Skin = *la piel*)

3. Give an account of a story you have read or heard about wolves, or other fierce animals.

9. WAR IN SOUTH AMERICA

A. *Translation into English*

Aquello era un infierno de fuego. El que no caía muerto, caía herido y el que sobrevivía a sus compañeros contaba por minutos la vida. De todas partes llovían balas. A los cinco minutos de estar el batallón en el fuego, sus pérdidas eran ya serias; muchos muertos y heridos yacían envueltos en su sangre. Recorriendo de un extremo a otro halló el comandante al cabo Gómez, herido en una rodilla; pero haciendo fuego hincado.

— Retírese, cabo — le dijo.

— No, mi comandante — le contestó. — Todavía estoy bueno — y siguió cargando su fusil y el comandante su camino.

Al regresar de la extrema derecha del batallón a la izquierda,

[1] —and was still walking. Tense ? [2] Use *quedar.* [3] *demasiado* is sufficient for 'only too well.' [4] Use *tocar.*

volvió a pasar por donde estaba Gómez. Ya no hacía fuego hincado, sino echado de barriga,[1] porque acababa de recibir otro balazo en la otra pierna.

— Pero, cabo, retírese, hombre, se lo ordeno — le dijo el jefe.

— Cuando Vd. se retire, mi comandante, me retiraré — repuso, y agregó — ¡ Paraguayos, ahora verán! — Y ebrio con el olor de la pólvora y de la sangre, hacía fuego y cargaba su fusil con la rapidez del rayo, como si estuviese ileso.

L. V. MANSILLA, *Excursión a los Indios Ranqueles*

Questions

1. ¿ Cómo era la batalla ?
2. ¿ Cómo halló el comandante al cabo Gómez ?
3. ¿ Por qué estaba hincado ?
4. ¿ Por qué no quiso retirarse ?
5. ¿ Cómo estaba Gómez la segunda vez que pasó el comandante ?
6. ¿ Cuántas heridas tenía ?
7. ¿ Cuándo se retiraría ?
8. ¿ Quiénes eran los enemigos ?
9. ¿ Qué excitaba a Gómez ?
10. ¿ Qué quiere decir "ileso" ?

B. *Translation into Spanish*

After the battle the first thing to[2] be done was to find out who had been killed or wounded. A review was held,[3] and it soon turned out that Gómez was not there. The hospitals had no news of him, and some of the soldiers said they had seen him lying on his face[4] when they left the trench. So he was given up for dead.[5] The army reoccupied its previous[6] position, and new battles and new perils began to efface the memory of the others. But one day an extraordinary thing happened. Certain men who had come out of the hospitals came back to the army and among them the major was astounded to see a familiar face. It was Corporal Gómez.

[1] 'lying face downward.'   [2] *que.*   [3] *se pasó.*   [4] *boca abajo.*
[5] *se le dio por muerto.*   [6] *primera.*

"But you can't be here," stammered the major. "You're dead!"

"Yes, sir," said Gómez, "so I am told. The fact is that I was captured by the enemy, and I was taken to one of their hospitals. When I recovered, I escaped, and here I am."

C. *Composition*

1. An incident in war-time.

2. Describe how Corporal Gómez was captured, and how he escaped.

3. A soldier is left lying on the battlefield, supposedly dead. He recovers consciousness. Describe his plight and how he eventually gets back to his regiment.

10. THE WELL

A. *Translation into English*

Todavía esta fuente tenía otro mérito y prestaba otro notable servicio, porque además de un gran pilar en que iban a beber todas las bestias de carga y de labor y los toros, vacas y bueyes, y además de otro pilar bajo, que solía ser abrevadero del ganado lanar y de cerda, llenaba con sus cristalinas ondas un espacioso albercón cercado de muros que lo ocultaban a la vista de los transeúntes, donde iban las mujeres a lavar la ropa, metidas en el agua hasta la rodilla, como por allí es uso, aun en el rigor del invierno. Frondosos y gigantescos álamos negros y pinos y mimbreras circundan la fuente, y hacen aquel sitio umbrío y deleitoso. Al pie de los mejores árboles hay poyos hechos de piedra y de barro y cubiertos de losas, en los cuales suelen sentarse los caballeros y las señoras que salen de paseo. Casi todas las tardes se arma allí tertulia y grata conversación, siendo los más constantes el escribano, el boticario, don Paco y el señor cura, quien, al toque de oraciones,[1] recita el Angelus Domini, al que responden todos, quitándose el sombrero y santiguándose.

JUAN VALERA, *Juanita la Larga*

[1] The church-bell ringing for the Angelus.

Questions

1. ¿Qué es una bestia de carga? ¿Cuáles son las más usuales?

2. ¿Para qué sirven los toros en España?

3. ¿Qué es un abrevadero?

4. ¿De qué animales se compone el ganado lanar? ¿Y el de cerda?

5. ¿Dónde se lava la ropa en Inglaterra?

6. ¿Por qué era el sitio tan deleitoso?

7. ¿Dónde estaban los poyos?

8. ¿Qué es una tertulia?

9. ¿De dónde salía el toque de oraciones?

10. ¿Por qué se quitaban el sombrero las personas de la tertulia?

B. *Translation into Spanish*

In this remote village the well played an important part in everyday life. Every evening, as twilight approached, the girls of the village would walk slowly down to the well, chattering gaily, each with a jar on her head. When they reached the ring of poplars which surrounded the well they went down the stone steps one after another and filled their jars. They stayed awhile, still talking and joking, saying good evening[1] to the old people for whom the well was a club where they met every day to sit on the benches at the foot of the trees, to smoke and talk and gaze at the landscape. It must be admitted that this last was their main occupation, and why not, after all? They had worked hard, and now it was their turn[2] to rest. As soon as darkness fell, all of them, old and young, would return slowly to the village, and the well would remain deserted until the next day.

C. *Composition*

1. Describe an English village square.

2. Describe an interesting place near your home.

3. You spend a fortnight's holiday in a remote country village. Say how you spend the time.

---

[1] *dar las buenas tardes.*   [2] *les tocaba.*

11. A SPANISH GARDEN

A. *Translation into English*

Apoyada en los barrotes de la reja,[1] Hortensia estaba al aire libre, suspendida entre cielos y tierra, como pájaro en jaula. Por un instante experimentó esa sensación, hasta el punto de creer que la reja se balanceaba. Había en el jardín orgía de luz. Apenas pasaba del mediodía; bajo los árboles se pintaban círculos intensísimos, y las matas bordaban sobre la arena imperceptibles festones. Ramas y hojas caían desmayadas y polvorientas; algunas rosas se esforzaban en vano por levantar sus corolas muertas de sed. Únicamente las malvas reales erguían sus pomposos y floridos tallos, desafiando al calor.

No hay pájaros; ocultos entre el ramaje o en los aleros del tejado esperan el fresco de la tarde para cantar; pero hay abejas, que van del romero a la adelfa, runruneando como amas de casa hacendosas y gruñonas, y hay mariposas que atraviesan el aire con vuelo incierto, tropezando en todas las flores. Y en lo alto, colgada en su reja, está también Hortensia, perdida, en la orgía de luz, convertida en un átomo más de todos aquellos infinitos átomos hipnotizados y adormecidos bajo el poder del sol.

G. MARTÍNEZ SIERRA, *Sol de la Tarde*

Questions

1. ¿Dónde estaba Hortensia?
2. ¿Para qué sirve una reja?
3. ¿Qué ilusión se hacía Hortensia?
4. ¿Cómo se sabe que es cerca de mediodía?
5. ¿Por qué caían las ramas?
6. ¿Qué flores había en el jardín?
7. ¿Por qué no cantaban los pájaros?
8. ¿Qué insectos se veían?
9. ¿Que árboles se encuentran?

[1] Projecting iron grille fixed over a window as a protection against intruders.

B. *Translation into Spanish*

The old couple had lived in the cottage for many years. Its whitewashed walls and tall chimney could be glimpsed through the great hedge that separated the garden from the road. There were really two gardens. The one[1] in front of the house was full of flowers. In the middle was a lawn with flower-beds round it, in which there were roses and hollyhocks, and stone pots full of carnations. This garden was always full of butterflies in the summer.

Behind the house was the vegetable-garden, where the old people grew nearly everything they needed. You could see carrots, potatoes, broad beans and haricots, melons, turnips, onions, and lettuce. There were also a few fruit-trees, which threw a welcome shade in the hot weather[2]: a pear-tree, an apple, a plum, two cherry-trees, a peach, an apricot, and even two or three orange-trees, which gave[3] the garden a certain distinction. The perfume of the orange-blossom[4] in spring filled the air, and while the fruit-trees were in bloom you[5] could always hear the murmuring of bees.

C. *Composition*

1. Describe an English garden.
2. Your mother sends you to do the shopping. Describe your visits to the greengrocer's and the florist's where you are buying flowers for your mother's birthday.
3. Describe the house in which you live.

12. A CHRISTMAS LETTER

A. *Translation into English*

Valencia, a 7 de enero de 1961

Muy apreciado amigo:

No puede figurarse la alegría con que recibí sus noticias después de tan largo silencio. Me apresuro a agradecerle su atento obsequio, ya que, créame, nada hubiese podido serme más grato que un libro.

---

[1] See Grammar p. 106 (*d*).   [2] Say 'when it was hot.'   [3] Use *prestar*.   [4] *el azahar*.   [5] Use impersonal reflexive.

Durante las pasadas fiestas conseguí un corto permiso de cinco días para estar en mi casa, junto a mi familia. En España, las fiestas de Navidad son, al igual que en Inglaterra, de tipo hogareño. Así, el día 24 de diciembre y el 25, los miembros de la familia procuran, aunque estén en el fin del mundo, congregarse para hacer juntos los honores a deliciosos ágapes. La Nochebuena marca el comienzo de la fiesta. Después de la cena hay muy amena sobremesa que se desarrolla entre los alegres comensales unidos por el parentesco. Si hay niños, se cantan villancicos ante el "Belén."[1] A medianoche la gente se va a la calle para asistir a la solemne misa del gallo,[2] que es la única que se celebra a las 12 de la noche. Después de la cual no queda sino meterse en la cama. Y esto voy a hacerlo yo en seguida, pues estoy muy cansado después de tan largo viaje.

Su servidor y amigo,

Manuel

Questions

1. ¿ Qué obsequios ha recibido Vd. por Navidad ?
2. ¿ Cuántos días de fiesta hay en Inglaterra ?
3. ¿ Qué fecha es (a) la Nochebuena ? (b) Navidad ? (c) el día de los Reyes ?
4. ¿ Quiénes son los comensales por Navidad ?
5. ¿ En qué consiste la comida de Navidad en su casa de Vd. ?
6. ¿ Qué quiere decir "sobremesa" ?
7. ¿ Qué personajes hay en el Belén ?
8. ¿ A qué hora se verifica la misa del gallo ?
9. ¿ Puede Vd. adivinar por qué tiene ese nombre ?
10. ¿ Qué se hace después de la misa ?

B. *Translation into Spanish*

Spanish children have never heard of[3] Santa Claus,[4] but they manage to enjoy themselves as much as English children do at Christmas. On Christmas Eve, instead of a Christmas tree,

[1] The crib, with figures representing the Holy Family, the Three Kings, the ox and the ass, etc.   [2] Midnight mass on Christmas Eve.   [3] *oir hablar de.*   [4] Use *el padre Noel.*

they have a crib, which is a miniature reproduction of the scene of Christ's birth. Some of these are very beautiful, others are clumsy, and may even be made of cardboard, according to the means of the family. There are little figures of shepherds, rivers made of silver paper, hens and ducks and sheep, and finally the doorway of the stable, with Joseph, Mary, the Child, and of course the traditional ox and ass. The children sing carols in front of the crib until they are[1] hoarse or until they fall asleep.

They get their presents on Twelfth Night, the 6th of January. On that night the children leave their shoes beneath an open window, and, while they are asleep, the Three Kings bring them gifts, as they did to that other Child, many centuries ago.

C. *Composition*

1. Write a letter to a friend, telling him how you usually spend Christmas.

2. Describe a Christmas tree in detail.

3. An adventure when out carol-singing.

13. CIVIL WAR[2]

A. *Translation into English*

Bajamos con los caballos a que bebiesen en el río, y al mirar tan cerca la otra orilla, sentí la tentación de arriesgarme. Consulté con mis hombres, y como unos se mostraban resueltos mientras otros dudaban, puse fin a tales pláticas, metiéndome río adentro con mi caballo. El animal ya nadaba con el agua a la cincha, cuando en la otra ribera asomó una vieja y comenzó a gritarnos. Al pronto supuse que nos advertía lo peligroso del paso. A mitad de la corriente, entendí mejor sus voces:

— ¡Teneos mis hijos! No paséis por el amor de Dios. Todo el camino está cubierto de negros alfonsistas.

En el mismo instante sonaron tiros, y pude ver en el agua el círculo de las balas que caían cerca de mí. Apresuréme para

---

[1] Use *ponerse*. [2] The two parties in the civil wars of the late nineteenth century were the *Carlistas* and the *Alfonsistas*.

ganar la otra orilla, y cuando ya mi caballo se erguía asentando los cascos en la arena, sentí en el brazo izquierdo el golpe de una bala. Mis jinetes ya trepaban al galope por una cuesta. Con los caballos cubiertos de sudor entramos en la aldea. Hice llamar a un médico que me puso el brazo entre cuatro cañas, y sin más descanso tomamos el camino de los montes.

R. DEL VALLE-INCLÁN, *Sonata de Invierno*

Questions

1. ¿ Por qué estaban cerca del río ?
2. ¿ Con qué motivo entró el jefe en el río ?
3. ¿ Por qué gritó la vieja ?
4. ¿ Cómo supieron que la vieja decía la verdad ?
5. ¿ Cómo fue herido el jefe ?
6. ¿ Qué es un jinete ?
7. ¿ Cómo se sabe que anduvieron rápidamente ?
8. ¿ Para qué puso las cañas el médico ?
9. ¿ Por qué no descansaron ?
10. ¿ Cuándo ocurrió la última guerra civil en España ?

B. *Translation into Spanish*

The pain from my wounded arm was so great that the soldiers of the escort, seeing my eyes bright with fever, maintained a respectful silence. When at last we came to a village my horse, who was running without my directing him, almost ran down[1] two women who were walking along together. As they moved quickly to one side of the road,[2] they stared at me, terror-stricken. One of them recognized me, and shouted my name. I turned towards her, almost blind with pain.

"What do you want, madam?"

"Don't you remember me?"

She came up to me, partly[3] uncovering her face, which was hidden by a mantilla. I saw a wrinkled face, and dark eyes. I tried to remember, and she came to my assistance: "Sor Simona! It seems impossible that you should forget me— you have seen me a hundred times when we were at the frontier with the King. But what ails you? Are you hurt?"

[1] *atropellar.* [2] to move to one side, *apartarse.* [3] *un poco.*

The Albufera lake, near Valencia. See page 58.

By kind permission of the Spanish Tourist Office

Peñíscola, on the Mediterranean coast
By kind permission of the Spanish Tourist Office

C. *Composition*

1. Continue the story.
2. A ride on horseback.
3. A headlong flight.

14. THE STAGE-COACH IS HELD UP

A. *Translation into English*

Ya están en la diligencia. Restalla el látigo del mayoral. El carruaje sube fatigoso una pendiente llena de revueltas entre altas rocas y monte de roble espeso.

— ¡ Alto !

La diligencia ha parado. Un hombre, con un pañuelo rojo atado por debajo de los ojos, asómase a la portezuela, y apuntando con un trabuco suplica cortés:

— Dígnense vuestras mercedes bajar.

Los viajeros descienden. Dos bandidos les ordenan que se coloquen en fila. Un tercer bandido apunta con el trabuco al mayoral. Uno de los bandidos salta al pescante y ata al mayoral y al zagal con cuerdas. Luego, en tanto este bandido permanece con el trabuco apuntado, los otros dos van registrando a los viajeros. El último de la fila es Urbano; el penúltimo, Simona. Ya se aproximan los bandidos a registrar a Simona. La sangre se agolpa en el cerebro de Urbano. Ahora los tres bandidos están casi juntos. Fuera de sí, arrójase Urbano sobre los dos bandidos más próximos, no sin antes derribar con un manotazo el trabuco que el otro tenía. Ya tiene a dos derrocados a sus pies. El otro se inclina a recoger el trabuco.

R. P. DE AYALA, *Los Trabajos de Urbano y Simona*

Questions

1. ¿ Qué es una diligencia?
2. ¿ Qué hace parar la diligencia?
3. ¿ Para qué servía el pañuelo rojo?
4. ¿ Qué diferencia hay entre una escopeta y un trabuco?
5. ¿ Cuántos bandidos había?

6. ¿ Por qué atan al mayoral y al zagal?

7. ¿ Por qué registran a los viajeros?

8. ¿ En qué momento ataca Urbano a los bandidos?

9. ¿ Qué hace con los bandidos?

10. ¿ Qué quiere decir "manotazo"? ¿ Conoce Vd. otras palabras semejantes?

B. *Translation into Spanish*

Suddenly Urbano remembered that he had with him two pistols, a present from his friend Pablo. One of these was not loaded, but of course the highwaymen didn't know that. "Halt!" cried Urbano, brandishing his pistols. "Don't touch that blunderbuss! If you move you will get a bullet through the heart. Now stand up. I want some of the passengers to untie the driver, and his assistant, and then to tie up these rogues with the same ropes. Tie them to that big oak-tree." No sooner said than done. Two of the passengers climbed on the box, and untied the driver, and within five minutes the three highwaymen were tightly bound to the tree. All that had been stolen[1] was returned to the passengers, who once more got into the stage-coach. Once again the driver cracked his whip, and the mules started off up the hill. Naturally all the travellers were very grateful to Urbano!

C. *Composition*

1. Tell this story in the first person, as if Urbano were telling it to his friend Pablo.

2. An adventure with a highwayman.

3. Contrast the transport of to-day with that of a hundred years ago.

15. TWO CHILDREN LOST IN THE FOREST

A. *Translation into English*

Ahora sí que anochecía de veras. Ya no sonaban a lo lejos los esquilones del ganado. Había que salir pronto de la selva, pero después de recoger la leña, para evitarse una riña al

---

[1] Use *lo* + past participle.

volver a casa. Buscaron al pie de los pinos, entre los matorrales, las ramas secas. Formaron apresuradamente dos
pequeños haces, y casi a tientas comenzaron la marcha. A los
pocos pasos la obscuridad era completa; apenas si los troncos
y los matorrales se destacaban como sombras más fuertes
sobre el lóbrego fondo.

Perdían la serenidad, no sabiendo ciertamente por dónde
marchaban. Estaban fuera del sendero; se hundían en
espinosos matorrales que les arañaban las piernas. Neleta
suspiraba de miedo, y de pronto dio un grito y cayó. Había
tropezado con las raíces de un pino cortado a flor de[1] tierra,
lastimándose un pie. La muchacha lloraba sordamente, como
si temiera alterar el silencio del bosque, atrayendo las horribles
bestias que poblaban la obscuridad.

El miedo de su compañera resucitó la energía de Tonet.
Había pasado un brazo por la espalda de la muchacha, la
sostenía, la animaba, preguntándole si podía andar, si quería
seguirle, marchando siempre adelante, sin que el pobre
muchacho supiera adónde.

V. BLASCO IBÁÑEZ, Cañas y Barro

Questions

1. ¿Por qué lleva esquilones el ganado?
2. ¿Dónde buscaron los niños? ¿Qué buscaban?
3. ¿Cuándo quisieron salir de la selva?
4. ¿Por qué no hallaron el camino?
5. ¿De qué tenía miedo Neleta?
6. ¿Cómo se lastimó ésta?
7. ¿Por qué temía hacer ruido?
8. ¿Qué bestias hay en una selva?
9. ¿Cómo pudieron seguir adelante?

B. *Translation into Spanish*

One autumn afternoon Tonet's mother said that instead of
worrying her, playing inside the house, the two children could
be useful to her for once, and she sent them to the forest to
gather firewood. They set off together, and soon reached the

'level with.'

first pine-trees on the edge of the forest. The thickets were
covered with flowers, and above them butterflies and dragon-
flies shone in the rays of sunlight. On the paths they found
fat caterpillars which they followed on all fours[1] until they
disappeared in the thickets. They had forgotten the firewood,
and thought only of going on. Suddenly Tonet noticed that
the shadows were growing darker and longer, and that he
was beginning to feel cold. The poor children had forgotten
the time as well as[2] the firewood. It was nightfall, and they
were very far from home. They started back[3] at once, but in
the twilight they could not find[4] the path. Tonet soon realized
that they had lost their way.[5]

C. *Composition*

1. Tell how the children find their way home.
2. Describe a wood in autumn, naming as many trees as
you can.
3. You are lost in a fog on a dark night. Relate your
experiences.

16. A YOUTHFUL SMUGGLER

A. *Translation into English*

A medida que el tren se aproximaba a la frontera, Nemesio
se azoraba. Al pensar en lo que contenía aquella maleta, se
puso cada vez más pálido, a tal punto que lo notó el viajero
de enfrente.

— ¡ Hombre ! — dijo éste — ¿ Está malo ?

— No — contestó Nemesio, avergonzado. — No es que esté
malo; pero le confieso que me hallo un poco acobardado
pensando en la aduana. Esta maleta . . . — No tuvo fuerzas
para terminar. Se sentía en la frente un sudor frío. El otro
sonrió.

— Pues   ¡ vaya !, pobrecito, — dijo.   — ¿ Quiere que me
encargue de su maleta ? Vd. toma la mía y todo queda
arreglado, ¿ verdad ?

---

[1] *a gatas.*   [2] *así como.*   [3] *emprender el camino de regreso.*   [4] *dar
con.*   [5] *extraviarse.*

— No puedo decirle cuanto le agradezco — balbuceó Nemesio. — Si verdaderamente no le molesta a Vd. . . . con muchísimo gusto.

Paró el tren y los viajeros fueron a la aduana.

— ¿ Nada que declarar? — preguntó el carabinero a Nemesio, que se había cargado con la maleta de su compañero. — Nada — respondió, tranquilo. Reparó en que tampoco habían reconocido la suya, ya en manos del otro viajero.

De vuelta ambos en el coche, el viajero devolvió la maleta. — Muchísimas gracias — dijo Nemesio. — En ésta tengo dos cajitas de puros para mi padre.

— ¿ De veras? — dijo el otro, socarrón. — ¡ Pues en la mía van doce!

Questions

1. ¿ Cuándo se perturbaba Nemesio?
2. ¿ Por qué pensaba el otro viajero que Nemesio estaba enfermo?
3. ¿ Por qué temía Nemesio a la aduana?
4. ¿ Cómo se sabe que su miedo era muy grande?
5. ¿ Qué le ofreció el viajero?
6. ¿ Dónde paró el tren?
7. ¿ Por qué ya no tuvo miedo Nemesio?
8. ¿ Cuándo se le devolvió su maleta a Nemesio?
9. ¿ Qué confesó Nemesio?
10. ¿ Qué contenía la maleta de su compañero?

B. *Translation into Spanish*

At this point the frontier passed through a region of high mountains; the road led to the customs-house, and, of course, the smugglers had no intention of going that way. They turned[1] left and took[2] a steep path which climbed towards the peaks. As they approached the frontier, Peter grew more and more frightened, thinking of all the tobacco in his sack. He grew so pale that one of his companions noticed it. "What's the matter?" asked the Basque. "Aren't you well? Or are you frightened?"

torcer a.   [2] *emprender.*

"I can't help thinking of the customs-men and their rifles," Pedro confessed. The other two laughed at him. "You won't see even one," they told him. "The way[1] we go, you won't see anything but mules and sheep. Perhaps a bear or a wolf, but they will be as frightened as you." Ashamed of himself, Pedro once more picked up his sack of cigars and cigarettes and followed the two men. They were right; he was too young for this. If only[2] he were at home in bed! This would be the last time!

C. *Composition*

1. Continue the story.
2. An amusing incident at the customs.
3. An adventure in a train at the frontier.

17. A BELATED GUEST

A. *Translation into English*

(The speaker has arrived very late for a party.)

Batí palmas, acudió el sereno,[3] le di unas monedas, entré y se cerró la puerta tras de mí. . . . Hasta que estuve dentro del ascensor no descubrí que me había olvidado de preguntar al sereno cuál era el cuarto en que vivía mi amigo. . . . Salí de la caja de hierro y cristal y comencé a subir la escalera. — El conflicto — iba cavilando — no es demasiado serio. Esta gente estará divirtiéndose; se cantará, se bailará. Acercaré el oído a las puertas, y donde haya bullicio, allí vivirá García.

La labor, pese a mis optimismos, no resultó fácil. En cada rellano había cuatro puertas que correspondían a otras tantas viviendas, y en las del primer piso ni siquiera escuché, porque placas metálicas fijas en las puertas cerradas anunciaban oficinas destinadas a diversos trabajos. Fue en el segundo donde comencé a encorvarme y a juntar la oreja con el ojo de las cerraduras.

---

[1] *por donde.*   [2] *ojalá* + subjunctive.   [3] The street-watchman, who has duplicate keys to all the houses in his area.

Silencio y quietud.

Estaba así, con el cuerpo doblado, las manos apoyadas en los muslos y la atención tensa, cuando se apagó la luz.[1] Subí a obscuras al otro piso y continué mis indagaciones. Pero resultaba difícil atinar con las cerraduras. . . . Entonces resolví encender la luz de la escalera.

W. FERNÁNDEZ FLÓREZ, *La Nube Enjaulada*

Questions

1. ¿ Por qué llamó al sereno?
2. ¿ En dónde entró primero?
3. ¿ Qué cosa importante ignoraba?
4. ¿ Cómo se propuso encontrar el piso de su amigo?
5. ¿ Qué había en el primer piso?
6. ¿ En qué piso comenzaban las viviendas?
7. ¿ Cómo buscó a su amigo?
8. ¿ Por qué no era fácil encontrarle?
9. ¿ Cuándo se apagó la luz?
10. ¿ Qué hizo después?

B. *Translation into Spanish*

I knew that the switch must be on the wall somewhere, and I stroked the walls for a long time, but I did not succeed in finding it. At last I felt a button under my fingers and pressed it. Nothing happened. I pressed it again, and suddenly I realized that a bell was ringing. I must be at some one's door! As quickly as I could in the darkness I ran up the stairs and waited. I heard the door open, and a voice called, "Who is there?"[2] A moment later, the light came on. "There's nobody here," the voice said, and the door closed. Too late, I realized that I should have asked where my friend lived. At any rate,[3] I could now see, and I went up to the nearest door and rang the bell.[4] After a time I heard footsteps, and

---

[1] The staircase-lights in blocks of flats are operated by a press-button on each landing which automatically switches off the lights after a few minutes. [2] — ¿ *Quién?* — [3] *de todas formas.* [4] *llamar* is sufficient.

a voice said, "Who is ringing at this time of night?"[1] And at that moment the light went out again.

C. *Composition*

1. Continue the story.
2. You arrive home late at night and discover that you have forgotten your key. Relate what follows.
3. A night in a haunted house (*una casa encantada*).

[Ghost = *el fantasma*, *el espectro*.]

18. IN JAIL

A. *Translation into English*

Entregaron los serenos a Martín en manos del alcaide, y éste le llevó hasta un cuarto oscuro con un banco y una cantarilla para el agua.

— ¡ Demonio ! — exclamó Martín —, aquí hace mucho frío. ¿ No hay sitio donde dormir ?

— Ahí tiene Vd. el banco.

— ¿ No me podrían traer un jergón y una manta para tenderme ?

— Si paga Vd.

— Pagaré lo que sea.[2] Que me traigan un jergón y dos mantas.

El alcaide se fue, dejando a oscuras a Martín, y vino poco después con un jergón y las mantas pedidas. Le dio Martín un duro, y el carcelero, amansado, le preguntó:

— ¿ Qué ha hecho Vd. para que le traigan aquí ?

— Nada. Venía, distraído, silbando por la calle. Y me ha dicho el sereno: "No se silba." Me he callado, y sin más ni más[3] me han traído a la cárcel.

— ¿ Vd. no se ha resistido ?

— No.

— Entonces será por otra cosa por lo que le han encerrado. Martín dijo que así se lo figuraba también él. Le dio las

---

[1] *a estas horas.*   [2] *lo que sea,* 'whatever it costs.'   [3] *sin más ni más,* 'without more ado.'

buenas noches el carcelero; contestó Martín amablemente, y se tendió en el suelo.

PÍO BAROJA, Zalacaín el Aventurero

Questions

1. ¿ Qué es un sereno?
2. ¿ Dónde estaba el cuarto oscuro?
3. ¿ Qué pedía Martín al alcaide? ¿ Por qué los quería?
4. ¿ Por qué habían traído a Martín a la cárcel?
5. ¿ Dónde se acostó Martín?
6. ¿ Cuántos muebles había en el cuarto? ¿ Qué faltaba?
7. ¿ Cuáles son los muebles de un comedor?
8. ¿ Y los de un dormitorio?

B. *Translation into Spanish*

When Martin awoke he saw a ray of sunlight entering by a high window. Soon the jailer arrived and asked him if he wanted breakfast, and Martin said he did.[1] When the jailer had gone Martin began to wonder how he could escape. The door was strong, and then there were the corridor and the stairs, and the risk of running into someone. The window was the only way.[2]

He pushed[3] the bench against the wall, climbed on it, and looked through the grating. He found[4] that it looked out on a square. If only[5] he had a rope! The bars were held in position[6] by a wooden frame, which was[7] worm-eaten at one end. Then he had an idea—the blankets. He still had his penknife in his pocket, and with this he would be able to cut the blankets into strips which he could tie to one another, and he would have the rope he needed. Without more ado he attacked the wood with his penknife.

C. *Composition*

1. Tell the story of Martin's escape.
2. Explain why Martin had really been put in jail.
3. An awkward conversation with a policeman.

---

[1] *dijo que sí.* [2] *recurso.* [3] Use *arrimar.* [4] Use *comprobar.*
[5] *ojalá* + subjunctive. [6] held in position, *sujeto.* [7] Omit.

19. A NIGHT IN THE TRAIN

A. *Translation into English*

Después de comer precipitadamente, tomé el tren correo[1] de Sevilla el día 4 de abril de 188–. Cuando hubieron cesado las despedidas, y el pito del jefe dio la señal de marcha y el prolongado tren salió de la estación, dirigí una mirada de examen a los que me acompañaban. El viajero que tenía enfrente era un hombre pálido, de cuarenta a cincuenta años, bigote negro; el que se sentaba más allá era un caballero gordo de ojos grandes y saltones, fisonomía abierta y risueña, mientras el otro parecía, por la expresión recelosa y sombría de sus ojos, hombre de carácter oscuro y malhumorado. Éste, cuando lo juzgó conveniente, hizo de la capa almohada y se tendió a lo largo, y no tardó en roncar. El tren corría ya por los campos de la Mancha cuando el segundo comenzó a dar cabezadas, pero sin decidirse a tumbarse.

Paró el tren. — Argamasilla, cinco minutos de parada — gritó una voz. Di un salto en el asiento y me apresuré a abrir la ventanilla.

— ¿Sabe Vd. que entra un fresquecito regular? — dijo el viajero malhumorado, despertándose.

— ¿Quiere Vd. que levante el cristal?

— Si Vd. no tiene inconveniente.

A. PALACIO VALDÉS, *La Hermana San Sulpicio*

Questions

1. ¿Qué es un tren correo?
2. ¿Quién dio la señal de marcha, y cómo?
3. ¿Cuántos viajeros estaban en el departamento?
4. ¿Cuáles durmieron?
5. ¿Cómo se veía que el segundo viajero dormitaba?
6. ¿En dónde paró el tren?
7. ¿Qué hizo el escritor?
8. ¿Por qué protestó el viajero malhumorado?

[1] Not a fast mail-train, as in England, but a slow, stopping train.

9. ¿ Qué rogó al escritor ?
10. ¿ Qué personaje célebre nació en la Mancha ?

B. *Translation into Spanish*

Soon after daybreak the train stopped at Baeza, and the fat man woke up and began to talk. He talked so much that I began to envy the bad-tempered man, who was fast[1] asleep, covered by his overcoat. But, just as[2] I was thinking this, the ticket-collector arrived at the door of the compartment, and woke him up and asked for his ticket. He was furious, but, as he was awake now, he got out of the carriage and walked away[3] along the platform. Five minutes later a bell rang, the porter shouted something, the guard's whistle sounded, and the engine replied. The fat man leaned out of[4] the window. "Good Heavens," he said, "the man's going to miss the train, and there are his coat and hat on the rack !" The porter shrugged his shoulders, and the train started.[5] "And there are his shoes," said the fat man. "He's only got his slippers on !"

C. *Composition*

1. Finish the story begun in A and B.
2. You are going on holiday by train. Describe the journey, starting at the house.
3. Describe the scene at a busy railway-station.

20. A JOURNEY IN THE RAIN

A. *Translation into English*

— ¿ Ocurre algo, Brión ?
— Que empieza a rayar el día, señor Marqués.
Bajé presuroso, sin cerrar la ventana que una ráfaga batió. Nos pusimos en camino con toda prisa.
Cuando partimos oí cantar los gallos de la aldea. De todas suertes no llegaríamos hasta cerca del anochecer. Hay nueve

---

[1] *profundamente.* [2] *en el momento que.* [3] *se alejó.* [4] *se asomó por.*
[5] *arrancar.*

leguas de jornada y malos caminos de herradura, trasponiendo
monte. Cuando salimos al campo empezaba la claridad del
alba. Vi en lontananza unas lomas yermas y tristes, y después,
otras. Traspuestas aquéllas, vi otras, y después otras. El
sudario ceniciento de la llovizna las envolvía: no acababan
nunca. Todo el camino era así. A lo lejos desfilaba una recua
madrugadora, y el arriero, sentado a mujeriegas en el rocín
que iba postrero, cantaba a usanza de Castilla. El sol empezaba a dorar las cumbres de los montes: rebaños de ovejas
blancas y negras subían por la falda, y sobre verde fondo de
pradera, larga bandada de palomas volaba sobre la torre
señorial. Acosados por la lluvia, hicimos alto en los viejos
molinos de Gundar, y como si aquello fuese nuestro feudo,
llamamos autoritarios a la puerta. Salieron dos perros flacos,
que ahuyentó el mayordomo, y después una mujer hilando.

R. DEL VALLE-INCLÁN, *Sonata de Otoño*

Questions

1. ¿ Por qué no cerró la ventana el Marqués ?
2. ¿ Cómo sabemos que salieron muy temprano ?
3. ¿ Cuánto tiempo duraría el viaje ?
4. ¿ Cuántos kilómetros hay en nueve leguas ?
5. ¿ Por qué era monótono el paisaje ?
6. ¿ Qué tiempo hacía ?
7. ¿ Qué quiere decir "a mujeriegas" ?
8. ¿ Qué animales vieron ?
9. ¿ Por qué hicieron alto ?
10. ¿ A quiénes vieron en el molino ?

B. *Translation into Spanish*

The bailiff greeted the woman, who replied politely enough.
Seeing us perished with cold, she told us to tie the mules
under the shed, and stood aside for us to enter the house.

"Come in and sit down by the fire," she said. "It's bad
weather for travellers."[1]

I went up to the hearth while the bailiff opened the saddlebags. The old woman put wood on the fire, which began to

[1] Say 'for travelling.'

smoke[1] and crackle, and stirred up the embers. The bailiff said, "Here is breakfast. We might take advantage of this breathing-space to eat it. If the rain really closes in[2] we shan't have another chance before nightfall."

The old woman set a trivet by the fire, and began to heat the food. Meanwhile I went to the door, and remained for a long time gazing at the grey curtain of rain which covered[3] the hills like a shroud. I heard at last the voice of the bailiff, respectful and yet[4] familiar: "Breakfast is ready when your honour pleases."[5]

C. *Composition*

1. A wet day in the town.
2. A picnic in the rain.
3. You go for a long walk, and are overtaken by a thunder-storm. You knock at a door and ask for shelter. The people in the house behave strangely. Relate what follows.

21. A WRETCHED INN

A. *Translation into English*

Gerardo se dejó conducir por un mozo a la fonda que le habían recomendado como la mejor, bajo una lluvia menuda y persistente, sumiéndose en unos soportales obscuros y cruzando unas calles angostas que sólo alumbraban las débiles luces de los escasos comercios que en ellas había. En la fonda, un caserón de huéspedes con pretensiones de gran hotel, una criada, descalza, resuelta, y picada de viruelas, le guió hasta un cuarto sórdido.

— Quiero otro mejor — dijo Gerardo, saliendo irritado al pasillo. — El mejor que haya.

— ¡ Ay, señor ! — contestó toda admirada[6] la criada. — Y luego, ¿ éste, qué tiene ? Pues le advierto que aquí paran viajantes de las mejores casas,[7] y nunca nada dijeron de los cuartos.

---

[1] NOT *fumar*; means 'to throw out smoke.' [2] *si cierra a llover.* [3] *envolver.* [4] *a la vez.* [5] *cuando a vuecencia bien le parezca.* [6] Careful ! NOT 'admiring.' [7] *i.e., casas de comercio,* 'firms.'

— Pero ¿ lo hay mejor o no? Pues si lo hay, lo quiero, y si no. . . .

— Haylo, señor, haylo — replicó la moza, y mirándole con cierta desconfianza añadió, previsora — Pero cuesta.[1]

— No he preguntado el precio — cortó secamente Gerardo. Lleváronle a otra habitación, una sala con alcoba, amueblada con pretensiones, a la moda de cincuenta años atrás, sin gusto ni comodidad. Sin embargo, se la ponderaron mucho y, con resignación, Gerardo tuvo que aceptarla.

A. PÉREZ LUGÍN, *La Casa de la Troya*

Questions

1. ¿ Qué tiempo hacía?
2. ¿ Cómo se sabe que ya era de noche?
3. ¿ Por qué quería Gerardo una habitación mejor?
4. ¿ Por qué se admiró la criada?
5. ¿ Qué motivo tenía la criada para desconfiar de Gerardo?
6. ¿ Cómo se sabe que Gerardo no era pobre?
7. ¿ Era mejor la segunda habitación?
8. ¿ Por qué tuvo que aceptarla Gerardo?
9. ¿ Qué contraste había entre la criada y las pretensiones del hotel?
10. ¿ Qué hace un viajante de comercio?

B. *Translation into Spanish*

When the maid had gone, and the porter who had brought his luggage from the station, Gerardo shut the door and looked round. The room was cold and unfriendly. He went to the balcony, opened the door and went out.[2] The balcony looked out on a very narrow street. It seemed that he could touch the house opposite merely by stretching out his arm. It was still raining; a gutter was spouting water into[3] the street. The sound was sad and monotonous, and seemed to make the ugly street uglier still. The cathedral clock was striking eight[4] when Gerardo suddenly noticed that a man

---

[1] 'it costs money.'   [2] *se asomó.*   [3] *a.*   [4] Say 'It was striking eight by (*en*) the cathedral clock.'

was standing at the street-corner. He was wrapped in a rain-coat and wore a black hat. He did not look up, but stood motionless beside a lamp-post, with his eyes fixed[1] on the ground. Gerardo's heart began to beat quickly. It was not the first time he had seen this man!

C. *Composition*

1. Complete the story.
2. Describe a hotel or boarding-house (*pensión*) at which you have stayed.
3. You are stranded in a seaside resort at the height of the holiday season. You cannot find accommodation. Say what you do.

22. AT MIDNIGHT

A. *Translation into English*

Sin hacer ruido, llegó don Paco a la casilla y vio que la puerta estaba cerrada. La luz salía por una ventana pequeña, donde, en vez de vidrios, había un trapo sucio. Don Paco se aproximó y reparó en el trapo tres o cuatro agujeros. Aplicó el ojo al más cercano, y lo que vio por allí le llenó de susto. Imaginó que veía a Lucifer en persona, aunque vestido de campesino andaluz. La cara del así vestido era casi negra, inmóvil, con espantosa y ancha boca y con colosales narices llenas de verrugas y en forma de pico de loro. Don Paco se tranquilizó, no obstante, al reconocer que aquello era una carátula de las que se ponen en las procesiones de Villalegre. El enmascarado guardaba silencio y estaba sentado en una silla, apoyados los codos en una vieja y mugrienta mesa de pino.

En otra silla estaba enfrente otra persona, en quien reconoció al punto don Paco a don Ramón, el tendero murciano de su lugar; notó además que tenía las manos atadas con un cordel a las espaldas.

— Hombre o demonio — decía don Ramón — quienquiera que seas, apiádate de mí y no me atormentes sin fruto.

JUAN VALERA, *Juanita la Larga*

[1] *clavados.*

Questions

1. ¿Por qué no quería hacer ruido don Paco?
2. ¿Cómo pudo ver la casilla?
3. ¿Cómo pudo ver dentro de la casilla?
4. ¿Qué asustó a don Paco?
5. ¿Por qué creía ver a Lucifer? ¿Quién es éste?
6. ¿Qué es una carátula? ¿Cuándo se usa?
7. ¿Quién había también en el cuarto, y cómo estaba?
8. ¿Qué es un tendero? *es el dueño de una tienda*
9. ¿Para qué sería retenido el tendero?
10. ¿Por qué cree Vd. que decía el tendero que el otro le atormentaba sin fruto?

B. *Translation into Spanish*

The little house in the middle of the heath had formerly belonged to an old gamekeeper who had just died. So that when don Paco saw a light in the window he was terrified. He at once thought of ghosts; nevertheless he plucked up courage[1] and set off to investigate (it). We have already related what he saw when he arrived. The masked man, who until now had kept silence, suddenly began to speak. "If you do not write me a paper," he said, "telling your wife to give me ten thousand *reales* I will kill you." The shopkeeper refused to do so. At[2] this the masked man threw himself on don Ramón and began to beat him. Don Paco could bear it no longer. He ran to the door, which was old and loose on its hinges,[3] and, letting loose on it a shower of kicks and blows from his cudgel,[4] succeeded in beating it down.

C. *Composition*

1. Finish this story.
2. A strange encounter at night.
3. An adventure with a burglar.

(no pudo   *could not)*

[1] *armarse de valor.*   [2] *con.*   loose on its hinges, *desvencijada.*
[4] *garrotazos.*

letting loose on it
sellándole

23. A PICTURESQUE CUSTOM

A. *Translation into English*

La playa de Boves era una media luna de pedrezuelas blancas, brillantes. De un lado el mar, del otro las verdes praderías. En uno de los cuernos de la luna asentaba sus chozas un pueblecito de pescadores. A la sazón de llegar la familia del Collado, volvían las lanchas pesqueras, tendida la vela triangular de lona blanca. A primera vista parecían navegar en desorden con la emulación de llegar la primera a la orilla. Mas no era así, sino que venían en orden geométrico, muy puntual.

— En cuña vienen, y yo estoy enterada del por qué — dijo Doña Rosita. — Miren la barca de la punta.

Ésta estaba empavesada, y en lo alto de la antena ondulaba un extraño pabellón, que no era sino un pañuelo de cintura de esos que usan las mozas de aldea. De pie en la proa estaba un marinero joven. Mujeres, niños, y ancianos acudían desde las chozas a recibir las barcas.

— Boda piden en la tripulación de Leonardo.

— ¿ Quién será el novio ?

— ¿ Quién será la elegida ?

— Catad al lienzo.[1]

— Es de Silvina.

— ¡ Viva la novia !

R. P. DE AYALA, *Luna de Miel, Luna de Hiel*

Questions

1. ¿ Qué acontecía cuando los del Collado llegaron a la playa ?
2. ¿ Qué es una lancha ?
3. ¿ Cómo se equivocaron al principio los del Collado ?
4. ¿ Explíquese "en cuña vienen." ?
5. ¿ Con qué se empavesan los barcos ?
6. ¿ Qué tiene de raro el pabellón de la primera barca ?
7. ¿ Qué significaba este pabellón ?
8. ¿ Quiénes eran los novios ?

[1] 'Look at the flag.'

B. *Translation into Spanish*

It is often forgotten, especially by English people, that Spain has a long coast-line, and that a great many Spaniards are sailors; the majority of these are fishermen. Not only in the Mediterranean, but also in the Bay of Biscay they go out in their small boats, which usually have a large triangular sail, known as a lateen sail. Their most important catches are[1] tunny and[1] sardines, which, contrary to what most children think, do not swim about[2] in tins! Most Spanish ports have a regatta once a year, when all the boats are dressed in bunting, and there are races in which there is a good deal of rivalry as to which[3] will come in first. Sometimes different quarters of the town choose a boat and a crew to[4] represent them, and then there is a fierce struggle to maintain the honour of their own quarter.

C. *Composition*

1. Describe any picturesque local custom of which you have knowledge.
2. A regatta.
3. A fishing-village you have visited.

24. A FIGHT WITH PIRATES

A. *Translation into English*

A eso de las once decayó el viento, y el buque quedó inmóvil en medio del mar hecho un espejo. El capitán, que desde el amanecer no dejaba de mirar hacia el sur, ahora se mostró más inquieto que nunca. De pronto se oyó un grito desde la proa; todos los que estaban en popa tendieron inmediatamente la vista hacia una isleta que estaba allí cerca; todos se pusieron muy pálidos. Se veían dos a modo de escarabajos que se aproximaban en el agua, pero muy grandes y, según parecía a Felipe, con un sinnúmero de patas.

— ¡ Hombre ! ¿ qué serán ? — preguntó al capitán.

— Galeras argelinas. — respondió éste. — Piratas. Hay que

[1] Insert *la de*. [2] Omit. [3] *sobre quién*. [4] *para que* + subjunctive.

defenderse si no queremos morir pronto, a menos que seamos esclavizados, lo que casi es peor.

— Pero, ¿ no es posible huir ?

El capitán torció el gesto, enseñándole las velas desmayadas. Luego mandó que se cargasen los cañones, que eran pocos y malos, y que se distribuyesen sables y pistolas, tanto a los pasajeros como a los tripulantes, y todos aguardaron silenciosos la llegada de las galeras, que ya no estaban muy lejos. Ahora vio Felipe que las patas eran remos que se balanceaban rítmicos como alas de gaviotas.

Questions

1. ¿ Por qué no pudo adelantar el buque ?
2. Explíquese "hecho un espejo."
3. ¿ Por qué estaba inquieto el capitán ?
4. ¿ Qué vieron los del buque cerca de la isleta ?
5. ¿ Qué ventaja tenían las galeras sobre el buque ?
6. ¿ De dónde venían las galeras, y por qué ?
7. ¿ Qué armas tenían a bordo del buque ?
8. ¿ Quiénes son los tripulantes ?
9. Descríbase una gaviota.
10. ¿ Cómo trataban los argelinos a sus esclavos ?

B. *Translation into Spanish*

As they approached, the two galleys separated, until there was a good distance between them. Then they attacked, one on each side of the ship. Felipe could see the sharp prows filled with soldiers, then all was hidden by smoke. It seemed as if[1] all the guns were fired together. Suddenly there was a crash, immediately followed by another, and armed men appeared as if by magic on the deck of the ship. They were Moors, dressed in turbans and short tunics, with scimitars in their hands. The Spaniards fought stubbornly, but the pirates were ten to[2] one, and the little band had to retreat slowly as far as the poop. When only ten of them were left, without powder for their pistols, or strength to use[3] their swords, they had to own defeat.[4] The Moorish captain[5] ordered them to be bound and carried on board one of the galleys.

[1] *que.* [2] *contra.* [3] *manejar.* [4] *darse por vencidos.* [5] *el arráez.*

C. *Composition*

1. Finish the story.
2. An adventure with pirates.
3. Tell the story of a film or book about pirates or of adventure at sea.

25. ON THE ASTURIAN COAST

A. *Translation into English*

Malia, después de contemplar un buen rato las olas, ha llenado su cubo de agua marina, y volviendo a ponérselo en la cabeza, emprende el camino de retorno. Malia es recia como un roble. Sostiene el cubo en alto y marcha con reposo, sin esfuerzo aparente. Es el camino pendiente y guijarroso, abierto en la roca brava.[1] Es casi mediodía; Malia se vuelve de vez en cuando para ver el mar y sentir en la cara el frescor de la brisa; luego el camino forma un recodo que oculta la playa; ya no se ven las olas, pero se escucha el rumor amansado de su ir y venir; tras el recodo hay una plazoleta; está sombreada por los castaños de dos huertos; a un lado del camino brota una fuente, y bañando las raíces en ella, álzanse cuatro álamos; los zarzales se espesan y hacen valla a los huertos, donde, sobre praderas, descabellan sus ramas los manzanos, cargados de fruta; pendiente arriba, una chicuela guarda una vaca. Allí, con el ruido del agua de la fuente, se apagan los rumores del mar; el aire pierde sus aromas marinos y empieza a saturarse de olor a montaña, sabroso y fragante.

G. MARTÍNEZ SIERRA, *Sol de la Tarde*

Questions

1. ¿Por qué descendió Malia a la playa?
2. ¿Cómo llevaba su cubo?
3. ¿Cómo se ha hecho el camino?
4. ¿Qué nos dice que hacía calor?
5. ¿Dónde estaba la plazoleta?
6. ¿Qué árboles la rodeaban?

[1] 'in the living rock.'

7. ¿ Por qué no se oía el mar desde la plazoleta ?
8. ¿ Por qué hacía falta guardar la vaca ?
9. ¿ Cómo se cambió el aire, pendiente arriba ?
10. ¿ Qué olores hay en la montaña ?

B. *Translation into Spanish*

We always spend our summer holidays at a village in the south-west of England. First come six hours in the train, then half-an-hour in the bus, which stops in the centre of the village in a little square. There is an old church with a square tower, and some beautiful old houses. This part of the village is on top of the cliffs. To get down to the beach you[1] turn[2] left by the post-office, and follow a steep, stony road with a few fishermen's cottages on one side until you come to a bend in the road. Here you see the sea for the first time, although you can hear it long before. When you reach the bottom of the cliffs you find that the beach is all sand, with very few pebbles. In summer the water is warm, and you can bathe all day or you can sit in the sun and watch the waves if you are as lazy as I am.

C. *Composition*

1. A holiday at the seaside.
2. Describe a town or village you have visited.
3. The little girl looking after some cows falls asleep, and the cows stray. Imagine their adventures.

26. A SPORTING DOG

A. *Translation into English*

El Canelo no era uno de esos perros frívolos que se ponen en dos patas así que se lo ordenan con imperio; ni se entretenía en buscar un pañuelo cuando se lo ocultaban adrede. Tampoco era un perro cominero que llevase la cesta al mercado y la bolsa de los cuartos y viniese muy tranquilo para casa con la carne y el pan sin tocar de ellos. Había formado opinión

---

[1] Use impersonal reflexive throughout.   [2] *torcer* (*ue*).

muy severa sobre todas estas niñerías que no tienen inconveniente en ejecutar los perros sietemesinos. Si alguien le
hubiera propuesto una cosa parecida, es seguro que lo hubiera
rechazado enérgicamente. Mas en lo que toca al cumplimiento
de las tareas que estaban encomendados a su cuidado, bien
puede decirse que ningún perro le ponía el pie delante.[1] Así
que sentía en el cuello el cascabel de caza y veía a su amo
tomar la escopeta, se le hinchaban las narices de contento y
empezaba a ladrar como un energúmeno . . . manifestando
por todos los medios posibles que el deber no era para él una
carga, antes por el contrario, estaba deseando ser útil en todo
lo que pudiera.

A. PALACIO VALDÉS, El Señorito Octavio

Questions

1. ¿ Por qué los llama el autor "frívolos" a unos perros ?
2. ¿ Y por qué los llama "comineros" a otros ?
3. ¿ Qué es, según Canelo, un perro serio ?
4. Descríbanse las tareas de un perro de caza.
5. ¿ Cómo sabía Canelo que su amo iba a cazar ?
6. ¿ Qué hacía para mostrar su alegría ?
7. ¿ Por qué llevaba un cascabel ?
8. ¿ Cómo es su perro de Vd. ?

B. *Translation into Spanish*

The next morning Señor Gómez got up early. It was the
first time he had been out[2] shooting, and he was determined
to learn. He took his gun from the corner of his bedroom,
filled his pockets with cartridges, and set out, with the gun-
dog which the owner of the house had lent him. The dog was
delighted and barked with joy. Soon they came to a small
wood. Señor Gómez made his way through the thickets which
hindered his progress. At last he saw a rabbit and fired his
gun, but the rabbit went on running. The dog looked at him
sadly. A little farther on he saw another, and fired again, but
again he missed.[3] This time the dog turned round and gazed

---

[1] 'surpassed him.'   [2] But he was going out now. Tense ?   to miss,
errar el golpe.

at him fixedly. Five minutes later he saw a third rabbit, sitting down this time. He fired, but the rabbit ran away unhurt. This time the dog sat down and howled, and refused to go any farther. So poor Señor Gómez had to go home.

C. *Composition*

1. You are taking your dog for a walk. He gets into a field full of cattle. Describe what follows.

2. The autobiography of a sheep-dog.

3. The misadventures of a would-be sportsman.

27. THE MAIL-BOAT

A. *Translation into English*

En el agua muerta, de una brillantez de estaño, permanecía inmóvil la barca-correo: un gran ataúd cargado de personas y paquetes, con la borda casi a flor de agua. La vela triangular, con remiendos obscuros, estaba rematada por un guiñapo incoloro que en otros tiempos había sido una bandera española y delataba el carácter oficial de la vieja embarcación.

Un hedor insoportable se esparcía en torno de la barca. Sus tablas se habían impregnado del tufo de los cestos de anguilas y de la suciedad de centenares de pasajeros. Los pasajeros, segadores en su mayoría, cantaban a gritos, pidiendo al barquero que partiese cuanto antes. ¡Ya estaba llena la barca! ¡No cabía más gente!

Así era; pero el hombrecillo, como si no les oyese, siguió esparciendo lentamente por la barca las cestas y los sacos que las mujeres le entregaban desde la orilla. Cada uno de los objetos provocaba nuevas protestas; los pasajeros se estrechaban o cambiaban de sitio, y los del Palmar que entraban en la barca recibían con reflexiones evangélicas la rociada de injurias de los que ya estaban acomodados. ¡Un poco de paciencia! ¡Tanto sitio que encontrasen en el cielo!

                    V. BLASCO IBÁÑEZ, *Cañas y Barro*

Questions

1. ¿Por qué estaba tan baja la borda?

2. ¿Dónde estaba la bandera?

3. ¿ Qué carácter oficial tenía la barca ?
4. ¿ Por qué olía tanto ?
5. ¿ Qué hace un segador ?
6. ¿ Por qué quería la gente partir de pronto ?
7. ¿ Qué hizo protestar a los pasajeros ?
8. ¿ Qué hacía el barquero ?
9. ¿ Cómo se sabe que éste no era muy alto ?
10. ¿ Cómo cabían tantos pasajeros ?

B. *Translation into Spanish*

Near Valencia lies the great lake of the Albufera. It is not all open lake; a great part of it consists of thick beds of reeds, and among the reeds are islets of clay, where rice is grown. A mail-boat ran[1] from Valencia to the island of El Palmar, across[2] the lake. The boatman always announced his arrival by blowing on a bugle.

This afternoon the boat was even more crowded than usual. It was full of passengers, of baskets of eels, parcels for the mail in Valencia, and bags of rice. It seemed that there really was no room for anyone else. Two men were already standing on the gunwale, clinging to the mast. But the boatman went on calmly sounding his bugle, in spite of the protests of the passengers. And at last there appeared the tavern-keeper, an enormously fat[3] man, who, complaining at every step, came slowly up to the boat, and began to hoist himself on board.

C. *Composition*

1. Continue the story.
2. An adventure in a boat (told in the first person).
3. Describe a ferry on which you have travelled, or a day-trip across the Channel.

[1] *hacer el trayecto.*   [2] Say 'crossing the lake.'   [3] Use absolute superlative.

28. A NIGHT RIDE

A. *Translation into English*

— ¿ Estás listo, Juan ?

— Sí.

— Vamos, pues, date prisa.

Los dos hombres entraron en el coche que ya estaba junto al encintado. Pedro, en el asiento del conductor, apretó el botón de arranque, y el coche echó a andar rápidamente hacia la oscuridad. Había poco tráfico por las calles; pronto habían pasado las afueras de la ciudad, y marchaban a buen paso por campo abierto. De vez en cuando, Juan echaba una ojeada a las manos de Pedro, asiendo firmemente el volante; luego, sus ojos se volvían hacia la carretera adelante, blanca cinta al resplandor de los faros. Cuando miraba arriba, no podía ver las estrellas. — Debe de estar muy nublado — pensó, y un momento después el parabrisas estaba cubierto de gotas de lluvia.

— Esto es una lata — dijo Pedro, rompiendo el silencio por vez primera. — Nos retrasará.

Apenas hubo acabado de hablar cuando el coche se desvió violentamente. Pedro frenó en seco y paró el coche al borde de la cuneta. Salieron e inspeccionaron las ruedas.

— Aquí está — dijo Juan. — El neumático ha reventado.

— ¡ No te extrañe ! — exclamó Pedro. — Hay vidrios rotos en la carretera.

— Pues tendremos que mojarnos y tratar de arreglarlo.

Questions

1. ¿ Cómo se pone en marcha un automóvil ?
2. ¿ Por qué no habría mucho tráfico ?
3. ¿ Cuándo pudieron andar a buen paso ?
4. ¿ A qué se parecía la carretera ?
5. ¿ Por qué no veían las estrellas ?
6. ¿ Cuándo rompió Pedro el silencio ?
7. ¿ Hacia dónde se desvió el coche ?
8. ¿ Qué es una cuneta ?

9. ¿Por qué tendrían que mojarse?
10. ¿Qué tendrían que hacer para "arreglarlo"?

B. *Translation into Spanish*

Juan took the spare wheel, and the two crouched down in[1] the rain and began their task. No sooner had they finished than the rain stopped, and the moon came out. They started off again. A short distance farther on[2] they saw ahead of them a narrow bridge. Pedro slowed down and changed gear —fortunately, for at that moment a big car came over the bridge at full speed, directly towards them. Pedro swerved violently to the right; the other driver braked hard, and his car skidded on the wet road, passing so close to them that the mudguards almost touched. Without even glancing at them, the driver went on his way and was soon out of sight.[3] "Did you see who it was?" exclaimed Juan, seizing Pedro by the arm. "Yes," he answered, frowning, "It was López. He tried deliberately to put us in the ditch. I wonder if that explains the broken glass, too? Come on, we must hurry."

C. *Composition*

1. Finish the story.
2. Describe a motor accident.
3. A drive through the country.

29. BOY MEETS GIRL

A. *Translation into English*

La tarde se encendía. Era un momento hermosísimo, propicio a la amistad.

Un pensamiento divirtió a Ignacio. ¿Qué demonios hacía allá, al lado de una muchacha cuyos pendientes bastarían para pagar su carrera[4] y aun sobraría[5] para que sus padres hicieran su tan suspirado[6] viaje a Mallorca? Ahí andaba él, por el Paseo central, opinando sobre marcas de automóvil, ajeno a los suyos, que eran aquellos magníficos gerundenses[7] que se

[1] *bajo.* [2] Omit. [3] *perderse de vista.* [4] *i.e.,* his university course. [5] Careful; this verb is impersonal. [6] 'sighed-for,' hence 'longed-for.' [7] people from Gerona.

volvían a la estación con la bolsa de la merienda vacía y la
piel de la espalda arrancada.[1]

Y, no obstante, se sentía satisfecho. Le parecía que todo
el mundo le miraba. Ana María debía de llamar la atención
con sus dos moños, una a cada lado, y las cintas de las alpar-
gatas[2] perfectamente cruzadas hasta media pierna. . . .
Tomaron asiento sobre una barca en la arena, riendo sin saber
de qué.

Ana María balanceaba sus piernas. Suspiró y dijo:

— Cuéntame cosas. . . .

Un pescador que pasaba oyó la frase.

— ¡Anda, hombre, cuénteselas!

Y la hora avanzaba. El crepúsculo era grandioso.

— Tienes una voz muy serena. Me gusta oírte.

— ¿De qué quieres que te hable?

— De lo que quieras.

Adapted from: J. M. GIRONELLA,
Los Cipreses creen en Dios

Questions

1. ¿Por qué se divirtió Ignacio?

2. Explique lo que son los pendientes. ¿Qué es una
pendiente?

3. ¿En dónde se hace la carrera?

4. ¿Puede usted explicar el verbo "sobrar"? Dé otro
ejemplo.

5. ¿Dónde está Mallorca?

6. ¿De qué ciudad viene Ignacio?

7. ¿Por qué le miraba todo el mundo?

8. ¿Qué les hizo reír?

9. ¿Qué hora sería?

10. Imagínese usted que está mirando un cuadro que
representa esta escena. Descríbalo.

B. *Translation into Spanish*

Ignacio's parents were not rich. For years they had been

---

[1] *i.e.*, peeling from sunburn.   [2] Rope-soled sandals with canvas
tops and long laces which cross over the instep and tie round the ankles.

dreaming of spending a holiday in Mallorca, but they never
had enough money. This year Ignacio, who was seventeen,
had the opportunity to spend a couple of weeks at the seaside,
on the Costa Brava, which is not far from Gerona, the town
in which he lived. He used to watch his friends from Gerona
arrive at the station in the morning, carrying bags containing
their lunch; then they toasted themselves on the beach all
day, and returned home in the evening. But he was lucky—
he didn't have to go home. For once he had time to spare[1] to
enjoy himself. One day, while he was swimming in the sea,
he met Ana María. She was pretty and intelligent, and they
got on with each other[2] at once. But it was obvious, when he
saw her clothes and her ear-rings, that her parents were well-
to-do people.[3] In spite of this, they became friends[4] and
several times they went for walks together on the beach and
watched the sun set.

C. *Composition*

1. Ignacio tells Ana María about his life at home.
2. If I were rich. . . . (Before you begin, read through
p. 138, 3.)
3. Give a detailed portrait of someone you know.

30. A SOUTHERN PORT

A. *Translation into English*

Era una mañana inmensa de oro. Lejos, encima del mar, el
cielo estaba blanco, como encandecido de tanta lumbre, y las
paradas aguas, que de tiempo en tiempo hacían una blanca
palpitación, ofrecían el sol infinitamente roto. Si pasaba una
lancha, silenciosa y frágil, los remos, al emerger, desgranaban
una espuma de luz.

Gritaban las gaviotas delirantes de alegría y de azul. Y en
las viejas barcas de carga, los gorriones picaban el trigo y el
maíz desbordando de los costales, y luego saltaban por la

---

[1] *le sobraba tiempo para.*   [2] *simpatizaron.*   [3] *gente acaudalada.*
[4] *trabar amistad.*

proa, dejando en la marina una impresión aldeana muy rara y graciosa.

Bajo las palmeras paseaban los enfermos, los ociosos, los que llegan de las tierras altas, hoscas y frías, buscando la delicia del templado suelo alicantino.[1]

Olía el pueblo a gentes de trabajo, a dinero y maderas, a vapores, a Mediterráneo; y traspasaba todas las emanaciones una fuerte y encendida, como un olor de sol, de semillas, de vida jugosa y apretada.

G. MIRÓ, *Libro de Sigüenza*

Questions

1. ¿Por qué dice que la mañana era de oro?
2. ¿Cómo se movían las lanchas?
3. Descríbase una gaviota.
4. ¿Qué barcas buscaban los gorriones, y por qué?
5. ¿Por qué daban al puerto una impresión aldeana?
6. ¿Quién era la gente que se paseaba?
7. ¿Qué diferencia hay entre el clima de las tierras altas y el de Alicante?
8. ¿Cómo sabemos que estamos en el Mediterráneo?

B. *Translation into Spanish*

About seven o'clock Pepito came out of the hotel and went down towards the pier. He realized, after running into Sánchez, that it was necessary that he should leave at once— it was too dangerous to linger here. He looked at the quiet waters of the little port, wondering how he could escape without leaving a trace. His enemies would keep watch on[2] the steamer, of course, but there, near the pier, was a small cargo-boat, with her red sails lowered. The skipper sat on a sack of wheat, smoking and watching the seagulls. Pepito knew that many of these small ships sailed to Africa, and that not a few were smugglers. If he paid enough money probably the skipper would hide him in the cargo after dark, and he would be asked no questions.[3] He thought for a moment, decided he had enough money, and that after dark he would approach the skipper and would ask him for a passage.

[1] *i.e.*, of Alicante. [2] *no perder de vista.* [3] *nada.*

64 A COMPREHENSIVE SPANISH COURSE

C. *Composition*

1. Finish the story.
2. Describe a fishing-port you know.
3. A visitor whom you have never seen arrives from abroad to stay with you and you meet him (her) at the port. You have both agreed to wear a white carnation, but so have several other people. Relate what follows.

31. A MADRID STREET

A. *Translation into English*

Madrid, a 29 de septiembre de 1951

Querido amigo:

Hablemos hoy de una calle de Madrid: la Gran Vía. En esta magnífica arteria se concentra todo el lujo y el esplendor de la ciudad. Aquí el fulgor de los anuncios de los "cines" de alto copete[1] te deslumbra; peligroso es, sin embargo, acercarse a la taquilla: una butaca de patio,[2] 80 pesetas. A un lado y a otro de la amplia calle, multitud de comercios ofrecen sus escaparates a la admiración de las gentes: las joyerías, las peleterías, las relojerías, los grandes almacenes, las librerías y, sobre todo, los confortables cafés, detrás de cuyas vidrieras muchos gozan del espectáculo del ir y venir apresurado de los transeúntes. Una cadena ininterrumpida de autos colma la calzada, destacando entre ellos los autobuses de dos pisos, iguales a los de Londres, pero pintados de azul y blanco. De trecho en trecho se abren las bocas del "Metro,"[3] que, alternativamente, tragan y vomitan público. Un par de rascacielos, los llamados "Telefónica" y "España," alzan sus moles de 20 o 25 pisos. La hora de congestión máxima es a las siete de la tarde, cuando millares de oficinas son abandonadas por los empleados. Y basta por hoy.

Te abraza tu amigo,

Manuel

Questions

1. ¿Para qué sirven los anuncios en los cines?
2. ¿Qué es una taquilla?

[1] 'high-class.' [2] 'pit stall.' [3] 'Underground.'

3. ¿ Qué se vende en las peleterías ?
4. ¿ Por qué entra la gente en los cafés ?
5. ¿ Qué diferencia hay entre los autobuses de Madrid y los de Londres ?
6. ¿ Qué quiere decir "Metro" ?
7. ¿ Qué es un rascacielos ?
8. ¿ Por qué hay congestión a las siete de la tarde ?
9. ¿ Cuál es la hora de congestión máxima en Inglaterra ?
10. ¿ Cuántos pisos tiene su colegio ? ¿ En qué piso está usted ahora ?

B. *Translation into Spanish*

London,
8th October, 1951

Dear Manuel,

Thank you very much for your letter, with its interesting description of a Madrid street. In return,[1] I will describe a London street for you. Let us choose Regent Street, which is one of the widest and most luxurious streets in London. It joins[2] Oxford Circus and Piccadilly Circus, and is always full of people, some of whom are shopping, but the majority are just[3] looking at the shop-windows. Here, too, there are many jewellers' shops, a few bookshops, some tailors, furriers, and department stores, but there are not many cafés. There is a Tube station at each end of the street, but none in the middle, and there is one cinema. The roadway is always packed with an interminable procession of cars and red two-decker buses. The rush-hour here is between five and six, when all the clerks and shop-assistants dash to the Tube and the buses.

Yours very cordially,

Dick

C. *Composition*

1. Write a letter to a friend in Spain, describing a street in your town in detail.
2. A bus journey in the rush hour.
3. You show a Spanish visitor the sights of London.

[1] *a mi vez.* [2] Use *unir.* [3] *no hacen más que.*

32. A VISIT TO AN AERODROME

A. *Translation into English*

El zumbido de motores se fue haciendo cada vez más intenso. Todavía no se veía el avión, pero se presentía que de un momento a otro haría su aparición en el espacio. Por fin, la plateada mole del cuatrimotor, reluciente bajo los rayos del sol, pasó majestuosamente sobre nuestras cabezas. La pista de aterrizaje del aeropuerto estaba despejada y pronta para recibir a la nave aérea. El aparato iba perdiendo altura, planeando en círculos concéntricos alrededor de donde nos encontrábamos. Ya se distinguían las aspas de las hélices al ir disminuyendo la velocidad de sus revoluciones. Próximo a tierra, del interior del aeroplano fueron surgiendo las ruedas del tren de aterrizaje. Poco a poco, suavemente, se posó. Los empleados del aeródromo acercaron una escalerilla a la portezuela de salida, empezando a salir los viajeros, que, hablando todas las lenguas del dilatado universo, recreaban el ambiente de la bíblica Babel. Por último, descendieron los tripulantes: pilotos, navegante, mecánico y una bella azafata, amén del radiotelegrafista. Mientras tanto, otros aviones hacían ejercicios en el aire, picando, elevándose velozmente, rizando el rizo. Algunos atraían más la curiosidad, por tratarse de modernísimos aparatos con turbopropulsión o propulsión a chorro.

Questions

1. ¿Por qué no se veía el avión?
2. ¿Cuántas aspas tienen las hélices?
3. Explíquese "la pista . . . estaba despejada."
4. ¿En qué consiste el tren de aterrizaje?
5. ¿Por qué hablaban los viajeros diversas lenguas?
6. Explíquese "Babel."
7. ¿Cuántos tripulantes había?
8. ¿Qué aparatos interesaban más a los curiosos?
9. ¿Por qué se necesitaba una escalerilla?
10. ¿Cuáles son los aviones más rápidos?

The Gran Vía in Madrid. See page 64.

By kind permission of the Spanish Tourist Office

Good Friday in Sevilla. The early morning procession. See page 67.

By kind permission of the Spanish Tourist Office

B. *Translation into Spanish*

It was eight o'clock in the morning when Archer got into the bus that was to take him to Heath Row. Near the river it was misty, but soon, as[1] he journeyed westward, he noticed with satisfaction that the mist was clearing,[2] and, by the time[3] the bus was entering the gates of the airport, the air was clear, and the runways were shining in the sun. The small group of passengers waited, looking across the vast space of the aerodrome, until the roar of engines warned them that the great four-engined machine was ready to receive them. One by[4] one they climbed the little stair and entered the aeroplane, where the air-hostess welcomed them and led them to their seats. The roar of the engines grew suddenly louder. They were moving,[5] faster and faster, until Archer realized that they were in the air, and that at last he was really going to South America.

C. *Composition*

1. A visit to an aerodrome in England.
2. Your first flight (real or imaginary).
3. The importance of air transport.

33. GOOD FRIDAY IN SEVILLE

A. *Translation into English*

Y llegó la madrugada del Viernes Santo, la madrugada en que la emoción religiosa de Sevilla llega al colmo. Al sonar las dos de la mañana, las pesadas puertas de la iglesia de San Lorenzo se abrieron de par en par, y la apiñada multitud que llenaba la oscura plazuela, el ánimo suspenso, contenida la respiración, afiebrados los ojos, hundió las miradas en las tinieblas del templo, fondo misterioso sobre el que se destacaban como fúlgidas apariciones en sus peanas de oro, plata y luz, el Cristo del Gran Poder y la Virgen del Mayor Dolor y Traspaso.[6] Las luces de los cirios parecían rutilantes estrellas;

---

[1] *a medida que.* [2] *disiparse.* [3] *cuando.* [4] *a.* [5] *en marcha.*
[6] Two famous images.

las llamas de los blandones, espíritus que vagaban en las sombras. En medio de un silencio solemne, empezaron a salir los negros encapuchados de dos en dos, el blandón de cera roja en la diestra enguantada, la cola de la túnica recogida sobre el brazo izquierdo, el paso majestuoso, el continente señoril. La mayoría iban desnudos de pies, otros con medias negras solamente, los menos con zapatos de cuero y hebilla de plata, y avanzaban llevando cada uno en su blandón encendido así como la llama lívida y sutil de un fuego fatuo.

CARLOS REYLES, *El Embrujo de Sevilla*

Questions

1. ¿Qué conmemora el Viernes Santo?
2. ¿Por qué estaba oscura la plazuela?
3. ¿Cómo se veían las imágenes en la oscuridad?
4. ¿A quiénes representaban éstas?
5. ¿Por qué parecen estrellas los cirios?
6. ¿Qué es un blandón?
7. ¿Cómo salían de la iglesia los encapuchados?
8. ¿Cómo estaban calzados?
9. ¿A qué se parecían los blandones?
10. ¿Dónde se ven los fuegos fatuos?

B. *Translation into Spanish*

As the procession slowly moved along[1] the narrow streets, it looked like a river of pale fire. On both sides were balconies, each one filled with watching people. All at once a woman's voice sounded loudly and clearly; she was singing a *saeta*, an improvised hymn. Others soon followed, answered by the deep voices of the crowd of people who lined the streets, taking off their hats as[2] the procession reached them. Among the penitents walked Pepe, carrying a lighted candle, and, as soon as they recognized him, the bystanders exclaimed in wonder at[3] seeing the bullfighter,[4] their idol, walking barefoot with the rest. Then they remembered his wound and his long

---

[1] *avanzar por.* [2] *cuando.* [3] *admirados de.* [4] N.B., NOT *toreador!*

illness and realized that he was giving thanks for his recovery. And still the procession continued: when the first of them[1] had reached Campana the last had not yet left the church. And it was not the only procession either,[2] for another was starting out from the Triana quarter.

C. *Composition*

1. Describe any procession you have seen.
2. Write an imaginary account of how Pepe received his wound.
3. Two processions meet at a crossroads, and neither will give way. Describe what follows.

34. ARRIVAL BY NIGHT

A. *Translation into English*

Era la primera vez que viajaba sola, pero no estaba asustada; por el contrario, me parecía una aventura agradable y excitante aquella profunda libertad en la noche. La sangre, después del viaje largo y cansado, me empezaba a circular en las piernas entumecidas y con una sonrisa de asombro miraba la gran Estación de Francia y los grupos que estaban aguardando el expreso y los que llegábamos[3] con tres horas de retraso.

Debía parecer una figura extraña con mi aspecto risueño y mi viejo abrigo que, a impulsos de la brisa, me azotaba las piernas, defendiendo mi maleta, desconfiada.

Uno de esos viejos coches de caballos que han vuelto a surgir después de la guerra[4] se detuvo delante de mí y lo tomé sin titubear, causando la envidia de un señor que se lanzaba detrás de él desesperado, agitando el sombrero. Enfilamos la calle de Aribau, donde vivían mis parientes, con sus plátanos llenos aquel octubre de espeso verdor y su silencio vívido de

---

[1] Omit 'of· them.'   [2] Say 'the procession was not the only (one).'   [3] 'those of us who were arriving.' Note this construction carefully; cf. *los españoles decís* . . . 'you Spaniards say . . .'   [4] *i.e.*, the Spanish Civil War of 1936–39.

la respiración de mil almas detrás de los balcones apagados.[1]
De improviso sentí crujir y balancearse todo el armatoste.
Luego quedó inmóvil.

— Aquí es — dijo el cochero.

After: CARMEN LAFORET, *Nada*

Questions

1. ¿Quién está hablando?
2. ¿Por qué tiene las piernas entumecidas?
3. ¿Qué hacía la gente en la estación?
4. ¿De quién desconfiaba?
5. ¿Cómo salió de la estación?
6. ¿Por qué se desesperaba el señor?
7. ¿Adónde iba la joven?
8. ¿Cómo sabemos que llegaba muy tarde?
9. ¿Por qué se detuvo el coche?
10. ¿A quién tendría que llamar antes de poder entrar en la casa?

B. *Translation into Spanish*

I looked up at the house opposite which the carriage had
stopped. Rows of balconies, exactly alike . . . I could not
guess which was my grandmother's. With a rather trembling
hand, I gave a few coins to the watchman who had appeared
while I was paying the driver. He opened the door, and, laden
with my suitcase, I began very slowly to climb the stairs. In
front of the door of the flat, I felt[2] a sudden fear of waking
these unknown people who were nevertheless my relations,
and I hesitated a while before ringing. At first, no one
answered, then I heard a trembling voice. "All right![3] All
right!" Then feet dragging themselves along[4] and clumsy
hands drawing[5] bolts. Everything seemed to me a nightmare.
At last a little old lady appeared, whispering, "Is[6] it you,
Gloria?" But my name was Andrea!

---

[1] 'whose lights were out'—*i.e.*, dark.   [2] *me acometió.*   [3] *¡Ya va!*
[4] Use *arrastrarse,* and omit 'along.'   [5] *descorrer.*   [6] Careful! What
person is this verb?

C. *Composition*

1. Finish the story.
2. You arrive late in a strange town. Say how you get to your destination.
3. You visit some relatives whom you have not seen for a long time. Imagine the conversation.

35. A SUNDAY OUTING

A. *Translation into English*

Terminó de pasar el mercancías y apareció todo el grupo de bicicletas al otro lado del paso a nivel. Paulina, al verlos, se puso a gritarles, agitando la mano:

— ¡ Miguel! ¡ Alicia! ¡ que estamos aquí!

— ¡ Hola, niños! — contestaban de la otra parte. — ¿ Nos habéis esperado mucho rato ?

Ya las barras del paso a nivel se levantaban lentamente. Los ciclistas entraron en la vía, con las bicis[1] cogidas del manillar.

— ¡ Y qué bien presumimos de moto![2] — dijo Miguel, acercándose a Sebastián y su novia.

Venían sudorosos. Las chicas traían pañuelos[3] de colorines, como Paulina, con los picos colgando. Ellos, camisas blancas casi todos. Uno tenía camiseta de rayas horizontales, blanco y azul, como los marineros. Se había cubierto la cabeza con un pañuelo de bolsillo, hecho cuatro nuditos en sus cuatro esquinas. Venía con los pantalones metidos en los calcetines. Otros en cambio traían pinzas de andar en bicicleta. Una alta, la última, se hacía toda remilgos por los accidentes del suelo, al pasar las vías, maldiciendo la bici:

— ¡ Ay, hijo, qué trasto[4] más difícil!

Tenía unas gafas azules que levantaban dos puntas hacia los lados, como si prolongasen las cejas, y le hacían un rostro místico y japonés.

— ¿ Habéis tenido algún pinchazo ? — preguntó Sebastián.

---

[1] Slang: 'bike.'   [2] 'Aren't we show-offs with our motor-bike!'
[3] *i.e.*, scarves over their heads.   [4] 'object,' 'thing,' 'gadget.'

— ¡Qué va!¹ Fue Mely que se paraba cada veinte metros, diciendo que nadie la obliga a fatigarse.

After: RAFAEL SÁNCHEZ FERLOSIO, *El Jarama*

Questions

1. Explique usted lo que es un paso a nivel.
2. ¿Quiénes habían sido los primeros en llegar?
3. ¿Dónde esperaban éstos a los demás?
4. ¿Cómo habían venido Sebastián y Paulina?
5. ¿Qué nos dice que hacía mucho calor?
6. ¿Cómo se preparaban los chicos para ir en bicicleta?
7. ¿Por qué se quejaba la chica alta?
8. ¿Cuándo se usan gafas azules?
9. ¿En qué se parecía la chica a una japonesa?
10. ¿Por qué pregunta Sebastián si han tenido un pinchazo?

B. *Translation into Spanish*

An engine roared suddenly, accelerated a couple of times, and the noise stopped outside the door of the café. Mauricio went out. A young man and a girl were there, dismounting from a motor-cycle. He recognised their faces.

"How are you, boy? Here again?"

"As² you see, we're coming to spend the day. Have the others arrived?"

"Oh, so you're³ not alone? No, nobody but you."

"There are eleven of us⁴ but the others are coming on bicycles. We'll wait for them here."

"What would you like to drink?"⁵

"I don't know; what about⁶ you, Pauline?"

"I had breakfast before starting out. I don't want anything."

"That's nothing,⁷ so did I! Have you any coffee?"

"Yes, I think there is some⁸ made in the kitchen. I'll go and see."

He came back a moment later with the coffee-pot. "Yes,

---

¹ 'Nothing of the kind!' ² *ya.* ³ Use *venir.* ⁴ Say 'we are eleven' and see note 3. ⁵ *tomar* ⁶ *y.* ⁷ *eso no hace* (slang). ⁸ *lo.*

I'll pour it out[1] for you at once. Put in[2] as much sugar as you like."

C. *Composition*

1. Continue the story told in B and A.
2. You are out cycling and have an accident. Say what happens and how you get home.
3. A meal in a country inn or café.

[1] *poner.*   [2] *echar.*

PART II

GRAMMAR SECTION

1. SOME PRELIMINARY REMARKS

Syllabification

1. A consonant between two vowels forms a syllable with the second.

  e.g., to|do, i|ra, a|vi|sar.

2. **ch, ll, rr,** are considered as single consonants.

  e.g., mu|cha|cho, bu|llir, pa|rra.

3. A consonant followed by **l** or **r** (except **rl, sl, tl, lr, nr, sr**) forms a syllable with it and the following vowel.

  e.g., ma|dre, si|glo, En|ri|que.

Stressing and Accentuation

1. All words ending in a vowel, or **n** or **s**, are stressed on the last syllable but one.

  e.g., correspondencia, crisis, examen, joven.

Note that when the strong vowels **a, e,** or **o** are preceded or followed by the weak vowels **i** or **u**, the combination forms only one syllable.

2. All other words are stressed on the last syllable.

  e.g., hablar, realidad, sencillez.

3. An accent (′) over a vowel indicates that the stress is exceptional.

  e.g., rápido, pálido, estación, francés.

4. In diphthongs (*i.e.*, when one of the strong vowels **a, e, o** combines with one of the weak vowels **i, u,** or when two weak

vowels combine) the stress falls on the strong vowel or on the second of the weak vowels.

    e.g., **ai, au, io, iu, ui.**

In triphthongs (*i.e.*, when a strong vowel stands between two weak vowels) the stress falls on the strong vowel.

    e.g., **iai, iei, uai (uay), uei (uey).**

5. The accent is also used:

  (*a*) to separate two vowels which would otherwise form a diphthong.

    e.g., **día, río.**

  (*b*) to distinguish words spelt the same which have different meanings.

    e.g., **mi** (my), **mí** (myself); **tu** (your), **tú** (you); **se** (himself), **sé** (I know); **de** (of), **dé** (give); **el** (the), **él** (he); **mas** (but), **más** (more), etc.

  (*c*) on all interrogative words and exclamations.

    e.g., **¿qué? ¿dónde? ¡qué bien!**

6. The diaeresis (¨) is used to show that the **u** followed by **e** or **i** must be pronounced.

    e.g., **averigüe, vergüenza.**

Note that some nouns which bear an accent in the singular do not require one in the plural and vice versa.

    e.g., **razón**, reason; **razones**, reasons.
           orden, order; **órdenes,** orders.

Punctuation Marks

Inverted question marks or exclamation marks are placed at the beginning of a question or exclamation.

    e.g., **¿Cómo está Vd.?** How are you?
       ¡Qué lástima! What a pity!

In dialogue a dash is generally used instead of quotation marks.

Capitalization

Capital letters in Spanish are not required with:

(*a*) nouns and adjectives indicating nationality and towns, etc., of origin.

> *e.g.*, **un francés**, a Frenchman.
> **un madrileño**, an inhabitant of Madrid.
> **un país hispano-americano**, a Spanish-American country.

(*b*) the days of the week, months, seasons.

> *e.g.*, **el lunes**, Monday; **mayo**, May; **la primavera**, Spring.

(*c*) titles (usually).

> *e.g.*, **el conde de Salamanca**: *but* **el Señor González**.

(*d*) **yo** (I).

"You" in Spanish

Usted (Vd.), **ustedes (Vds.)** are used to people one does not know, to elders and to superiors as a mark of respect, to waiters, porters, servants, etc., to keep the relationship formal.

Tú (pl. **vosotros, vosotras**) is used between members of a family, between people of the same age, or social equals; it is invariably used between children and between young people generally. Adults always address children (and animals) as **tú.** It is no longer a mark of intimacy, only of equality—for instance, people in their teens or early twenties call each other **tú** practically on sight.

2. THE ARTICLE

		Definite				*Indefinite*	
		Singular	*Plural*			*Singular*	*Plural*
Masc.		el	los	*Masc.*		un	unos
Fem.		la	las	*Fem.*		una	unas

Notes. **El** is used instead of **la** before a noun beginning with stressed **a** or **ha**. Similarly, **un** is used instead of **una**.

> *e.g.*, **el agua; el hambre; un ala.**

A el becomes **al; de el** becomes **del.**

> *e.g.*, **al pupitre,** to the desk; **del perro,** of the dog.

The neuter article **lo** is used before an adjective used as a noun.

> *e.g.*, **lo bello,** beauty (that which is beautiful).

The *Definite Article* is used:

1. With nouns used in a general sense.

> *e.g.*, **Me gusta el azúcar,** I like sugar.

2. With abstract nouns.

> *e.g.*, **La pereza es un vicio,** laziness is a vice.

3. With names of languages, except after **hablar.**

> *e.g.*, **Enseño el español,** I teach Spanish.
> **Habla francés,** he speaks French.

4. With titles, except in direct address.

> *e.g.*, **el Señor Ruiz,** Mr Ruiz; **el rey Jaime,** King James.

Note that the title **Don, Doña,** is an exception.

> *e.g.*, **Don Pedro, Doña Sol.**

Similarly, **San, Santo (-a).**

> *e.g.*, **San Juan, Santo Tomás.**

5. Before a proper noun qualified by an adjective.

> *e.g.*, **La pobre Rosita está enferma,** poor Rosita is ill.
> **El África central,** Central Africa.

6. With parts of the body, articles of clothing, personal attributes or characteristics (unless they are the first words in a sentence), instead of the possessive adjective.

> *e.g.,* **Juan bajó la voz,** John lowered his voice.
> **He perdido el sombrero,** I have lost my hat.
> **Me llamó la atención . . .,** he attracted my attention.

Note constructions like: **me duelen los dientes,** my teeth ache; **se lavó la cara,** he washed his face.

7. Instead of the English 'a' or 'an' in expressions of space, time, weight, measure, etc.

> *e.g.,* **Dos veces al mes,** twice a month.
> **Una peseta la botella,** one peseta a bottle.

8. With the names of certain countries—**el Brasil, el Canadá, la India, el Japón, el Perú, el Uruguay, el Ecuador,** etc.

> *e.g.,* **Va al Canadá la semana que viene,** he is going to Canada next week.

> *But* **Francia es un país hermoso,** France is a beautiful country.

The *Definite Article* is omitted in Spanish in the following cases:

(*a*) Between the name and number of a king or ruler.

> *e.g.,* **Jorge quinto,** George the Fifth.

(*b*) Usually before a noun in apposition.

> *e.g.,* **Murió en Madrid, capital de España,** he died in Madrid, the capital of Spain.

The *Indefinite Article* is omitted in Spanish in the following cases:

(*a*) After **ser, hacerse,** etc., before nouns denoting nationality, trade, profession, calling, etc.

> *e.g.,* **Es abogado,** he is a lawyer.
> **Se hizo médico,** he became a doctor.
> **Es inglés,** he is an Englishman.

(b) Before: **otro,** another; **cierto,** a certain; **cien(to),** a hundred; **mil,** a thousand; **tal, semejante,** such (a).

> *e.g.,* **otro día,** another day.
> **cierto hombre,** a certain man.
> **mil libros,** a thousand books.
> **tal cosa,** such a thing.
> **semejante asunto,** such a matter.

(c) After ¡ **qué!** and **sin.**

> *e.g.,* ¡ qué color tan hermoso !, what a pretty colour !
> **sin sonrisa,** without a smile.

N.B. (i) The indefinite article is always used in Spanish, contrary to English usage, before an abstract noun qualified by an adjective.

> *e.g.,* **Manifestó un valor extraordinario,** he showed extraordinary courage.

(ii) As in English, no article in Spanish is required before a noun used in a partitive sense.

> *e.g.,* **Compro chocolate,** I am buying chocolate.
> **No tengo tinta,** I haven't any ink.

Note also the following idiomatic construction with the neuter article **lo:**

> **¿Sabe Vd. lo inteligente que es?,** do you know how clever he is?
> **Vd. no sabe lo egoístas que son mis hermanas,** you don't know how selfish my sisters are.
> **¡ Lo hermosa que es (ella) !,** how beautiful she is !

N.B. The adjective must agree with its noun or pronoun in this construction.

Exercises

1. Do you like chocolate? 2. Captain Ruiz is not here. 3. He bowed his head. 4. Kindness is a virtue. 5. The apples are two pesetas a pound. 6. Have you visited France? *Las visiledo* 7. French is a difficult language. 8. I have left my hat in the *He dejado mi sombrero*

hall. 9. My brother is a schoolmaster. 10. What a pretty
tie! 11. A certain man told me so. 12. We are not going to
Spain this year. 13. I have never made such a journey.
14. I have cigars and tobacco but no cigarettes. 15. In such
a case I should write to the doctor. 16. She washed her hair
and put on her hat. 17. Do you know San Sebastián, a
pleasant town on the north coast of Spain? 18. Why don't
you wear your gloves? 19. Paquita has to visit the dentist
twice a month. 20. I have done it a thousand times. 21. You
can't imagine how lazy she is. 22. My grandfather has
wonderful patience. 23. Your friend has big feet, hasn't he?
24. You don't know how strong my brothers are. 25. He
revealed wonderful skill.

3. PLURAL OF NOUNS AND ADJECTIVES

1. Words ending in a vowel add -s.

   e.g., **las hojas verdes,** green leaves.
   los pájaros hermosos, beautiful birds.

2. Words ending in a consonant add -es.

   e.g., **las lecciones útiles,** useful lessons.
   los profesores jóvenes, young masters.

3. Words ending in -z change -z into -ces.

   e.g., **el lápiz** (pencil) becomes **los lápices** (pencils).
   la nariz (nostril) becomes **las narices** (nostrils).

4. Words ending in -s preceded by an unstressed vowel
remain the same.

   e.g., **la crisis** (crisis) becomes **las crisis** (crises).

5. Words ending in a stressed vowel (other than e) add -es.

   e.g., **el rubí** (ruby), **los rubíes** (rubies).

(Exceptions: **sofá, sofás; mamá, mamás; papá, papás.**)

4. GENDER OF NOUNS

1. Names of male and female beings are masculine and feminine as in English.

2. Names of rivers, mountains, oceans, trees, winds, cardinal points, years, months, and days of the week are masculine.

> *e.g.*, **el Támesis**, the Thames; **los Andes**, the Andes; **el Pacífico**, the Pacific; **el manzano**, apple-tree; **el poniente**, the west wind; **el oeste**, West; **el año**, year; **agosto**, August; **el martes**, Tuesday, etc.

3. Names of countries ending in -a are feminine (with the exception of **el Canadá**). All others are masculine.

Genders by Endings

Feminine. (*a*) Nouns ending in **-a**. (Exceptions include such nouns as **el día, el mapa, el tranvía, el clima, el tema, el dilema, el programa,** etc.)

(*b*) Most nouns in **-z**. (Exceptions include **el lápiz, el juez.**)

(*c*) Nouns ending in **-dad, -tad, -tud,** and **-umbre.**

(*d*) Nouns ending in **-ción.**

(*e*) Most nouns ending in **-is**. (Exceptions include **el paréntesis.**)

(*f*) Most nouns ending in **-d**. (Exceptions include **el césped, el huésped.**)

Masculine. (*a*) Nouns ending in **-o** except **la dínamo, la mano, la radio,** etc.

(*b*) Most nouns ending in **-l**. (Exceptions include **la cárcel, la col, la hiel, la miel, la piel, la sal, la señal,** etc.)

(*c*) Most nouns ending in **-r**. (Exceptions include **la coliflor, la flor, la labor.** N.B. **mar** is usually masculine but may be feminine when used figuratively—*e.g.*, **Tengo la mar de cosas que hacer,** I have heaps of things to do.)

Note. A few words differ in meaning according to gender.

e.g., **el capital,** capital (money); **la capital,** capital (city).

el cura, parish priest; **la cura,** cure.

el pendiente, ear-ring; **la pendiente,** slope, etc.

N.B. When learning nouns it is essential to learn the noun with its article.

5. DIMINUTIVES AND AUGMENTATIVES

Certain suffixes are commonly added to the noun (and occasionally to adjectives and adverbs) in Spanish to give a different meaning to the noun. These suffixes frequently indicate size, but other ideas can be expressed by them as well. The student is advised not to form diminutives or augmentatives for himself but to note them as they occur and use only those he knows to be correct. Their use is determined by precedent, colloquial usage, and sometimes euphony.

Diminutive Suffixes

-ito, -(e)cito (and feminine forms). These express, in addition to smallness, affection, pity, etc.

e.g., **la casa,** house; **la casita,** small house.

el pueblo, town; **el pueblecito,** small town.

el papá, papa; **el papaíto,** papa (term of endearment).

poco, little; **poquito,** very little.

-illo, -(e)cillo (and feminine forms). These express smallness and also indifference or ridicule.

e.g., **el secreto,** secret; **el secretillo,** little secret.

un autor, author; **un autorcillo,** petty author.

-uelo, -(e)zuelo (and feminine forms). These express smallness and sometimes ridicule and scorn.

e.g., **la plaza,** square; **la plazuela,** little square.

el rey, king; **el reyezuelo,** petty king.

N.B. The forms, **-cito, -cillo,** and **-zuelo** are usually only added to words of more than one syllable ending in **-n** or **-r.**

> *e.g.,* **jovencito, autorcillo,** etc.

Note that if the word ends in **-e,** the addition is **-cito (-a).**
> *e.g.,* **madrecita**

Augmentative Suffixes

-ón (-ona), -azo (-aza). These often express, in addition to largeness, awkwardness or grotesqueness.

> *e.g.,* **silla,** chair; **sillón,** armchair.
> **mujer,** woman; **mujerona,** big, strapping woman.

-ote. This suffix usually expresses largeness in a deprecia-tory sense.

> *e.g.,* **lugar,** place; **lugarote,** ugly village.

N.B. **un ratón,** mouse; **un islote,** a small barren island.

Other augmentative suffixes are **-ajo, -acho, -uco, -ucho.** These often express contempt or poor quality.

> *e.g.,* **cuarto,** room; **cuartucho,** miserable room.
> **vino,** wine; **vinacho,** poor wine.

Exercises

1. The Thames passes through London, the capital of England. 2. The tribes wandered through the country. 3. Do you like my aunt's flowers? 4. We have had many crises lately. 5. The tram always stops here. 6. You should obey the laws of your country. 7. The guide sent me to the parish priest. 8. I shall explain the difficulty. 9. Little John often breaks his pencils. 10. My cousin lives in a delightful little square in a small town in Andalusia. 11. Rubies are red, emeralds are green. 12. The driver was a huge man who had a loud voice. 13. Apple-trees sometimes have small roots. 14. Our bees give us a lot of honey. 15. You can buy cigar-ettes in that little shop. 16. Can you speak German? Just a little. 17. I like that new arm-chair in the little drawing-room.

18. Daddy, may I listen to the wireless to-night? 19. Every day aeroplanes fly over our house. 20. There are Frenchmen, Spaniards, and Germans in this hotel.

6. PERSONAL "A"

The preposition **a** is used before a direct object of a verb when that object is:

(*a*) A noun which denotes a definite person or personified thing.

> *e.g.,* **Conozco a sus padres,** I know your parents.
> **Teme a la Muerte,** he fears Death. (But, if there is no personification of the idea of death, it would be: *Teme la muerte.*)

(*b*) A noun which denotes a specific intelligent animal.

> *e.g.,* **He perdido a mi perro,** I have lost my dog. (But *he perdido mi perro* might be used.)

(*c*) Any of the following pronouns referring to a person or persons: **alguien, alguno, uno, ninguno, ambos, cada uno, cualquiera, cuantos, los demás, otro, todo, cual, quién, quien, éste,** etc.; **ése,** etc.; **aquél,** etc.; **el que (la que,** etc.); **el cual (la cual,** etc.); **nadie.**

> *e.g.,* ¿**Ha visto Vd. a alguien? A nadie,** have you seen anyone? No one.
> ¿**A quién ha encontrado Vd.?,** whom have you met?

(*d*) A collective noun representing persons. (This rule is not always strictly observed.)

> *e.g.,* **Vi a una muchedumbre cerca de la iglesia,** I saw a crowd near the church.

Exercises

1. I don't know your elder sister. 2. Did you recognize my friend, Henry? 3. Help that poor old man who has fallen

down. 4. I love my little dog. 5. I am looking for a good servant. 6. I sent Peter to talk to you. 7. He dreamt he saw Death. 8. I didn't hit John but his brother. 9. Mother often scolds my little sister. 10. Whom did you see. at the theatre? 11. You ought to listen to your father. 12. We are going to send Federico away. 13. Stop that thief! Call a policeman! 14. We found someone who spoke Spanish. 15. I left the others. Then I met an old friend.

7. NUMBERS

Cardinal Numbers

0	cero	30	treinta
1	un(o), -a	31	treinta y un(o), -a
2	dos	40	cuarenta
3	tres	50	cincuenta
4	cuatro	60	sesenta
5	cinco	70	setenta
6	seis	80	ochenta
7	siete	90	noventa
8	ocho	100	ciento
9	nueve	101	ciento un(o), -a
10	diez	102	ciento dos
11	once	200	doscientos, -as
12	doce	300	trescientos, -as
13	trece	400	cuatrocientos, -as
14	catorce	500	quinientos, -as
15	quince	600	seiscientos, -as
16	dieciséis	700	setecientos, -as
17	diecisiete	800	ochocientos, -as
18	dieciocho	900	novecientos, -as
19	diecinueve	1000	mil
20	veinte	100,000	cien mil
21	veintiun(o), -a	1,000,000	un millón
22	veintidós	2,000,000	dos millones

Notes. 1. dieciséis to diecinueve can be written diez y seis, etc., and similarly, veintiuno to veintinueve may be written veinte y uno, etc., but this is very old-fashioned.

2. **Uno** becomes **un** before a masculine singular noun and **ciento** becomes **cien** before any noun but not before a number.

> *e.g.*, **un libro**, one (*or* a) book; **cien lápices**, a hundred
> pencils; **cien plumas**, a hundred pens.
> *But* **ciento cincuenta y cuatro**, a (*or* one) hundred and
> fifty-four.

3. **Ciento** and **mil** can be used in the plural as collective nouns, although **centenar** and **millar** are also used.

> *e.g.*, **cientos** (or **centenares**) **de hombres,** hundreds of
> men.
> **miles** (or **millares**) **de hombres,** thousands of men.

N.B. **un millón de hombres,** a million men.

4. Note carefully that counting by hundreds does not go beyond the nine hundreds.

> *e.g.*, **mil quinientos,** fifteen hundred; **mil novecientos
> sesenta,** 1960.

5. Note **veintiún días,** twenty-one days. **Veintiuna
semanas,** twenty-one weeks.

6. Note that **y** is only used between tens and units.

> *e.g.*, **ciento cuarenta y tres,** a hundred and forty-three.

7. **Ó** meaning 'or' bears a written accent following a number ending in zero.

> *e.g.*, 1700 **ó** 1800 **hombres,** seventeen or eighteen
> hundred men.

Ordinal Numbers

1st	**primer(o), -a, -os, -as**	9th	**noveno, -a, -os, -as**
2nd	**segundo**	10th	**décimo**
3rd	**tercer(o)**	11th	**undécimo**
4th	**cuarto**	12th	**duodécimo**
5th	**quinto**	13th	**décimotercero**
6th	**sexto**	19th	**décimonono**
7th	**séptimo**	20th	**vigésimo**
8th	**octavo**	30th	**trigésimo**

Notes. 1. **Primero** and **tercero** drop the ending **-o** before a masculine singular noun.

> *e.g.,* **el primer ejercicio,** the first exercise; **el tercer capítulo,** the third chapter.

2. The Spanish ordinals above **duodécimo** are rarely used. The tendency is to use the cardinals even from **segundo** to **duodécimo.** Cardinals thus used follow the noun.

> *e.g.,* **el siglo quince,** the fifteenth century.

3. With names of kings, etc., the ordinals are not used after **décimo.**

> *e.g.,* **Enrique octavo,** Henry the Eighth.
> **Luis quince,** Louis the Fifteenth.

Collective Nouns

The following are the most commonly used: **un par,** a pair; **una docena,** a dozen; **una centena** (or **un centenar**), a hundred; **un millar,** a thousand; **una gruesa,** a gross.

N.B. All these collectives require **de** with a noun.

> *e.g.,* **un par de guantes,** a pair of gloves.
> **una docena de lápices,** a dozen pencils.

Fractions

$\frac{1}{2}$, **un medio;** $\frac{1}{3}$, **un tercio;** $\frac{1}{4}$, **un cuarto;** $\frac{1}{5}$, **un quinto** (or **la quinta parte**); $\frac{1}{10}$, **un décimo** (or **la décima parte**).

N.B. **una vez,** once; **dos veces,** twice, etc.; **sendos,** one apiece.

Time, Dates, Age, Measure, Weather

Time

> **¿Qué hora es?** what time is it?
> **Es la una,** it is one o'clock.
> **Son las dos,** it is two o'clock.

Es la una y cinco, it is five (minutes) past one.
Son las seis y cuarto, it is a quarter past six.
Son las ocho y media, it is half-past eight.
Son las nueve menos veinte, it is twenty (minutes) to nine.
Son las diez menos cuarto, it is a quarter to ten.

Note these expressions:

A las ocho de la mañana, at eight in the morning (a.m.).
A las tres de la tarde, at three in the afternoon (p.m.).
A eso de las siete, at about seven o'clock.
Son cerca de las once, it is nearly eleven o'clock.
A (or al) mediodía, at noon.
A (or a la) media noche (medianoche), at midnight.
A las doce (del día) en punto, at twelve sharp.
Está dando la una, it is striking one.
Están dando las cuatro (de la tarde), it is striking four.
De día, in the daytime.
De noche, by night.
Al amanecer, at dawn.
Al anochecer, at nightfall.
Al atardecer, al caer de la tarde, at dusk.

Days of the Week

el domingo, Sunday
el lunes, Monday
el martes, Tuesday
el miércoles, Wednesday
el jueves, Thursday
el viernes, Friday
el sábado, Saturday

The Months

enero, January	**julio,** July
febrero, February	**agosto,** August
marzo, March	**septiembre,** September
abril, April	**octubre,** October
mayo, May	**noviembre,** November
junio, June	**diciembre,** December

The Seasons

    el invierno, winter   **la primavera,** spring
    el verano, summer   **el otoño,** autumn

Notes. 1. English 'on' is never expressed in Spanish before days or dates.

    e.g., **Salieron (el) martes,** they left on Tuesday.
        Salían los martes, they used to leave on Tuesdays.

2. Cardinal numbers, except for the 1st (**el primero**), are used for days of the month in Spanish.

    e.g., **el primero de agosto,** (on) the 1st of August.
        el once de enero de mil novecientos sesenta, (on) January 11th, 1960.

Note these expressions:

¿A cuántos (or a cómo) estamos hoy?   what day of the month is it?
¿Qué día del mes tenemos?

Hoy estamos a dos (de marzo), to-day is the 2nd (of March).
El sábado pasado, last Saturday.
Anoche, last night.
Mañana, to-morrow.
Pasado mañana, the day after to-morrow.
Mañana por la mañana, to-morrow morning.
Mañana por la tarde, to-morrow evening.
Ayer, yesterday.
Anteayer, the day before yesterday.
La víspera, the day before (the eve).
Al otro día, the next day.
Al día siguiente, the next day.
Ocho días, a week.
Quince días, a fortnight.
Muchos años ha, many years ago.

Age

    ¿Cuántos años tiene Vd.? how old are you?
    ¿Qué edad tiene Vd.? how old are you?

Tengo veinte años, I am twenty (years old).

Su (día de) cumpleaños es el primero de mayo, his birthday is on the 1st of May.

Dimension

La habitación tiene siete metros de alto (or **de altura**)**, quince metros de largo** (or **de longitud**) **y diez metros de ancho** (or **de anchura**)**,** the room is seven metres high, fifteen metres long and ten metres wide.

una habitación de diez metros de ancho (or **de anchura**)**,** a room ten metres wide.

Weather

¿Qué tiempo hace? what is the weather like?

Hace (mucho) calor, it is (very) hot.

Hace (mucho) frío, it is (very) cold.

Hace buen tiempo, it is fine (**el tiempo es bueno** is also possible).

Hace fresco, it is cool.

Hace viento, it is windy.

Hace mal tiempo, it is bad weather.

Hace un tiempo muy feo, it is dirty weather.

Hace un tiempo encantador, it is glorious weather.

Hay sol, it is sunny.

Hay luna, the moon is shining.

Hay niebla, it is foggy.

Hay neblina, it is misty.

Hay polvo, it is dusty.

Hay lodo, it is muddy.

Exercises

1. Fifteen hundred people were present at the ceremony. 2. One hundred thousand people have visited France this summer. 3. Millions of pupils drink milk at school. 4. I know nothing about the sixteenth century. 5. Twenty-one days have passed since the accident. 6. Hundreds of aeroplanes flew over the town. 7. It is striking seven; I must get

up. 8. On the twenty-first page there is a portrait of Louis
the Fifteenth. 9. It is now twenty-seven minutes to eight.
10. I am going to meet my friend at a quarter to one sharp.
11. At about half-past six last night the telegram arrived.
12. In the hall we found a dozen pairs of gloves. 13. Two
years ago, we were living in London. 14. It was very foggy
the next day. 15. The meeting will take place on Thursday
at 8.30 P.M. 16. To-day is the twenty-first of August. 17.
To-morrow morning we shall study the first chapter. 18. They
will spend at least a week on the coast. 19. On the first of
March, the day after to-morrow, I shall have news. 20.
Several years ago I always used to wake up at dawn. 21.
When is your birthday? It is on Tuesday, the sixteenth of
July. 22. I was eighteen on Friday, the day before yesterday.
23. The garage is ten metres long and six metres wide. 24. It
was very hot at noon but it was quite cold at midnight.
25 I shall play tennis to-morrow if it isn't too windy.

8. ADJECTIVES

Formation of Feminines

With adjectives ending in -o, -o becomes -a.

> *e.g.,* **rojO** becomes **rojA.**

Other adjectives do not change, except as in (*a*) and (*b*)
below.

> *e.g.,* **una ciudad tropical,** a tropical town.

Note. (*a*) Adjectives of nationality add -a.

> *e.g.,* **español** becomes **española.**
> **inglés** becomes **inglesa.**

> (*b*) Adjectives ending in -án, -ón, -or, -ín, add -a
> (except comparatives).

> *e.g.,* **malgastador** becomes **malgastadora.**
> *But* **la mejor alumna,** the best pupil.

Agreement of Adjectives

Adjectives agree with nouns in gender and in number.

e.g., **Las cosas interesantes,** interesting things.
Los lápices azules, blue pencils.

When the same adjective is used to qualify two or more nouns of different genders, it is normally masculine.

e.g., **El hombre y la mujer están cansados,** the man and the woman are tired.

Comparison of Adjectives

Comparative: **más** plus adjective.
Superlative: **el(la) más** plus adjective.

e.g., **hermoso,** beautiful; **más hermoso(-a),** more beautiful; **el(la) más hermoso(-a),** most beautiful.

N.B. If the superlative follows the noun the article is omitted.

e.g., **Los libros más divertidos que he leído** (NOT **los más divertidos**), the most amusing books I have read.

The 'Absolute' Superlative

When there is no comparison the superlative is expressed by **muy** plus adjective, or by adding **-ísimo** (**-ísima,** etc.) to the stem of the adjective.

e.g., **Esta historia es muy triste,** this story is very sad.
Un regalo utilísimo, a very (or most) useful present.

N.B. There are spelling changes in certain superlatives in **-ísimo(-a).**
noble: nobilísimo(-a). rico: riquísimo(-a).

Note. (*a*) After a superlative 'in' is translated by **de.**

e.g., **Ella es la alumna más bonita de la clase,** she is the prettiest pupil in the class.

(*b*) 'Most,' followed by a noun, is **la mayor parte de.**

e.g., **La mayor parte de las manzanas están maduras,** most of the apples are ripe.

Irregular Comparisons

grande, big	**mayor,** bigger	**el(la) mayor,** biggest
pequeño, small	**menor,** smaller	**el(la) menor,** smallest
bueno, good	**mejor,** better	**el(la) mejor,** best
malo, bad	**peor,** worse	**el(la) peor,** worst
alto, high	**más alto,** higher **superior**	**el(la) más alto(-a),** highest **el(la) superior**
bajo, low	**más bajo,** lower **inferior**	**el(la) más bajo(-a),** lowest **el(la) inferior**

Note that ALL the irregular comparisons also have a regular form. Either (**el**) **mayor** or (**el**) **más grande** may be used for 'bigger, biggest.' (**El**) **mayor** also means 'older, oldest.'

(**El**) **menor** is less frequently used than (**el**) **más pequeño** in the sense of 'smaller, smallest.' In speaking of children, either can be used to mean 'younger, youngest,' but in speaking of adults, (**el**) **más joven** is more usual.

Position of Adjectives

Adjectives usually follow the noun.

e.g., **un perro negro,** a black dog.

Bueno, malo, grande (when not referring to size) precede the noun.

e.g., **una buena historia,** a good story.

An adjective which has no distinguishing force usually precedes the noun.

e.g., **la blanca nieve,** the white snow.

The following adjectives have different meanings according to whether they precede or follow the noun:

	Preceding	*Following*
bueno	good	worthy
cierto	(a) certain	sure, true
grande	great, fine	large
nuevo	fresh	new
pobre	poor (expressing pity)	poor (meaning impecunious)

Comparisons of Equality and Inequality

tan . . . como, $\begin{cases} \text{so . . . as.} \\ \text{as . . . as.} \end{cases}$

> *e.g.*, **Es tan perezoso como su hermano,** he is as lazy as his brother.

tanto (-a, -os, -as) . . . como, $\begin{cases} \text{so much, many . . . as.} \\ \text{as much, many . . . as.} \end{cases}$

> *e.g.*, **No tengo tantas plumas como mi hermana,** I haven't as many pens as my sister.

más . . . que, more . . . than.
menos . . . que, less . . . than.

> *e.g.*, **Bebe más agua que yo,** he drinks more water than I.
> **Soy menos inteligente que él,** I am not so (less) clever as he (is).

Note. When the second term of the comparison is a clause, **del (de la, de los, de las) que** is used instead of **que** if the comparison is made with a noun.

> *e.g.*, **Tiene más dinero del que dice,** he has more money than he says.

De lo que is used instead of **que** if there is no noun acting as a point of comparison.

> *e.g.*, **Tiene más de lo que dice,** he has more than he says.
> **Es más valiente de lo que creía,** he is braver than I thought.

Note. After **más** and **menos** before a numeral (when no comparison is made) 'than' is translated by **de**. In the negative, however, **no . . . más que** is practically always used.

> *e.g.*, **Juan tiene más de mil sellos,** John has more than a thousand stamps.
> **No tengo más que dos,** I haven't more than two, I have only two.

Note the following:

cuanto (-a, -os, -as) más (menos) . . . tanto (-a, -os, -as)
más (menos), the more (less) . . . the more (less).

> *e.g.,* **Cuantas más plumas tiene, tantas más (plumas)
> pierde,** the more pens he has, the more he loses.

Adverbially this construction becomes:

$$\text{cuanto }\genfrac{}{}{0pt}{}{\text{más}}{\text{menos}} \ldots \text{tanto }\genfrac{}{}{0pt}{}{\text{más.}}{\text{menos.}}$$

> *e.g.,* **Cuanto más tiene, (tanto) más quiere,** the more he
> has, the more he wants.

Cada vez más renders 'more and more.'

> *e.g.,* **Se hace cada vez más frío,** or **Hace cada vez más
> frío,** it is getting colder and colder.

Apocopation of Adjectives

**Uno, primero, tercero, alguno, ninguno, bueno, malo,
postrero,** drop the ending **-o** when they immediately precede
a masculine singular noun.

> *e.g.,* **el primer ejercicio,** the first exercise.
> **no tengo ningún amigo,** I have no friend.

N.B. **Grande** drops the **-de** and **cualquiera** the **-a** before
any singular noun.

> *e.g.,* **un gran soldado,** a great soldier; **una gran caja,**
> a big box; **cualquier hombre,** any man.

Ciento drops the **-to** before a noun.

> *e.g.,* **cien lápices,** a hundred pencils; **cien plumas,** a
> hundred pens.

Santo becomes **San** before a proper noun (except before
Domingo, Tomás, Tomé).

> *e.g.,* **San Pablo,** Saint Paul, *but* **Santo Tomás,** Saint
> Thomas.

Exercises

1. The English actress; Spanish wine; German cars.
2. Red flowers; lazy children; blue pencils. 3. An English
boy and girl arrived yesterday. 4. She is ugly like her young
sister. 5. I am reading an interesting and amusing book.
6. A long story; a longer story; the longest story. 7. The
trees give cool shade in summer. 8. Ripe apples and pears
are delicious. 9. The prettiest child in the class. 10. Conchita
is younger than Teresa but older than Rosita. 11. I haven't
as many ties as you but I have more than five hundred stamps.
12. What a wonderful harvest after so much rain. 13. The
more letters you write, the more you receive. 14. The white
snow fell on the green fields. 15. She is getting fatter and
fatter. 16. He put a hundred postcards in a big box. 17.
There are more than ninety apples on that apple-tree. 18. It
was a great day for the great general. 19. Most of the guests
came on the third day. 20. St Peter was a fisherman. 21. She
is as lazy as her friend. 22. I haven't learnt as many poems
as you. 23. You have more hats than you need. 24. There
is no light in the small room. 25. His uncle has more horses
than he says.

9. ADVERBS

Formation

Add -mente to the feminine singular of the adjective.

> *e.g.*, **ligero,** light; **ligeramente,** lightly.
> **insolente,** insolent; **insolentemente,** insolently.
> **rápido,** quick; **rápidamente,** quickly.

> *Note.* (a) Some adjectives are also used as adverbs.

> *e.g.*, **bajo,** low; **barato,** cheap, cheaply; **bastante,**
> quite, fairly, enough; **pronto,** quick, soon.

> (b) **Con** with a noun is often preferred to the form
> in -mente.

> *e.g.*, **Con orgullo** (proudly) may be used instead of
> **orgullosamente.**

Comparison

The Superlative adverb is formed with **lo,** but the **lo** is generally omitted.

> *e.g.,* **fácilmente,** easily; **más fácilmente,** more easily; **(lo) más fácilmente,** most easily:

Irregular Formations

bien, well	**mejor,** better, best
mal, badly	**peor,** worse, worst
mucho, much	**más,** more
poco, little	**menos,** less, least

The 'Absolute' Superlative

Add -**mente** to the feminine singular of the 'absolute' superlative adjective.

> *e.g.,* **fortísimamente,** very strongly, most strongly.
> **riquísimamente,** very richly, most richly.

These adverbs are sometimes very long, *e.g.,* **impacientísimamente,** and forms like **muy impacientemente** or **con mucha impaciencia** are often preferred.

Comparisons of equality and inequality: as adjectives.

Some Notes on Adverbs

1. When two adverbs follow each other, only the last one takes -**mente.**

> *e.g.,* **Escribe lenta y legiblemente,** he writes slowly and legibly.

2. **Recientemente** becomes **recién** before a past participle used as adjective or noun.

> *e.g.,* **un paquete recién llegado,** a parcel recently come.
> **el recién llegado,** the new arrival.

3. **Ya** usually means 'already,' 'presently,' 'now,' but it is often used for emphasis or to round off a phrase, and then it cannot adequately be translated into English.

e.g., **Ya he acabado mi trabajo,** I have already finished
my work.

Ya entiendo, now I understand.

Ya veremos, we'll see presently.

¡Ya lo creo! of course!

4. **Muy** translates 'very' (or 'much') before adverbs and
adjectives. It is never used alone.

e.g., **Estoy muy enfermo,** I am very ill.

Escribe muy mal, he writes very badly.

Estoy muy agradecido, I am much obliged.

But **Parece muy perezoso. Sí, mucho.** He seems very
lazy. Yes, very.

Mucho translates 'much' and also translates 'very' in
expressions where Spanish has a noun instead of an adjective.

e.g., **Juan es mucho más grande que yo,** John is much
bigger than I am.

Tengo mucha hambre, I am very hungry.

Hace mucho calor, it is very hot.

Muchísimo translates 'very much.'

e.g., **Me gusta muchísimo el español,** I like Spanish very
much (indeed).

5. **Demasiado** (meaning 'too much') renders in Spanish the
English 'too' before an adjective. (N.B. **demasiado** is sometimes used as an adjective.)

e.g., **Estoy demasiado cansada para trabajar,** I am too
tired to work.

Tiene demasiados libros, he has too many books.

6. **Donde** (meaning 'where'), when used with a verb of
motion, is usually preceded by a preposition.

e.g., **¿Adónde va Vd.?** where are you going?

No sabíamos de dónde llegaban, we didn't know
where they were coming from.

¿Por dónde va Vd.? which way are you going?

N.B. **Adonde** is generally written as one word nowadays.

A block of flats in Madrid in baroque style
By kind permission of the Spanish Tourist Office

Lastres, on the Asturian coast. See page 54.
By kind permission of the Spanish Tourist Office

Note the following adverbial expressions:

a (la) derecha, on the right
a (la) izquierda, on the left
al fin, at last
de pronto, suddenly
de veras, really
por lo tanto, consequently
de vez en cuando, from time to time
poco a poco, little by little
aquí dentro, in here
tal vez, perhaps
he aquí, here is, here are
ahora mismo, right now
ahí mismo, right there
tanto tiempo, so long
raras veces, seldom

a menudo, often
muchas veces, often
mucho tiempo, a long time
hace poco (tiempo), a short time ago
ayer mismo, only yesterday
de buena gana, willingly
hoy día, nowadays
por supuesto) of course
desde luego) of course
cuando más, at most
cuando menos, at least
cuanto antes, as soon as possible
allí arriba, up there
más arriba, farther up

Position of Adverbs

Adverbs usually follow verbs but may precede the verb for emphasis.

e.g., **Ella está a menudo perezosa,** she is often lazy.
Siempre escribe cartas, she is *always* writing letters.

Exercises

1. Antonio reads worse than his younger brother. 2. He speaks clearly, but not so clearly as his sister. 3. I like this story very much indeed. 4. He always works very slowly. 5. He often plays the piano better than you. 6. She does little, he does less. 7. Now I understand; you have explained it much better. 8. He finished it only yesterday. 9. He works more diligently than his elder brother. 10. My friend stupidly replied: "Yes!" 11. He always speaks slowly and carefully. 12. The recently arrived guest is my father's cousin. 13. Luis is too sad to say very much. 14. Nowadays, of course, everybody has to do more than before. 15. Really, I don't know where he has come from.

10. POSSESSIVE ADJECTIVES AND PRONOUNS

ADJECTIVES			PRONOUNS		
Singular	*Plural*	*English*	*Singular*	*Plural*	*English*
mi	mis	my	el mío la mía	los míos las mías	mine
tu	tus	your	el tuyo la tuya	los tuyos las tuyas	yours
su	sus	his, her, its your	el suyo la suya	los suyos las suyas	his, hers, its, yours
nuestro (-a)	nuestros (-as)	our	el nuestro la nuestra	los nuestros las nuestras	ours
vuestro (-a)	vuestros (-as)	your	el vuestro la vuestra	los vuestros las vuestras	yours
su	sus	their, your	el suyo la suya	los suyos las suyas	theirs, yours

Notes. (a) To avoid ambiguity, **su, sus** with a noun can be replaced by the definite article with the noun followed by **de él** or **de ella** or **de Vd.** (also plural forms).

> *e.g.,* **Su libro** means 'his, her, their, *or* your book,' but **el libro de él** means 'his book,' **el libro de ella** means 'her book,' etc. **Su libro de él,** etc. may also be used.

(b) The pronouns agree in gender and number with the nouns for which they stand. Thus for each pronoun there are four forms, **el mío, la mía, los míos, las mías,** etc.

> *e.g.,* **mi amigo y el suyo,** my friend and his (hers, yours).
> **mi amiga y la suya,** my friend and his (hers, yours).

N.B. To avoid ambiguity, **el (la,** etc.**) de él (de ella,** etc.**),** are often used for **el suyo (la suya,** etc.**).**

e.g., **mi amigo y el de él,** my friend and his.
   mi amiga y la de ella, my friend and hers, etc.

(*c*) The article is often omitted after **ser.**

e.g., **Estos zapatos son míos,** these shoes are mine.

(*d*) The pronoun form without the article is used when directly addressing a person and to express the English 'of mine,' 'of yours,' etc. When thus used they follow the noun.

e.g., **muy señores míos,** dear Sirs (in letters).
   un amigo suyo, a friend of yours (of his, of hers).
   cierto vecino nuestro, a certain neighbour of ours.

(*e*) **Lo mío** renders 'what is mine,' my property, etc.; **los míos** means 'my people,' *i.e.*, my relatives; **los suyos** means 'his men,' etc.

Exercises

1. My friends are here, yours are coming later. 2. You must do your homework and help Carmen do hers. 3. Here are some shoes: they are not mine, are they his? 4. Her parents have invited our class to have tea with them. 5. A friend of mine has just arrived from Canada. 6. Your children are not as tall as mine. 7. Our school and yours are very different. 8. My cousins and hers live in the same street. 9. I can't read her writing but yours is very clear. 10. My uncle gave the beggar some clothes of his. 11. I don't know that neighbour of yours. 12. Send me that photograph of his! 13. Our dog is more intelligent than theirs. 14. These books are mine; yours are there. 15. "Finish your exercise, Anita," said her teacher.

11. PERSONAL PRONOUNS

Subject		Direct Object		Indirect Object		Prepositional Form	
yo	I	me	me	me	to me	(para) mí	(for) me
tú	you	te	you	te	to you	ti	you
él	he, it	le, lo	him, it	le ⎫	to him	él	him
ella	she, it	la	her, it	le ⎪	to her	ella	her
Vd.	you	le, la	you	le ⎬	to it	Vd.	you
				le ⎭	to you	sí	himself (etc.)
nosotros (-as)	we	nos	us	nos	to us	nosotros (-as)	us
vosotros (-as)	you	os	you	os	to you	vosotros (-as)	you
ellos	they	los ⎫	them	les	to them	ellos	them
ellas	they	las ⎬		les		ellas	them
Vds.	you	les ⎭	you	les	to you	Vds.	you

Notes. (*a*) 3rd person Direct Object Pronouns, *i.e.*, 'him,' 'her,' 'it,' 'them,' 'you,' (with **usted(es)**):

Singular	*Plural*
Masc. **le**—for persons	**les** or **los**—for persons
lo—for things	**los**—for things
Fem. **la**—for persons or things	**las**—for persons or things

N.B. Spaniards do not agree on this rule and tend to use the 3rd person Object Pronouns rather indiscriminately. The above represents the best guidance that can be offered.

(*b*) Note that, although **a** appears before the personal noun-object (see Personal **a**, *p*. 84), when a pronoun is substituted it is generally the Direct Object form that is used before the Verb, not the Indirect.

e.g., **La vi**, I saw her (*not* **le vi**).

(*c*) Reflexive pronouns are the same as the Direct Object pronouns, except of the 3rd person, singular and plural, **se**. The corresponding prepositional form is **sí**.

(*d*) Personal Object pronouns usually precede the verb but when the verb is an Infinitive, a Present Participle, or a positive Imperative (or Subjunctive used imperatively), the Object Pronoun follows the verb and is joined to it.

> *e.g.*, **Voy a enviarlo** (or **lo voy a enviar**), I am going to send it.
> **Estoy escribiéndolo** (or **lo estoy escribiendo**), I am writing it.
> **¡ Envíelo (Vd.) !**, send it !

(*e*) When an Indirect Object noun of a person follows the verb an Indirect Object pronoun is used as well with the verb.

> *e.g.*, **Le dije a mi padre las noticias**, I told my father the news.

Similarly, when a Direct Object noun precedes the verb a Direct Object Pronoun is used as well with the verb.

> *e.g.*, **Todas las dificultades de Vd. las comprendo perfectamente**, I understand all your difficulties perfectly.

(*f*) **Ello** [neuter, meaning 'it'] as subject is rarely used except in the expression, **ello es que . . .**, the fact is that . . . .
Ello after a preposition translates 'it' (indefinite).

> *e.g.*, **No pienso en ello**, I don't think of it.

Position of Object Pronouns

When two pronouns are used with a verb, the indirect object always precedes the direct object.

> *e.g.*, **Vd. me lo da**, you are giving it to me.

When two pronouns of the 3rd person are used with the verb, the first is changed to **se**.

> *e.g.*, **Vd. se lo da**, you are giving it to him (to her, to them).

N.B. To avoid ambiguity or for emphasis, **a él, a Vd., a ellos, a ellas**, may be added.

> *e.g.*, **Vd. se lo da a él**, you are giving it to him.

The prepositional form of the personal pronoun is chiefly used after a preposition. **Entre,** however, is usually followed by the subject pronouns.

> *e.g.,* **con ella,** with her.
> **para Vd.,** for you.
> **sin mí,** without me.
> **entre Vd. y yo,** between you and me.

This form is also used to emphasize a subject or object pronoun.

> *e.g.,* **Me lo enviaron a mí, no a él,** they sent it to me, not to him.

N.B. **conmigo,** with me; **contigo,** with you; **consigo,** with himself, herself, themselves.

Note the following uses of the neuter pronoun **lo:**

(a) It replaces the adjective complement of a verb.

> *e.g.,* **Su cara está sucia y lo estaba ayer,** your face is dirty and was (so) yesterday.

(b) It replaces the noun complement of **ser.**

> *e.g.,* **¿ Es ella enfermera? Lo es.** Is she a nurse? She is.

It is commonly found that certain authors add the object pronouns to the verb in all tenses of the Indicative. This practice is a matter of style and is best avoided by the student.

> *e.g.,* **Hiciéronlo así** instead of **Lo hicieron así,** they did it in that way.

Exercises

1. I shall send it to him to-morrow. 2. Where is my new tie? You have left it in the shop. 3. I must return it to her. 4. We don't like repeating it too often. 5. He hasn't yet given the present to his father; he will give it to him to-morrow. 6. Please send them to me as soon as possible. 7. Lend it to us! don't lend it to them! 8. Speak to me

softly! I will listen to you. 9. Picking it up, he fell down.
10. Don't make fun of me! 11. Come with me and help me
to finish it! 12. They shouldn't have sent it to us, but to
them. 13. Between you and me, he cannot do it. 14. "Did
you bring the letter with you?" her father asked her. 15.
Don't worry her! She is cutting it. 16. They approached us
quietly, smiling at us. 17. Listen to me! Don't show it to
her yet! 18. Let us not tell them anything! They never tell
us. 19. I cannot help you to do it without him. 20. I should
like to tell him so but I dare not. 21. She was a school-
mistress, it seems? Yes, she was. 22. You are pale to-day,
and were yesterday. 23. Is your brother a doctor? Yes, he
is. 24. Do you know my sister who is a shop-assistant?
Yes, I know her well. 25. I am giving it back to her, without
telling her why.

12. DEMONSTRATIVE ADJECTIVES AND PRONOUNS

Adjectives

Singular		Plural		Singular		Plural	
Masc.	este this	estos these	ese aquel } that		esos aquellos } those	
Fem.	esta this	estas these	esa aquella } that		esas aquellas } those	

Note. **Ese,** etc., means that which is near or referring to
the person addressed, 'that, just there.'

Aquel, etc., means that which is away from the speaker and
from the person addressed, 'that, over there, over yonder.'

Pronouns

(a) The pronoun form is the same as the adjective except
that it bears an accent on the stressed vowel.[1]

Éste, etc., means 'this one'; **ése,** etc., means 'that one';
aquél, etc., means 'that one.'

[1] The *Nuevas Normas* of 1959 make this optional in some cases, but
the student is advised to retain the accent.

(*b*) The neuter forms **esto, eso, aquello** (N.B. no accent), refer to an indefinite antecedent and not to any definite noun used previously.

> *e.g.,* ¿**Le gustaría a Vd. ver aquello?** would you like to see that?

(*c*) **Éste** (**ésta,** etc.) often means 'the latter'; **aquél** (**aquélla,** etc.) often means 'the former.'

(*d*) 'That of,' 'the one of,' etc., is rendered by:

> **el** (**la, lo, los, las**) **de** followed by a noun.
> **el** (**la, lo, los, las**) **que** followed by a clause.

> *e.g.,* **La silla de acero y la de madera,** the steel chair and the wooden one.
> **Esta niña es la que Vd. buscaba,** this girl is the one you were looking for.
> **Mi sombrero y el de Juan,** my hat and John's.

N.B. 'He who,' 'she who,' etc., are also rendered by **el que, la que,** etc.

> *e.g.,* **El que trabaja mucho, merece el éxito,** he who works hard deserves success.

(*e*) **Esto de, eso de, aquello de,** renders the English 'the fact of,' 'the fact that,' 'the matter of,' etc.

> *e.g.,* **Esto del gusto es muy difícil,** this matter of taste is very difficult.

Exercises

1. This house is larger than that one opposite. 2. These apples are sweeter than those. 3. You cannot deny that, can you? 4. I like that poem, it is shorter than this one. 5. Peter's cousin and Mary are here; the latter is younger than the former. 6. Those stamps are more valuable than these, aren't they? 7. Pilar knows that girl who lives near that aunt of yours. 8. This is good. I like listening to this. 9. Those soldiers you saw belong to that regiment from the South. 10. The silk dress and the cotton one are in my room.

11. Go and fetch the glass jug and the porcelain one. 12. He who said that is very stupid. 13. Not that cup! Bring the one I described to you. 14. Those who do nothing don't need rest. 15. This matter of homework is very difficult.

13. RELATIVE PRONOUNS AND ADJECTIVES

(a) **Que** (pronoun) translates 'who,' 'whom,' 'which,' 'that.'

> *e.g.*, **El profesor que hablaba,** the master who was speaking.
> **La historia que Vd. oyó,** the story (which, that) you heard.

N.B. The relative pronoun must never be omitted in Spanish as it often is in English.

(b) After a preposition, **quien, quienes** is used for persons; or the following pronouns can be used for persons and things:

> **el cual, la cual, los cuales, las cuales.**
> **el que, la que, los que, las que.**

There is no difference in use between these pronouns except that after **sin, por, tras,** and any preposition of more than one syllable, **el cual** tends to be preferred to **el que.**

> *e.g.*, **El hombre del que (de quien, del cual) hablamos,** the man of whom we are speaking.
> **Los edificios en los que estaba trabajando,** the buildings on which he was working.
> **La iglesia enfrente de la cual se reunió la muchedumbre,** the church in front of which the crowd gathered.

Note that when any of these pronouns is an object referring to a person, it must be preceded by **a.**

> *e.g.*, **El hombre al que (a quien, al cual) buscamos,** the man we are looking for.

After **en** and **de, que** may be used instead of **el cual,** or **el que,** but in modern Spanish there is an increasing tendency to use the latter forms instead.

(c) **Cuyo (-a, -os, -as)** (adjective) translates 'whose.'

> e.g., **Los obreros cuyas herramientas estaban perdidas . . .,** the workmen whose tools were lost . . . .

(d) **Lo que** and **lo cual** translate 'what.' **Todo lo que** and **todo lo cual** translate 'all,' 'all that.'

> e.g., **No escuché lo que dijo,** I didn't listen to what he said.
> **Todo lo que sé es que . . .,** all I know is that . . . .

N.B. **Lo que** (or **lo cual**) translates 'which' referring to a whole clause.

> e.g., **Ella llora siempre, lo que** (or **lo cual**) **es extraño,** she is always weeping, which is strange.

(e) **Cuanto** (neuter) translates 'all that'; **cuantos (-as)** translates 'all (those) who.'

> e.g., **Quería decirle a Vd. cuanto he hecho,** I wanted to tell you all I have done.
> **Quería enviarlo a cuantos lo han merecido,** I wanted to send it to all who have deserved it.

Exercises

1. The oranges you bought were very dear. 2. The girl I saw yesterday in the train was very like your sister. 3. The man for whom you work is very young. 4. The museum in which you saw those fine statues no longer exists. 5. I know whom you met at the cinema—my father! 6. The daughter of a neighbour of mine who often visits us sings very well. 7. The square, around which there are some very old houses, is nearly always empty. 8. I am afraid of that dog whose teeth are so big. 9. That village, in whose main street there is an old monument, is very well-known. 10. I always do

what I can to help you. 11. Do you know what I must do
to get a ticket? 12. I want to inform you of all I have heard.
13. The owners of this restaurant, who live in Italy, are very
rich. 14. My uncle, who is not at home and without whom
I cannot do anything, will write to you. 15. All those who
wish to go with me are here. 16. It is still raining, which is
a pity. 17. There is a hill near here from which you can see
the whole village. 18. What they say or what they do doesn't
interest *me*. 19. Our neighbours often go and see my mother
in hospital, which is very kind. 20. The country through
which I walked yesterday was very beautiful.

14. INTERROGATION AND EXCLAMATIONS

(*a*) In exclamations ¡qué! means 'what (a) . . .!,' 'how
. . . !'

> *e.g.*, ¡Qué canción tan (or más) hermosa! What a
> beautiful song!
> ¡Qué cansado está! How tired he is!

(*b*) ¿qué? (adjective and pronoun), which?, what?

> *e.g.*, ¿Qué libro busca Vd.? Which book are you looking
> for?
> ¿Qué hace? What is he doing?

(*c*) ¿quién? (¿quiénes?), who?

> *e.g.*, ¿Quiénes han llegado? Who have arrived?

(*d*) ¿cuál? (¿cuáles?), which? (of two or more).

> *e.g.*, ¿Cuál de los niños lo ha tomado? Which of the
> boys has taken it?

N.B. ¿Cuál? (¿cuáles?) is hardly ever used adjectivally.

(*e*) ¿de quién?, whose?

> *e.g.*, ¿De quién es ese gato? Whose is that cat?

(*f*) ¿cuánto (-a, -os, -as)?, how much? how many?

> *e.g.*, ¿Cuánto dinero ha gastado Vd.? How much money
> have you spent?

Note. All interrogative adjectives and pronouns require the accent, even when they introduce indirect questions.

> *e.g.,* **Me preguntó cuánto dinero me había dado Vd.**, he asked me how much money you had given me.

(g) ¿qué clase de?
¿qué tal (qué tales)? } what kind of?
¿a qué? for what purpose? why?

> *e.g.,* ¿**Qué clase de obrero es el Señor Ruiz?** What kind of workman is Mr Ruiz?
>
> ¿**Qué tales son esas flores?** What kind of flowers are they?
>
> ¿**A qué todas estas lágrimas?** Why all these tears?

Note. ¿**Qué tal?** how are you?

Exercises

1. Which word do you mean? 2. What shall we do now? 3. How are you? What a lovely day! 4. How ill he looks! 5. Who has forgotten his exercise-book? 6. Who have remembered to bring their pens? 7. Which of the sisters is a school-mistress? 8. Whose hat is that? 9. How much butter do you need? 10. To what does he owe his success? 11. She asked me which of the photographs I preferred. 12. Whose is that dog which is barking so furiously? 13. I didn't ask him what he wanted. 14. Which of the books have you chosen? 15. Whose is that new car? 16. What kind of pronoun is this? 17. Why so many sighs, Juanita? 18. How many times have I told you that? 19. I want to know which of the pupils threw the apple. 20. Tell me with whom you went to the theatre last night.

15. INDEFINITE ADJECTIVES AND PRONOUNS

alguno (-a, -os, -as), some, a few
cada (*invar.*), each, every
mismo (-a, -os, -as), same, self

algo, something
alguien, somebody, any-body, anyone

mucho (-a, -os, -as), much, many

ninguno (-a, -os, -as), none, no

otro (-a, -os, -as), other, another

poco (-a, -os, -as), little, few

tal, such, such a

tanto (-a, -os, -as), as (so) much, many

todo (-a, -os, -as), all, every

uno (-a, -os, -as), one, some, a few

ambos (-as), both

los (las) dos, both

cada uno (-a), each one

los demás, the rest

sendos, each his own

todo (*invar.*), everything

nada, nothing

nadie, nobody

cualquiera (cualesquiera), any (one) at all, whatever

quienquiera (quienesquiera), whoever

dondequiera, wherever

cuandoquiera, whenever

Note. (*a*) **Alguno** and **ninguno** apocopate before a masculine singular noun.

> *e.g.*, **algún chico,** some boy or other.
> **ningún amigo mío,** no friend of mine.

(*b*) **Cualquiera** becomes **cualquier** before a noun.

> *e.g.*, **Cualquier hombre sabe hacer eso,** any man can do that.

(*c*) The Subjunctive is required in a subordinate clause depending on **cualquiera,** etc., **quienquiera,** etc., used in the main clause.

> *e.g.*, **Cualquiera que sea su fé . . .,** whatever your faith may be . . . .
> **Quienquiera que sea . . .,** whoever you may be . . . .

(*d*)   **el mismo día,** the same day.
      Ella misma me lo contó, she herself told me.

(*e*)   **Tengo poco dinero,** I have little money (*i.e.*, not much).
      Voy a darte un poco de dinero, I will give you a little money.

Exercises

1. Somebody is whistling upstairs. 2. I spoke to each one of the children. 3. You must practise each day. 4. Both have decided to return. 5. The rest are going for a walk. 6. Ask any pupil in the school! 7. You can tell it to whoever you like. 8. Few people know many languages. 9. I myself told my father everything. 10. Something strange happened the other day. 11. So many people tell such lies. 12. I am going to give you a little money to spend. 13. He does the same work every day of his life. 14. Few young people could do as much. 15. Whatever your fears are, you must forget them.

16. NEGATION

(*a*) 'Not' is expressed by using **no** before the verb. **No** also translates the English 'no' standing alone, or 'not' in phrases.

> *e.g.,* ¿**No lo ha enviado Vd.? No.** Have you not sent it? No.
>
> **Ahora no,** not now.
>
> **Aquí no,** not here.

(*b*) **No** is used before the verb to complete the negation with:

> **nada** (nothing), **nadie** (nobody), **ninguno** (no), **nunca** (never), **jamás** (never), **ni . . . ni** (neither . . . nor, not . . . or), **ni** (not even), **ni siquiera** (not even), **tampoco** (not . . . either, nor . . . neither), **sino** (not . . . but)

when these negatives follow the verb. If, however, they are used without a verb or precede the verb, the **no** is omitted.

> *e.g.,* **No ha venido nadie,** nobody has come.
>
> **Nadie ha venido,** nobody has come.
>
> **No lo dije nunca,** I never said it.
>
> **Nunca lo dije,** I never said it.
>
> ¿**Queda algún dinero? Ni un penique siquiera,** Is there any money left? Not even a penny.

No he acabado mis deberes. — Ni yo tampoco, I
haven't finished my homework. — Nor have I.
No tengo ni plumas ni tinta, I haven't pens or ink.
No conozco a su hermana, sino a su hermano,
I don't know your sister, but your brother.

(c) 'Only' is rendered by: no . . . más que or no . . . sino.

    e.g., No tengo más que mi cuaderno, I have only my
    exercise book.
    No hace sino quejarse, he does nothing but
    complain.

Note that más que after other negatives means 'except,'
'but.'

    e.g., Nadie más que su mejor amigo sabía el secreto, no
    one except his best friend knew the secret.

(d) ¿No es verdad? (often just ¿verdad?) corresponds to the
English 'doesn't it?', 'isn't it?', 'won't you?', 'will they?',
etc., when the subject of the interrogative part is the same
as the subject of the statement.

    e.g., Llueve, ¿no es verdad? It is raining, isn't it?
    Vd. viene ahora, ¿verdad? You are coming now,
    aren't you?
    But Él va a hablar, ¿y Vd.? He is going to speak;
    aren't you?

Note that in modern usage ¿no es verdad? is increasingly
shortened to ¿no?

    e.g., Ya te lo he dicho, ¿no? I've already told you,
    haven't I?

(e) Note that sin is followed by a negative pronoun.

    e.g., Volvió sin encontrar a nadie, He returned without
    meeting anyone.

Exercises

1. I said nothing; nobody said anything. 2. We have no fuel, not even a piece of firewood. 3. You have never done that, have you? 4. I didn't send him a card either. 5. Neither my father nor my mother knew the truth. 6. He lit the fire, didn't he? 7. If he comes he will only quarrel with us. 8. I didn't say that, but this. 9. Never have I seen such a dirty house. 10. I have told nobody the good news except my mother. 11. They haven't any paper or envelopes. 12. We didn't send her a present. —Nor I, either. 13. Haven't you ever visited a museum? —No, not yet! 14. Do you want a chocolate? —Not now. 15. Without saying anything, he left the room.

17. PREPOSITIONS AND CONJUNCTIONS

Some Notes on Prepositions

'Por' and 'Para'

Por usually means 'by,' 'through,' 'along.'

> *e.g.,* **Don Quijote fue escrito por Cervantes,** *Don Quixote* was written by Cervantes.
> **El gato entró por la ventana,** the cat entered through the window.
> **Cuando le vi, se paseaba por el camino,** when I saw him, he was walking along the road.

Por also means 'for the sake of,' 'on account of,' 'in exchange for.'

> *e.g.,* **Yo haría todo por ella,** I would do everything for her.
> **Le alabé por haber hecho tan bien el trabajo,** I praised him for having done the work so well.
> **No pagaré veinte duros por el libro,** I shall not pay twenty dollars for the book.

Para translates 'for' in most other cases.

e.g., **Carlos trabaja ahora para su padre,** Charles is now working for his father.

Para translates 'in order to' with an infinitive.

e.g., **Él lo hace para ganar dinero,** he is doing it to (in order to) earn money.

With verbs of motion, **para** indicates destination, **por** indicates route.

e.g., **Salgo para París, viajando por Calais,** I am leaving for Paris, passing through (going via) Calais.

'*A*'

A indicates distance from a place and must never be omitted in Spanish. It often renders the English 'away.'

e.g., **Vivo a dos millas de la escuela,** I live two miles (away) from the school.

See also *Personal 'a'* (p. 84).

A denotes 'motion to'; **en** 'rest in' a place.

e.g., **Se va pronto a España,** he is going away soon to Spain.
Estaremos mañana en casa, we shall be at home to-morrow.

The following are some of the common compound prepositions formed with **a**:

conforme a, according to.
en cuanto a, as for.
frente a, opposite (to).
tocante a, in regard to.

Distinguish carefully between the following:

antes de, before (time).
delante de, before (place).
después de, after (time).
detrás de, after (place).

hacia, towards.

hacía, 3rd person singular of the Imperfect of hacer.

hasta, up to, as far as (until).

N.B. *All* prepositions are followed by an infinitive.

> *e.g.*, antes de salir, before leaving.
>
> > después de haber trabajado, after having worked.
> >
> > No pienso en escribir cartas, I am not thinking about writing letters.

. Note also the construction al with an infinitive.

> *e.g.*, Al despertarme, oí un ruido, on waking up (*or* when I woke up) I heard a noise.

Some Notes on Conjunctions

Y becomes e before initial i- or hi-, but not before hie-, and not when it is the first word of a question.

O becomes u before initial o- or ho-.

> *e.g.*, madre e hija, mother and daughter.
>
> > plata u oro, silver or gold.

Pero and mas translate 'but'; sino renders 'but' after a negative statement.

> *e.g.*, No voy a Francia sino a España, I am not going to France but to Spain.

Note the following correlative conjunctions:

> apenas . . . cuando, hardly . . . when.
>
> no bien . . . cuando, no sooner . . . than.
>
> no sólo . . . sino (que), not only . . . but.
>
> o . . . o, either . . . or.
>
> ni . . . ni, neither . . . nor.
>
> (o) ya . . . (o) ya, whether . . . or, sometimes . . . sometimes.
>
> que . . . o que, whether . . . or.
>
> sea . . . sea, whether . . . or.
>
> siquiera . . . siquiera, whether . . . or.

Note the following idiomatic phrases with **que:**

creo que sí, I think so.
creo que no, I think not.
digo que sí, I say so.
claro que sí, of course.
claro que no, certainly not.

Exercises

1. I shall be in Madrid until the 15th of June. 2. Don't go along this street, take the other one! 3. I thanked him for his kindness. 4. Suddenly our dog jumped through the window. 5. I did it entirely for my aunt. 6. He bought the car for less than a thousand pounds. 7. They left for Madrid last Thursday and intended to travel through Paris. 8. They used to live five miles away from our house. 9. I shall be there before one o'clock. 10. Hardly had they entered the room when the bell rang. 11. Either you do it now or you won't ever do it. 12. Not only did he refuse to listen but he even walked away. 13. He replied: "Certainly not, I never play cards." 14. As for father and son, they always spend their holidays in Germany. 15. I don't think so, you should go through here.

18. INTERJECTIONS

It is almost impossible to give exact English equivalents to the Interjections listed below. Some Interjections can express, for example, joy at one time and sorrow at another.

¡**ay!** oh! alas! bah! tut! pooh!

¡**chito!** ¡**chitón!** Ssh! hush!

¡**hola!** hallo! now then!

¡**ojalá!** would to God! if only!

¡**caramba!** ¡**caracoles!** heavens!

¡**cuidado!** mind! take care!

¡**oiga!** listen! I say! look here!

¡**quita!** get along with you!

¡**toma!** there!

¡**vamos!** now then! well! why! come (now)! etc.

¡**vaya!** indeed! now then! well, I never!

¡**viva!** hurrah!

¡por favor! please!
¡fuego! fire!
¡silencio! silence!
¡socorro! help!
¡bravo! ¡bravísimo! bravo!
¡dale! bother it!
¡hombre! dear me! well!
¡quieto! be quiet!
¡anda! is it really!
¡calle! you don't say!

¡otro! encore!
¡fuera! out with him!
¡ya! ¡ya! quite so! yes yes!
¡diantre! the deuce!
¡Jesús! dear me!
¡qué va! oh no, really! (protest)
¡mira! look!
¡olé! hurrah!

Certain phrases are commonly used as Interjections, such as:

¡Dios mío! dear me!
¡qué lástima! what a pity!
¡Virgen santísima! heavens above!

¡Válgame Dios! bless me!
¡Santos cielos! bless my soul! etc.

19. WORD ORDER

The order of words in Spanish is, generally speaking, freer than in English. Note the following differences:

(a) The subject of an affirmative sentence or clause may precede the verb or follow it. If the subject consists of a number of words it usually follows the verb.

> *e.g.*, **Siento mucho que su padre esté enfermo,** I am very sorry your father is ill.
>
> **Siento mucho que esté enfermo su padre,** I am very sorry your father is ill.
>
> **No ha llegado aún el presidente de una de las Repúblicas sudamericanas,** the president of one of the South American Republics has not arrived yet.

(b) Inversion of subject and verb is compulsory when a verb like **decir, responder,** etc., is used parenthetically.

> *e.g.*, — **Óigame — dijo mi madre,** "Listen to me," my mother said.

(c) In interrogative sentences the subject regularly follows the verb. Note that the auxiliary and the past participle in a compound tense are not separable as in English and French.

> *e.g.*, ¿No ha vuelto su hermana del teatro? Hasn't your sister returned from the theatre?
> ¿Ha estado Vd. enfermo? Have you been ill?

(d) In questions a noun object generally precedes a noun subject, unless the object is the longer of the two.

> *e.g.*, ¿Ha acabado la carta su amigo? Has your friend finished the letter?
> ¿Ha acabado su amigo todas aquellas cartas? Has your friend finished all those letters?

(e) Inversion is commonly found to enable the relative pronoun to follow immediately after its antecedent.

> *e.g.*, Acaban de llegar los obreros que no vinieron a trabajar ayer, the workmen who didn't come to work yesterday have just arrived

(f) For the position of adverbs, see p. 99.

(g) For the position of adjectives, see p. 93.

Exercises

1. Mind! There is a step at the end of the passage. 2. Dear me! What a dark night! 3. Heavens! What will happen now? 4. "I say!" Pedro said. "What is it?" I replied. 5. Look! I can do it myself. 6. What a pity! Such a nice boy! 7. Help! I am drowning. 8. Come now! It's no fault of mine. 9. Hurrah! The holidays have come at last. 10. Bother it! I have forgotten something. 11. The window which looked on to the garden slowly opened. 12. At that moment the leader of the group spoke. 13. "I say! Has your mother read that new book?" 14. Suddenly some one shouted: "Fire!" 15. Is Mr Perez lending my father all those

illustrated periodicals? 16. "Come now!" the teacher said, "the lesson has begun." 17. The headmaster of the grammar school in the town then rose. 18. "Bless my soul!" my mother replied. "What a lot of luggage!" 19. The man then gave my friend a small wooden box. 20. Have you done all the grammar exercises in this book?

PART III

VERB SECTION

1. TENSE ENDINGS

Infinitive	-ar		-er		-ir	
Present Participle	-ando		-iendo			
Past Participle	-ado		-ido			
Present Indicative	-o -amos -as -áis -a -an		-o -emos -es -éis -e -en		-o -imos -es -ís -e -en	
Imperative	-a, -ad		-e, -ed		-e, -id	
Future	(Add to infinitive)	-é -emos -ás -éis -á -án				
Conditional	(Add to infinitive)	-ía -íamos -ias -íais -ía -ían				
Imperfect	-aba -ábamos -abas -abais -aba -aban		-ía -íamos -ías -íais -ía -ían			
Preterite	-é -amos -aste -asteis -ó -aron		-í -imos -iste -isteis -ió -ieron			
	Pretérito Grave -e -imos -iste -isteis -o -ieron					
Present Subjunctive	-e -emos -es -éis -e -en		-a -amos -as -áis -a -an			
Imperfect Subjunctive	-ase -ásemos -ases -aseis -ase -asen		-iese -iésemos -ieses -ieseis -iese -iesen			
	*-ara -áramos -aras -arais -ara -aran		*-iera -iéramos -ieras -ierais -iera -ieran			

* This form of the Imperfect Subjunctive can conveniently be called the Conditional Subjunctive for reference.

2. FORMATION OF TENSES

1. The stem of a verb is obtained by taking off the endings -ar, -er, -ir of the infinitive (*e.g.*, habl-ar, aprend-er, escrib-ir). By adding the endings listed above, all tenses of Regular verbs can be formed, except the Future and Conditional which use the infinitive itself as a stem.

2. Some Irregular verbs form their Preterite with an irregular stem and with the endings unaccented. (See list of Irregular Verbs, p. 127.) This is called the *Pretérito Grave*.

> *e.g.*, Preterite of tener: tuve, tuviste, tuvo, tuvimos, tuvisteis, tuvieron.

3. The stem of the Present Subjunctive of all verbs with the exception of dar, estar, haber, ir, saber, ser (see Irregular Verb list, p. 127) is that of the 1st person singular of the Present Indicative.

> *e.g.*, tener: 1st person of the Present tense: *tengo*.
> Stem of the Present Subjunctive: teng-
> (1st person Present Subjunctive is tenga).

4. The stem of the Imperfect Subjunctive of all verbs is taken from the 3rd person plural of the Preterite.

> *e.g.*, saber: 3rd person plural Preterite: supieron.
> Stem of Imperfect Subjunctive is sup-
> (1st person Imperfect Subjunctive is supiese or supiera).

5. Progressive or Continuous tenses are formed by adding the Present Participle of the verb to the required tense of estar (ir and quedar are also used).

> *e.g.*, estamos hablando, we are talking.
> estábamos hablando, we were talking.

6. All compound tenses are formed by adding the Past Participle of the verb to the appropriate tense of haber.

e.g., Perfect tense: **he hablado,** I have spoken.
Pluperfect tense: **había hablado,** I had spoken.
Past Anterior tense: **hube hablado,** I had spoken.
Future Perfect tense: **habré hablado,** I shall have
spoken.
Conditional Perfect: **habría hablado,** I should
have spoken.
Perfect Subjunctive: **haya hablado,** I have spoken.
Pluperfect Subjunctive:
hubiese hablado ⎱ I had spoken.
hubiera hablado ⎰

7. The following are the only common regular or radical-changing verbs with irregular Past Participles:

abrir (to open): **abierto**
cubrir (to cover): **cubierto**
descubrir (to discover): **descubierto**
escribir (to write): **escrito**
volver (to return): **vuelto**
resolver (to resolve): **resuelto**
morir (to die): **muerto**

Note. For verbs having both a regular and an irregular Past Participle, see Participles, p. 134 (*d*).

8. The Future Subjunctive is rarely used in modern Spanish. It occurs chiefly in proverbs and legal expressions. It has been replaced by the Present Subjunctive. The student should on no account try to use it, except in an accepted idiom, such as **sea lo que fuere,** 'be it what it may,' etc.
The endings of this tense are:

-ar verbs: **-are, -ares, -are, -áremos, -areis, -aren.**
-er, -ir verbs: **-iere, -ieres, -iere, -iéremos, -iereis, -ieren.**

3. THE FOUR PILLARS OF SPANISH

Infinitive: **TENER,** to have. Participles: **TENIENDO,** having; **TENIDO,** had.

Present Indicative I have, etc.	*Singular:* **tengo, tienes, tiene** *Plural:* **tenemos, tenéis, tienen**
Imperfect Indicative I had, etc.	*Singular:* **tenía, tenías, tenía** *Plural:* **teníamos, teníais, tenían**
Preterite Indicative I had, etc.	*Singular:* **tuve, tuviste, tuvo** *Plural:* **tuvimos, tuvisteis, tuvieron**
Future Indicative I shall have, etc.	*Singular:* **tendré, tendrás, tendrá** *Plural:* **tendremos, tendréis, tendrán**
Conditional Indicative I should have, etc.	*Singular:* **tendría, tendrías, tendría** *Plural:* **tendríamos, tendríais, tendrían**
Present Subjunctive	*Singular:* **tenga, tengas, tenga** *Plural:* **tengamos, tengáis, tengan**
Imperfect Subjunctive	(1) **tuviese,** etc. (2) **tuviera,** etc.
Imperative	*Singular:* **ten (tú), tenga Vd.,** (have) *Plural:* **tengamos,** (let us have) **tened (vosotros),** (have) **tengan Vds.,** (have)

Infinitive: **HABER,** to have. Participles: **HABIENDO,** having; **HABIDO,** had.

Present Indicative I have, etc.	*Singular:* **he, has, ha** *Plural:* **hemos, habéis, han**
Imperfect Indicative I had, etc.	*Singular:* **había, habías, había** *Plural:* **habíamos, habíais, habían**
Preterite Indicative I had, etc.	*Singular:* **hube, hubiste, hubo** *Plural:* **hubimos, hubisteis, hubieron**
Future Indicative I shall have, etc.	*Singular:* **habré, habrás, habrá** *Plural:* **habremos, habréis, habrán**
Conditional Indicative I should have, etc.	*Singular:* **habría, habrías, habría** *Plural:* **habríamos, habríais, habrían**
Present Subjunctive	*Singular:* **haya, hayas, haya** *Plural:* **hayamos, hayáis, hayan**
Imperfect Subjunctive	(1) **hubiese,** etc. (2) **hubiera,** etc.
Imperative	*Singular:* **(he), haya Vd.,** (have) *Plural:* **hayamos,** (let us have) **habed (vosotros),** (have) **hayan Vds.,** (have)

Infinitive: **ESTAR**, to be. Participles: **ESTANDO**, being; **ESTADO**, been.

Present Indicative I am, etc.	*Singular:* **estoy, estás, está** *Plural:* **estamos, estáis, están**
Imperfect Indicative I was, etc.	*Singular:* **estaba, estabas, estaba** *Plural:* **estábamos, estabais, estaban**
Preterite Indicative I was, etc.	*Singular:* **estuve, estuviste, estuvo** *Plural:* **estuvimos, estuvisteis, estuvieron**
Future Indicative I shall be, etc.	*Singular:* **estaré, estarás, estará** *Plural:* **estaremos, estaréis, estarán**
Conditional Indicative I should be, etc.	*Singular:* **estaría, estarías, estaría** *Plural:* **estaríamos, estaríais, estarían**
Present Subjunctive	*Singular:* **esté, estés, esté** *Plural:* **estemos, estéis, estén**
Imperfect Subjunctive	(1) **estuviese,** etc. (2) **estuviera,** etc.
Imperative	*Singular:* **está (tú), esté Vd.,** (be) *Plural:* **estemos,** (let us be) **estad (vosotros),** (be) **estén Vds.,** (be)

Infinitive: **SER**, to be. Participles: **SIENDO**, being; **SIDO**, been.

Present Indicative I am, etc.	*Singular:* **soy, eres, es** *Plural:* **somos, sois, son**
Imperfect Indicative I was, etc.	*Singular:* **era, eras, era** *Plural:* **éramos, erais, eran**
Preterite Indicative I was, etc.	*Singular:* **fui, fuiste, fue** *Plural:* **fuimos, fuisteis, fueron**
Future Indicative I shall be, etc.	*Singular:* **seré, serás, será** *Plural:* **seremos, seréis, serán**
Conditional Indicative I should be, etc.	*Singular:* **sería, serías, sería** *Plural:* **seríamos, seríais, serían**
Present Subjunctive	*Singular:* **sea, seas, sea** *Plural:* **seamos, seáis, sean**
Imperfect Subjunctive	(1) **fuese,** etc. (2) **fuera,** etc.
Imperative	*Singular:* **sé (tú), sea Vd.,** (be) *Plural:* **seamos,** (let us be) **sed (vosotros),** (be) **sean Vds.,** (be)

4. IRREGULAR VERBS

In the following list of Irregular verbs it will be noted that only the Infinitive, the Present and Past Participles, the Present tense (in full), the 1st person of the Preterite (and other persons, if irregular), and the 2nd person singular of the Imperative, if irregular, are given. Under the heading *Notes* will be found the 1st person singular of irregular Futures and of irregular Present Subjunctives. All other tenses can be formed from the parts given. (See Formation of Tenses, p. 122, and Tense Endings on p. 121.)

Apart from obvious abbreviations for names of tenses, note that *F.* stands for Future and *P.G.* for Pretérito Grave.

Infinitive	Participles	Present Tense	Preterite	Imperative	Notes
andar to go, walk	andando andado	ando, andas, anda andamos, andáis, andan	anduve (P.G.)		
asir to grasp	asiendo asido	asgo, ases, ase asimos, asís, asen	así		
caber to be contained in	cabiendo cabido	quepo, cabes, cabe cabemos, cabéis, caben	cupe (P.G.)		*F.* cabré
caer to fall	cayendo caído	caigo, caes, cae caemos, caéis, caen	caí *3rd Persons.* cayó, cayeron		
dar to give	dando dado	doy, das, da damos, dais, dan	di, diste, dio dimos, disteis, dieron		*Pres. Subj.* dé *1st & 3rd Pers.*
decir to say	diciendo dicho	digo, dices, dice decimos, decís, dicen	dije (P.G.)	di	*F.* diré
hacer to make, do	haciendo hecho	hago, haces, hace hacemos, hacéis, hacen	hice *3rd Pers. Sing.* hizo (P.G.)	haz	*F.* haré
ir to go	yendo ido	voy, vas, va vamos, vais, van	fui *3rd Persons.* fue, fueron	ve, id *1st Pers. Pl.* vamos	*Pres. Subj.* vaya
oir to hear	oyendo oído	oigo, oyes, oye oímos, oís, oyen	oí *3rd Persons.* oyó, oyeron	oye	

Infinitive	Participles	Present Tense	Preterite		Imperative	Notes
poder to be able	**pudiendo** **podido**	puedo, puedes, puede podemos, podéis, pueden	pude	(P.G.)		F. podré
poner to put	**poniendo** **puesto**	pongo, pones, pone ponemos, ponéis, ponen	puse	(P.G.)	pon	F. pondré
querer to wish, want	**queriendo** **querido**	quiero, quieres, quiere queremos, queréis, quieren	quise	(P.G.)	quiere	F. querré
saber to know	**sabiendo** **sabido**	sé, sabes, sabe sabemos, sabéis, saben	supe	(P.G.)		F. sabré Pres. Subj. sepa
salir to set out	**saliendo** **salido**	salgo, sales, sale salimos, salís, salen	salí		sal	F. saldré
traer to draw, carry	**trayendo** **traído**	traigo, traes, trae traemos, traéis, traen	traje	(P.G.)		
valer to be worth	**valiendo** **valido**	valgo, vales, vale valemos, valéis, valen	valí		val (vale)	F. valdré
venir to come	**viniendo** **venido**	vengo, vienes, viene venimos, venís, vienen	vine	(P.G.)	ven	F. vendré
ver to see	**viendo** **visto**	veo, ves, ve vemos, veis, ven	vi			
yacer to lie	**yaciendo** **yacido**	yazco (yazgo, yago) yaces, yace yacemos, yacéis, yacen	yací		yace or yaz	

5. SOME NOTES ON THE USE OF TENSES AND PARTICIPLES

Present Tense

1. The *Present* tense in Spanish has three English meanings.

> *e.g.,* **hablo:** I speak; I am speaking; I do speak.

2. It is used in Spanish instead of a *past* tense in English to express an action (or state) which began in the past and is still continuing in the present.

> *e.g.,* **Hace una hora que le espero,** I have been waiting for him for an hour (and am still waiting).
> **Estoy aquí desde hace un mes,** I have been here a month (and am still here).

3. The *Present* tense is sometimes used in Spanish instead of the *Past* tense in English to add vividness to a narrative.

4. For the use of the *'Continuous' Present,* see Progressive or 'Continuous' Tenses, p. 131.

Future Tense

1. The *Future* tense in Spanish has two meanings in English.

> *e.g.,* **hablaré:** I shall speak; I shall be speaking.

2. It often denotes in Spanish probability or conjecture in present time.

> *e.g.,* **¿Qué hora es? Será la una.** What time is it? It is probably one o'clock.
> **Se habrá marchado,** he must have gone.

Conditional Tense

1. The *Conditional* tense in Spanish has two English meanings.

> *e.g.,* **hablaría:** I should speak; I should be speaking.

2. It often denotes probability or conjecture in past time.

e.g. ¿**Qué hora era? Sería la una.** What time was it?
It was probably one o'clock. (Sometimes in
English, 'it would be about one o'clock'.)
¿**Estaría enferma?** Could she be ill?

Past Tenses

1. *The Preterite Tense*

This tense is the ordinary past tense in Spanish and is used
to indicate what happened once at a definite time in the past.
It renders the simple English past.

e.g., **fui,** I went; **vieron,** they saw; **ella vino,** she
came, etc.
El rey vio ayer a su primer ministro, the king saw
his prime minister yesterday.

N.B. This tense is used in conversation, letters, etc., unlike
the use of the Past Historic in French.

2. *The Imperfect Tense*

This tense is used to translate the English 'was (were) -ing'
or 'used to . . .' (sometimes 'would'). It expresses an action
or state of indefinite duration.

e.g., **fumaba,** he was smoking *or* he used to smoke (or
'he smoked' when the latter meaning can be
rendered by 'was smoking' or 'used to smoke').
Era verdad, it was true. (One doesn't know (*a*)
when it started being true, (*b*) when it finished
being true, (*c*) how long it continued being true.)
Trabajaba cuando le vi, he was working when I
saw him.
Cuando era joven, yo vivía en el campo, when I
was young, I lived in the country.
**Yo daba un paseo todas las mañanas cuando estaba
en casa de mi tía,** I would go for a walk every
morning when I stayed with my aunt.

It is also used in Spanish instead of the *Pluperfect* tense in
English to express an action or state which began in the past

An old street in Toledo. See page 170.

130

Getting water from the pump in a street in Seo de Urgel,
Lérida

Photo R. Ayerst

and was still continuing in the past when something else happened.

> *e.g.*, **Yo le esperaba desde hacía una hora cuando empezó a llover** (*or* **Hacía una hora que le esperaba cuando . . .**), I had been waiting for him an hour (and was still waiting) when it started to rain.

Progressive or 'Continuous' Tenses

The tenses of **estar** (or **ir, venir, andar,** and **quedar**) may be used with the *Present Participle* of the verb (just as 'to be' is used with the Present Participle in English) to express continuity of action.

> *e.g.*, **¿Dónde está su padre? Está trabajando** (or **trabaja**) **en el jardín.** Where is your father? He is working in the garden.
>
> **Siempre estaba trabajando** (or **trabajaba**) **cuando vivía en su casa,** he was always working when I lived in his house.
>
> **Va corriendo hacia la escuela,** he is (goes) running to school.

N.B. These forms cannot be used with **ir** and **venir**.

The Imperative Mood

The *Imperative Mood* is used to express a command. The **Vd.** (and **Vds.**) form of the Imperative is taken from the Present Subjunctive. The Imperative of the 1st person plural can be expressed by the Present Subjunctive or rendered by **vamos a** + Infinitive.

> *e.g.*, **¡cante Vd.!** sing!
>
> **¡canten Vds.!** sing!
>
> **¡cantemos!** or **¡vamos a cantar!** let us sing!

For the familiar forms (**tú** and **vosotros**) see Tense Endings, p. 121.

N.B. All negative Imperatives are expressed by the Present Subjunctive.

> *e.g.,* — **Busca tu pluma, Juanito, dijo su madre,** "Look for your pen, John," said his mother.
>
> *But* — **¡ No busques tu libro ahora! dijo su madre.** "Don't look for your book now," said his mother.

Note. 1st person plural Imperative. With Reflexive verbs the Present Subjunctive is seldom used except in literary style. In the negative, the Subjunctive should always be used in theory, but in practice there is a strong tendency in conversation to use the Indicative instead.

Compound Tenses

The *Pluperfect* tense has two English meanings.

> *e.g.,* **había dicho:** I had said; I had been saying.
>
> **Yo sabía que Vd. había decidido salir,** I knew that you had decided to leave.
>
> **Yo no había hablado, pero mi profesor gritó:** — **¡ Calla, Juan !,** I hadn't been speaking, but my master shouted, "Be quiet, John !"

The *Past Anterior* replaces the *Pluperfect* tense in Spanish in the subordinate clause of a compound sentence when the verb in the main clause is in the Preterite tense and the subordinate clause is introduced by a conjunction of time (such as: **apenas,** scarcely; **cuando,** when; **luego que,** after; **no bien,** no sooner; **así que, tan pronto como, en cuanto,** as soon as, etc.).

> *e.g.,* **Cuando hubo acabado de leer, salió,** when he had finished reading he went out.
>
> **Apenas hubo entrado el profesor, cuando se abrió la puerta,** the master had scarcely come in when the door was opened.

In modern Spanish this tense is little used, and is generally replaced by the Preterite.

The *Perfect Tense* is used to translate the English 'has' or 'have' with a Past Participle.

e.g., **Él no ha estado nunca aquí,** he has never been here.

No han llegado todavía, they have not arrived yet

Note. The *Perfect* tense is sometimes used to express an action which took place at an indefinite, unspecified time in the immediate past.

e.g., **Recientemente he visitado a mi abuelo,** recently I visited my grandfather.

but **Ayer por la tarde vi a mi abuelo,** yesterday evening I saw my grandfather.

The Participles

The *Present Participle* is always invariable in Spanish. It is chiefly used verbally or to form 'continuous' tenses with the verb **estar (quedar, ir,** etc.).

(*a*) The Present Participle cannot be used as a verbal noun in Spanish. Its place is taken by the Infinitive.

e.g., **Ver es creer,** seeing is believing.

(*b*) "By" followed by the Present Participle in English is usually rendered by the Present Participle in Spanish.

e.g., **Vd. me hará muy feliz haciéndolo,** you will make me very happy by doing it.

Note. The Present Participle ending in **-ando** or **-iendo,** being invariable, can only be used verbally, and never as an adjective agreeing with a noun. If an adjectival use is required, it is replaced by another form, **-ando** becoming **-ante,** **-iendo** becoming **-iente.**

e.g., **Hay agua corriendo por la calle,** there is water running down the street.

Hay agua corriente en los dormitorios, there is running water in the bedrooms.

The *Past Participle* in Spanish may be used as an adjective or to form compound tenses with **haber.**

(*a*) Past Participles used as adjectives or in an 'absolute' construction vary like ordinary adjectives.

> *e.g.*, **Las niñas, muy cansadas, se acostaron temprano,** the little girls, very tired, went to bed early.
>
> **Hechos sus deberes, salieron,** having finished their homework, they went out.

(*b*) Past Participles conjugated with **haber** in compound tenses are invariable, but agree in gender and number with the subject of the sentence when conjugated with **ser** (in the Passive) or **estar**.

> *e.g.*, **La criada fue herida en el accidente,** the servant was injured in the accident.
>
> **Ella no está hoy tan agitada,** she isn't so excited to-day.
>
> **Mis abuelos nos han visitado varias veces esta semana,** my grandparents have visited us several times this week.

(*c*) **Tener, llevar, quedar,** etc., are used with the Past Participle of a verb to indicate that the action is finished and done with. The Past Participle agrees with the object in this construction.

> *e.g.*, **Tengo (llevo) escritas todas las cartas,** I have written all the letters.

(*d*) Some verbs, such as **prender, romper, oprimir, suprimir,** etc., have two Past Participles, a regular and an irregular form. The irregular form is now chiefly used as adjective.

> **prender** (to take) has **prendido** and **preso.**
> **romper** has **rompido** and **roto.**
> **oprimir** has **oprimido** and **opreso.**
> **suprimir** has **suprimido** and **supreso.**
> **freír** has **freído** and **frito.**

Note. **Roto** and **frito** are commonly used to form compound tenses with **haber.**

> *e.g.*, **Se ha roto la pierna,** he has broken his leg.

Exercises

1. We have been living here for two years now. 2. I shall write to-morrow. 3. It must be ten o'clock; I shan't wait any more. 4. I knew he would return early. 5. By helping me, you will be helping others. 6. Many years ago she used to work in the country. 7. I would often spend a week at the seaside when I lived in London. 8. She had been waiting for nearly half an hour when I arrived. 9. I thought it would be fine to-day. 10. As I was leaving the house, some one called me. 11. He is always smoking a pipe when I see him. 12. My uncle was working in the garden all the morning. 13. I hadn't been writing more than ten minutes when Pablo came in. 14. "Don't look for your bag now, Rosita! Listen to me!" 15. They hadn't been sleeping well for a long time. 16. Scarcely had he hidden the money, when some one shouted. 17. You haven't told me what you did. 18. Being a pupil of this school, you can obtain tickets. 19. Studying is a pleasure for some people. 20. I have prepared all my lessons for to-morrow. 21. Having finished the task, the workmen sat down to rest. 22. She has such a fine voice; I think she must go on singing. 23. Rosa always hurries; she is running up the street now. 24. I thought you knew the result last week. 25. As soon as we had finished dinner, we went out.

6. THE SUBJUNCTIVE MOOD

In *Main Clauses* the *Present Subjunctive* is used

(a) to express the Imperative with **Vd., Vds.** and 1st and 3rd persons.

> *e.g.*, ¡**hable Vd.**! speak! ¡**hablen Vds.**! speak!
> ¡**hablemos**! let us speak! ¡**que hable**! let him speak!

(b) to express a wish.

> *e.g.*, ¡**que seas feliz**! may you be happy!
> ¡**ojalá (que) viniera**! if only he would come!

(c) to express all negative Imperatives.

> e.g., ¡vé (tú)!—go! *but* ¡no vayas!—don't go!
> ¡id (vosotros)!—go! *but* ¡no vayáis!—don't go!

In *Dependent Clauses* the *Subjunctive* is used:

1. In *Noun clauses* after the following verbs:

(a) Verbs of wishing, asking, ordering, allowing, forbidding, preventing, denying: **querer que,** to wish that; **rogar que,** to ask that; **preferir que,** to prefer that; **aconsejar que,** to advise that; **mandar que,** to order that; **permitir que, dejar que,** to permit, allow, that; **prohibir que,** to forbid that; **impedir que,** to prevent that; **negar que,** to deny that; etc.

> e.g., **Aconsejamos que Vd. lo haga,** we advise you to do it.
> **Mandaron que saliese,** they ordered him to leave.

(b) Verbs of emotion expressing sorrow, fear, hope, pleasure, doubt, surprise, etc.: **sentir que,** to be sorry that; **temer que,** to fear that; **esperar que,** to hope that; **alegrarse de que,** to be glad that; **extrañarse que,** to wonder that; **sorprenderse de que,** to be surprised that; etc.

> e.g., **Siento que Vd. no esté aquí,** I am sorry you will not be here.
> **Me alegraba de que hiciese buen tiempo,** I was glad it was fine weather.

Note. **Extrañar que,** 'to be surprised that,' is nowadays used impersonally as a general rule. Similarly **sorprender que.**

> e.g., **Me extraña que haya venido tan temprano,** I am surprised that he has come so early.

(c) Verbs of saying, thinking, used negatively: **decir que,** to say that; **creer que,** to believe that; **pensar que,** to think that; **ver que,** to see that, etc., and verbs of doubt and denial used affirmatively: **dudar que,** to doubt that or whether; **negar que,** to deny that.

Note. **Dudar si,** 'to doubt whether,' is followed by the Indicative.

> *e.g.,* **No pienso que sea verdad,** I don't think that it is true.
>
> **Dudamos que lo supiese,** we doubted whether he knew it.

(*d*) Impersonal verbs, except those implying certainty or fact: **hace falta que, es preciso que,** it is necessary that; **importa que,** it is important that; **conviene que,** it is proper that; **es posible que,** it is possible that; **puede que,** it may be that; etc.

> *e.g.,* **Importa que Vd. llegue temprano,** it is important that you arrive early.
>
> **No es cierto que venga,** it isn't certain he will come.
>
> *But* **Es cierto que viene hoy,** it is certain he is coming to-day.

2. (*a*) In *Adverbial Clauses* after the following conjunctions when future time, uncertainty, or supposition is implied: **cuando,** when; **hasta que,** until; **luego que, así que, en cuanto, tan pronto como,** as soon as; **mientras que,** as long as; **después (de) que,** after; **aunque,** although, even if.

> *e.g.,* **Cuando vea Vd. a mi padre, dígale lo que he dicho,** when you see my father, tell him what I said.
>
> *But* **Cuando viene a verme, siempre me trae chocolate,** when he comes to see me, he always brings me chocolate.
>
> **No puedo hacerlo, aunque Vd. me ayude,** I can't do it, even if you help me.
>
> *But* **No pude hacerlo, aunque trabajé toda la noche,** I couldn't do it, although I worked all night.

(*b*) The following conjunctions are always followed by the Subjunctive: **para que, a fin de que,** in order that; **con tal que, siempre que,** provided that; **a menos que,** unless; **antes de que,** before; **sin que,** without (that); **dado que,** granted that; **por miedo de que,** for fear that; **de modo que, de manera que,** in such a way that.

e.g., **Hay que reparar el techado, para que no entre la
lluvia,** it is necessary to repair the roof, in order
that the rain doesn't come in.

**Subieron sin ruido, por miedo de que se despertasen
los niños,** they went up quietly, lest they should
wake (up) the children.

3. In *'if' clauses*. The Subjunctive is used in an 'if' clause
where the action of the verb did not, in fact, take place, or is
incapable of realisation.

e.g., **Si yo fuera rey, tu serías mi reina,** if I were king,
you would be my queen (but I am not the king).
Si lo hubiese sabido, habría ido, if I had known, I
should have gone (but I didn't know).

Note that the Conditional Indicative may be replaced, at
all times, by the Conditional Subjunctive, particularly with
certain verbs such as **quisiera,** I should like; **debiera,** I ought,
etc.

Note that **si,** meaning 'if,' is never followed in Spanish by
the Present Subjunctive, Future Indicative, and Conditional
Indicative. When **si** means 'whether,' it can be followed by
any tense.

e.g., **No sé si vendrá,** I don't know whether he will
come.

Table for sequence of tenses in conditional sentences:

Main Clause	*'If' Clause*
Present, Future Indicative	Present Indicative
Conditional (Indicative or Subjunctive)	Imperfect (Indicative or Subjunctive)
Conditional Perfect (Indicative or Subjunctive)	Pluperfect (Indicative or Subjunctive)

4. In *Adjectival Clauses* introduced by a relative pronoun:

(*a*) After an indefinite or negative antecedent.

e.g., **No he encontrado a nadie que le conozca,** I have
not met anyone who knows you.

> **Busco un hombre que hable español,** I am looking
> for a man who speaks Spanish.
>
> *but* **Busco a ese hombre que habla español,** I am
> looking for that man who speaks Spanish
> (**hombre** here is a definite person).

(*b*) After the following:

> **quienquiera que,** whoever; **cualquiera que,** whatever
> **comoquiera que,** however; **por . . . que,** however
> **cuandoquiera que,** whenever; **dondequiera que,** wherever

Note. See p. 111 for **quienquiera** and **cualquiera.**

> *e.g.,* **Quienquiera que sea . . .,** whoever he is . . . .
> **Cualesquier libros que Vd. tenga . . .,** whatever
> books you have . . . .
> **Cualquiera que sea la dificultad . . .,** whatever
> may be the difficulty . . . .
> **Dondequiera que Vd. vaya . . .,** wherever you
> go . . . .
> **Por bueno que Vd. sea . . .,** however good you
> are . . . .

7. SEQUENCE OF TENSES WITH THE SUBJUNCTIVE

When the verb in the main clause is in the *Present* or
Future or *Imperative*, the *Present* or *Perfect Subjunctive* is
used in the dependent clause, according to the sense.

> *e.g.,* **Querré que Vd. cante esta tarde,** I shall want you
> to sing this evening.
> **No creo que él haya vuelto,** I don't think he has
> returned.

Note. But if the action of the Subjunctive clause is defi-
nitely *Past* the *Imperfect Subjunctive* is used.

> *e.g.,* **Es posible que no estuviese allí,** it is possible he
> wasn't there.

When the verb in the main clause is in *any other tense*, the *Imperfect (Conditional)* or *Perfect* or *Pluperfect Subjunctive* is used according to the sense.

> *e.g.*, **Yo esperaba que él viniese,** I was hoping he would come.
>
> **Dudábamos que él hubiese dicho la verdad,** we doubted whether he had told the truth.

Avoidance of Subjunctive

If the subject of the main clause is the same as the subject of the dependent clause, the *Infinitive* is preferred.

> *e.g.*, **Siento mucho llegar tarde,** I am sorry I am late.

If the conjunction introducing the Subjunctive has a corresponding prepositional form, the *Infinitive* is used after the latter when the subjects of both clauses are the same.

Conjunction	*Preposition*
para que, in order that	**para,** in order to
a fin de que, in order that	**a fin de,** in order to
en caso de que, in case (that)	**en caso de,** in case
por miedo de que, for fear that	**de miedo de,** for fear that
sin que, without	**sin,** without
cuando, when	**al,** when
hasta que, until	**hasta,** until
antes (de) que, before	**antes de,** before
después (de) que, after	**después de,** after

> *e.g.*, **Quiero hacer muchas cosas antes de irme,** I want to do a lot of things before I go away.
>
> **Al recibir su carta, se la enseñaré a mi profesor,** when I receive your letter, I shall show it to my master.

Note. This rule is very freely interpreted in practice and the Infinitive is often used even where the subjects are not the same.

> *e.g.*, **Salimos antes de llegar las cartas,** we left before the letters arrived.

Exercises

1. "Don't speak to me now! Tell me about it later." 2. May you be clever—as clever as your father! 3. If only you could help me! 4. "Go to bed, Maria," said her mother. "Don't read any more." 5. I forbid you to sing in class. 6. We were glad you were able to come. 7. They doubted whether John had done it. 8. I am not sure it is true, but it is possible you are right. 9. It is important that you send it to him at once. 10. As soon as he returns the book, I will lend it to you. 11. Unless you make up your mind to work hard, you will not succeed. 12. I paid for the broken window without his knowing. 13. Although I waited two hours, he never came. 14. If I were older, I shouldn't say such silly things. 15. If you had arrived earlier, you would have met my cousin. 16. I shouldn't run if I were ill. 17. We found no one who was going to town that day. 18. Do you know a person who teaches Russian well? 19. Whatever your reasons are, I do not agree with you. 20. Whoever they are, they are always very polite. 21. Luisa is afraid she has lost her watch. 22. They left suddenly without giving me warning. 23. We should like you to remember what we have done. 24. I want you to believe that we have never regretted our action. 25. Even if you went back, you might not find it. 26. I shall think of you wherever you are. 27. Whatever you say, say it so that all can hear it. 28. Don't forget to give him the news before you leave. 29. We don't believe you have picked it up. 30. He was sorry so many people in the town were ill.

8. THE USES OF **ESTAR** AND **SER**

ESTAR	SER
1. Expresses what is temporary or accidental. *e.g.*, **Estoy cansado hoy,** I am tired to-day	1. Expresses what is permanent or inherent. *e.g.*, **Es perezoso,** he is lazy.
2. Indicates place. *e.g.*, **Él está en su cuarto,** he is in his room.	2. Indicates profession or essential quality. *e.g.*, **Es profesor,** he is a schoolmaster. **El pupitre es de madera,** the desk is wooden.
3. The 'false' Passive. *e.g.*, **La puerta estaba abierta,** the door was open.	3. Forms the *Passive Voice* with the *Past Participle* of the verb. *e.g.*, **He sido disuadido de ir,** I have been dissuaded from going.

> *e.g.*, **Ayer estaba triste,** yesterday I was sad (temporarily).
>
> **Este hombre es triste,** this man is sad (permanently).

Note. Pupils may find the following distinction useful:

> **ESTAR** tells 'how' and 'where' (*i.e.*, how it is, the state of affairs).
> **SER** tells 'who,' 'when,' 'what.'

9. THE PASSIVE VOICE

The *Passive Voice* is formed from **ser** + the Past Participle of the verb. **Por** translates 'by' except after verbs of feeling, when **de** is used.

> *e.g.*, **La criada fue acusada por su ama,** the servant was accused by her mistress.
>
> **El profesor era temido de sus alumnos,** the master was feared by his pupils.

The Passive expresses an *action*. It must not be confused with the 'false' Passive, which expresses a *state resulting*

from an action. In this case **estar** is used with the Past
Participle of the verb.

> *e.g.*, **La puerta fue abierta por la criada,** the door was
> opened by the servant. (Action.)
>
> **La puerta estaba abierta,** the door was open.
> (State—action already over.)

N.B. The Past Participles used with **ser** and **estar** always
agree with the subject of the sentence.

The *Passive Voice* is avoided, whenever possible, in Spanish
by using:

    (*a*) the reflexive form of the verb

or   (*b*) the 3rd person plural of the Active Voice of the verb.

(*a*) The reflexive construction may be (i) personal (in which
case the verb is used transitively, having the reflexive pronoun
for object), or (ii) impersonal (in which case the verb may be
transitive or intransitive).

> *e.g.*, (i) **Cuando salí, el cielo se llenaba de estrellas,**
> when I left, the sky was filled with stars.
>
> (ii) **Se dice . . .,** one says, you say, we say, they
> say, people say, it is said.
>
> **Se me dice que está enfermo,** I am told that he
> is ill.
>
> **Se vio al hombre en el tejado,** the man was seen
> on the roof.

Note that (ii) corresponds to the French use of '*on*' with an
active verb.

(*b*) The last example could be expressed thus:

> **Vieron al hombre en el tejado,** the man was seen
> on the roof.

Note that if the subject of the sentence is personal, and an
agent is expressed, **ser** with a Past Participle *must* be used.

> *e.g.*, **El ladrón fue descubierto por un policía,** the thief
> was discovered by a policeman.

Exercises

1. Because I came home very late last night, I am very tired to-day. 2. I don't think he is just lazy, he is stupid as well. 3. I believe he is a doctor, but he might be a dentist. 4. He was saying that the watch was a gold one. 5. You have been advised to stay at school. 6. I never know whether you are unhappy or not. 7. I can't read this book because it is written in German. 8. He is always smoking, which isn't good for his health. 9. You must have been consulted before me. 10. I am often unwell; yesterday I was very ill. 11. They told me the ring was platinum but I think it is silver. 12. The table on which he put the gramophone was broken. 13. It is said that she is nearly blind. 14. The books were returned by a small boy. 15. It was said he had been wounded by a bullet. 16. The boys were sent by the headmaster to his study. 17. It is believed that the burglar entered by a window. 18. Your friend was seen at the pictures with his mother. 19. Portuguese is spoken in one of the South American republics. 20. When I was young, I was very mischievous. 21. One never knows what is going to happen. 22. The matter was reported to me by a small boy. 23. Our guests were taken to the station by my brother. 24. Our doctor is esteemed by all his patients. 25. The workman was found lying on the ground, seriously hurt.

10. REFLEXIVE VERBS

(*a*) Reflexive Pronouns are the same as the conjunctive object pronouns except **se**, which means 'himself,' 'herself,' 'itself,' 'themselves,' 'yourself,' 'yourselves.'

(*b*) Reflexive Pronouns follow the same rules as to position as other object pronouns. Se, however, always precedes any other object pronouns.

> *e.g.*, **Se las metió en el bolsillo,** she put them in her pocket.
> **Me lo compraré,** I shall buy it (for myself).

N.B. In the plural of the *Imperative* affirmative, 1st and 2nd persons only, the final **s** or **d** of the verb is dropped (except **irse, idos**).

> *e.g.,* **sentémonos,** let us sit down.
> ¡ **sentaos!** sit down !

(*c*) **mismo** (sometimes **propio**) may be used to emphasize the reflexive pronoun.

> *e.g.,* **Después de lavar a los niños, se lavó a sí misma,** after washing the children, she washed herself.

(*d*) Reflexive verbs are used to express reciprocity.

> *e.g.,* **se hablan** means either 'they are talking to themselves' or 'they are talking to each other' (or 'to one another').

N.B. If ambiguity arises, the reciprocal meaning of the pronoun can be made clear by using after the verb **uno** (**-a, -os, -as**) and **otro** (**-a, -os, -as**) preceded or not by the definite article and with the preposition required by the verb inserted between them. (**Mutuamente** or **recíprocamente** may be used instead.)

> *e.g.,* **Se hablaban (los) unos a (los) otros,** they were talking to one another.
> **Se reían el uno del otro,** they were making fun of one another.

(*d*) Any transitive verb can be used reflexively, if the meaning warrants it.

> *e.g.,* **cortar,** to cut; **cortarse,** to cut oneself.

(*e*) Some verbs are only used in the reflexive form.

> *e.g.,* **atreverse,** to dare; **abstenerse,** to abstain, refrain from; **arrepentirse,** to repent; **condolerse,** to condole; **desvergonzarse,** to speak or act impudently; **dignarse,** to condescend, deign; **jactarse,** to boast; **quejarse,** to complain; **ausentarse,** to stay away; etc.

(*f*) Some verbs have different meanings in the simple and in the reflexive form.

e.g., acordar, to agree   acordarse (de), to remember

hallar ⎫
encontrar ⎭ to find   hallarse ⎫
encontrarse ⎭ to be

hacer, to make   hacerse (followed by noun or adjective), to become

poner, to put   ponerse (followed by adjective), to become

ponerse a, to begin to

Other examples showing a slight difference of meaning when used in the reflexive form.

e.g., ir, to go   irse, to go away

comer, to eat   comerse, to eat up

perder, to lose   perderse, to get lost

alegrar ⎫
regocijar ⎭ to gladden   alegrarse ⎫
regocijarse ⎭ to be happy, rejoice

levantar, to lift   levantarse, to rise, get up

acostar, to put to bed   acostarse, to go to bed

llamar, to call, knock   llamarse, to be called

sentir, to feel, regret   sentirse (followed by adjective), to have a feeling (within oneself)

dormir, to sleep   dormirse, to go to sleep

volar, to fly   volarse, to fly away

Exercises

1. He himself complained to the manager. 2. "Sit down, children, and don't make a noise." 3. We are going away to live with some relatives. 4. After putting the children to bed, she went to bed herself. 5. The young people talked to each other all the evening. 6. I am going to introduce myself; my name is Dr Truata. 7. My grandparents often sing to themselves. 8. We found one another near the exit. 9. "Rosita, don't go to sleep," said Mrs González. 10. They were sent home because they spoke impudently in class.

11. He became a great lawyer, I am told. 12. I am sure you will be glad when you hear the news. 13. I usually get up at six o'clock and have my breakfast before seven. 14. They boasted to each other of their skill at games. 15. I am beginning to feel tired, so I shall go to bed.

11. ORTHOGRAPHIC-CHANGING VERBS

The following classes of verbs change their spelling so as to retain the sound which the consonant of the stem has in the infinitive.

Infin. Ending	Change	Tenses Affected	Examples	
-car	c + e > qu	*Pret. 1st Sing.* and *Pres. Subj.*	buscar	busqué busque
-gar	g + e > gu		pagar	pagué pague
-zar	z + e > c	*Pret. 1st Sing.* and *Pres. Subj.*	comenzar	comencé comience
-guar	gu + e > gü		averiguar	averigüé averigüe
consonant + { -cer -cir	c + a, o, > z	*Pres. 1st Sing.* *Pres. Subj.*	vencer	venzo venza
vowel + { -cer -cir	c + a, o, > zc	*Pres. 1st Sing.* *Pres. Subj.*	conocer	conozco conozca
+ { -ger -gir	g + a, o, > j	*Pres. 1st Sing.* *Pres. Subj.*	coger	cojo coja
-guir	gu + a, o, > g	*Pres. 1st Sing.* *Pres. Subj.*	distinguir	distingo distinga
-quir	qu + a, o, > c	*Pres. 1st Sing.* *Pres. Subj.*	delinquir	delinco delinca

Notes. The principal exceptions to the 'vowel + -cer, -cir,' group are: **cocer**, to cook; **escocer**, to smart; **mecer**, to rock; and the following irregular verbs: **hacer** (and compounds), to make; **decir** (and compounds), to say.

Verbs ending in **-ducir** besides changing c to zc also form preterites with **j**, *e.g.*, **conducir**: 1st person Preterite is **conduje**.

Other Peculiarities

1. As unaccented **i** cannot stand between two vowels, note the changes necessary with the following verbs:

> **creer:** creyendo (for cre-iendo); creyó (for cre-ió)
> creyeron (for cre-ieron)
> **concluir:** concluyendo; concluyó; concluyeron; etc.

Like **creer** is: **leer.** Like **concluir** are: **destruir; huir; construir.**

2. When the stem ends in -**ll** or -**ñ**, the **i** of the endings -**ie**-, -**ió**, disappears.

> **bullir:** bullendo; bulló; bulleron
> **gruñir:** gruñendo; gruñó; gruñeron

3. A certain number of verbs whose root ends in the vowel **i** and **u** take an accent on the **i** or **u**, in the 1st, 2nd, and 3rd persons singular and 3rd person plural of the Present Indicative, in the Present Subjunctive and also in the Imperative singular.

> **criar**   *Pres. Tense:* **crío, crías, cría; crían**
> to bring up: *Pres. Subj.:* **críe, críes, críe; críen**
>   *Imperative:* **cría**
> **continuar**   *Pres. Tense:* **continúo,** etc.
> to continue: *Pres. Subj.:* **continúe,** etc.
>   *Imperative:* **continúa**

Note. Like **criar** are: **enviar,** to send; **fiar** (and compounds), to trust; **guiar,** to guide; **liar,** to bind; **telegrafiar,** to telegraph; **vaciar,** to empty; etc.
Like **continuar** are **situar,** to situate; **insinuar,** to insinuate; **perpetuar,** to perpetuate; **puntuar,** to punctuate; etc.

Exercises

1. I want you to pay me for the book before you go. 2. I took out my watch and showed it to him. 3. "I want you to

catch this apple, Enrique. Don't drop it!" 4. The king has ordered that we should conquer this enemy. 5. He empties the box and then destroys it. 6. I began my homework at half-past six and finished at nine. 7. Before your brother sends me the parcel, bind it with rope! 8. Let us distinguish between the true and the false. 9. The servant led me along the dark corridor. 10. I don't believe you will recognise my father after his illness. 11. They concluded the concert by singing the school song. 12. He didn't believe them when they told him what they had heard. 13. We do not wish his body to lie in a foreign land. 14. I played the piano all the morning until lunch-time. 15. It is necessary that the soldiers advance quickly.

12. RADICAL-CHANGING VERBS

CLASS 1. Certain -**ar** and -**er** verbs.

When the radical vowel is stressed: $\begin{Bmatrix} e > ie \\ o > ue \end{Bmatrix}$

Example:

Infinitive	Pres. Tense	Pres. Subj.	Imperative
despertar	despierto	despierte	
	despiertas	despiertes	despierta
	despierta	despierte	
	despertamos	despertemos	
	despertáis	despertéis	despertad
	despiertan	despierten	
mostrar	muestro	muestre	
	muestras	muestres	muestra
	muestra	muestre	
	mostramos	mostremos	
	mostráis	mostréis	mostrad
	muestran	muestren	
perder	pierdo, etc.	pierda, etc.	pierde, perded

CLASS 2. Certain -**ir** verbs.

Besides the changes in CLASS 1, these verbs also change **e** to **i**, **o** to **u**, when stressed -**a**, -**ie**, or -**ió** follows.

Example:

Infin.	Pres. Part.	Pres. Tense	Pres. Subj.	Imper.	Pret.
sentir	sintiendo	siento	sienta		sentí (1st Pers.
		sientes	sientas	siente	Sing.)
		siente	sienta		sintió (3rd Pers.
		sentimos	sintamos		Sing.)
		sentís	sintáis	sentid	sintieron (3rd Pers.
		sienten	sientan		Plur.)
dormir	durmiendo	duermo	duerma		dormí (1st Pers.
		duermes	duermas	duerme	Sing.)
		duerme	duerma		durmió (3rd Pers.
		dormimos	durmamos		Sing.)
		dormís	durmáis	dormid	durmieron (3rd
		duermen	duerman		Pers. Plur.)

CLASS 3. Certain **-ir** verbs.

These verbs change the vowel in exactly the same *places* as CLASS 2, but have only one kind of change, **e** to **i**, for all of them.

Example:

Infin.	Pres. Part.	Pres. Tense	Pres. Subj.	Imper.	Pret.
pedir	pidiendo	pido	pida		pedí (1st Pers.
		pides	pidas	pide	Sing.)
		pide	pida		pidió (3rd Pers.
		pedimos	pidamos		Sing.)
		pedís	pidáis	pedid	pidieron (3rd Pers.
		piden	pidan		Plur.)

The following are some of the commonest radical-changing verbs.

CLASS 1

acertar, to hit the mark
acordarse de, to remember
acostarse, to lie down
almorzar, to lunch
aprobar, to approve (to pass exam.)
atravesar, to cross
calentar, to warm
cerrar, to shut
colgar, to hang up

comenzar, to begin
confesar, to confess
consolar, to console
contar, to count, relate
costar, to cost
defender, to defend; forbid
demonstrar, to prove, show
descender, to descend
devolver, to give back
doler, to hurt, pain

empezar, to begin

encender, to light

encerrar, to enclose, shut up

encontrar, to find, meet

entender, to understand

enterrar, to bury

envolver, to wrap up, enfold

errar, to wander

forzar, to force

gobernar, to govern

helar, to freeze

llover, to rain

merendar, to have a snack

morder, to bite

mostrar, to show

mover, to move

negar, to deny

nevar, to snow

oler, to smell

pensar, to think

perder, to lose

probar, to try, test, prove

quebrar, to break

recordar, to recall

resolver, to determine, solve

rogar, to request

sembrar, to sow

sentarse, to sit down

soler, to be accustomed to

soltar, to loosen, release

sonar, to sound

soñar, to dream

temblar, to tremble

tender, to stretch (out)

tentar, to tempt, try

tronar, to thunder

tropezar, to stumble

volar, to fly

volver, to return

Notes. (a) **Jugar** and the following -ir verbs: **adquirir, concernir, discernir, inquirir,** belong to this class.

(b) Consonant changes occur where applicable (*e.g.,* **tropezar**) (see Orthographic-changing verbs).

(c) In **errar** and **oler** accented **e** and **o** become **ye** and **hue** respectively.

			Singular	*Plural*
e.g., **errar:**	*Pres. T.:*		**yerro**, etc.	**erramos**, etc. **yerran**
	Pres. Subj.:		**yerre**, etc.	**erremos**, etc. **yerren**
	Imperative:		**yerra**	**errad**
oler:	*Pres. T.:*		**huelo**, etc.	**olemos**, etc. **huelen**
	Pres. Subj.:		**huela**, etc.	**olamos**, etc. **huelan**
	Imperative:		**huele**	**oled**

(*d*) The Past participle of verbs in -olver is irregular (*e.g.*, volver: vuelto).

CLASS 2

advertir, to warn	herir, to wound
arrepentirse, to repent	hervir, to boil
conferir, to confer, grant	mentir, to tell a lie
consentir, to consent, agree	morir, to die
convertir, to convert	preferir, to prefer
diferir, to differ, defer	referir, to refer, relate
divertir, to amuse, turn aside	sentir, to feel, regret
dormir, to sleep	sugerir, to suggest
erguir, to erect	

Notes. (*a*) The Past participle of **morir** is irregular: **muerto**.

(*b*) In **erguir** the Present tense is **yergo** (or **irgo**), etc., but the 1st person plural is **erguimos**; the Present Subjunctive is **yerga** (**irga**), etc.

CLASS 3

ceñir, to gird	regir, to rule
conseguir, to obtain, achieve	reír, to laugh
corregir, to correct	rendir, to yield
despedir, to dismiss, send away	reñir, to scold
elegir, to elect, choose	repetir, to repeat
freír, to fry	seguir, to follow, continue
gemir, to moan, groan	sonreír, to smile
impedir, to hinder, prevent	teñir, to dye, stain
medir, to measure	vestir, to clothe, dress

Notes. (*a*) Consonant changes occur where applicable.

> *e.g.*, **corregir** and **seguir**:
>> **corrijo, sigo** (Present Indicative)
>> **corrija, siga** (Present Subjunctive)

(*b*) In verbs ending in -ñir, -ie and -ió lose their i after ñ.

e.g., **reñir:** *Preterite* (*3rd person sing. and pl.*): **riñó, riñeron.**
Present Participle: **riñendo.**

(c) In **freír, reír,** and **sonreír,** the **i** of the stem and the **-ie**
and **-ió** endings coalesce.

e.g., **reír:** *Preterite* (*3rd person sing. and pl.*): **rió, rieron.**
Present Participle: **riendo.**

Exercises

1. It always snows and freezes here in the winter. 2. I am
sure that bicycle costs more than ten pounds. 3. Do you
dream a lot? Not usually, but I always dream if I sleep in the
afternoon. 4. I am afraid that your mother will scold you.
5. My legs are aching and my feet are beginning to ache as
well. 6. "Isabel, return that pencil at once to your brother!"
said her sister. 7. "Sit down and wait! It is raining outside."
8. He amused me because he went on laughing. 9. "Don't
close the door! My friend is following me." 10. I deny that
she trembles when I speak to her. 11. The oil-lamp we
bought the other day still smells. 12. He prefers to remain
unknown in this company. 13. Too many soldiers died last
year from that illness. 14. He repented too late. 15. She
always falls asleep when she is listening to the wireless. 16.
They dressed hurriedly and went downstairs to have breakfast.
17. She smiled and then repeated what I had said. 18. We
want you to ask for the money. 19. I am not suggesting that
you correct the mistake. 20. They return to-day. I hope it
doesn't rain. 21. I don't believe he ever tells lies. 22. "Follow
me and don't smile if the manager scolds you!" 23. He
laughed and said: "I am sorry." 24. I suggest that you
amuse yourself now. 25. "Don't move, as I am going to take
your photograph."

13. PREPOSITIONS AFTER VERBS

The Use of Prepositions after Verbs before a Following Verb

1. The following is a list of the more commonly used verbs taking a direct Infinitive:

aconsejar, to advise to
acostumbrar, to be in the habit of
afirmar, to affirm
amenazar, to threaten to
anhelar, to long to
asegurar, to assure, claim to
confesar, to confess to
conseguir, to manage to, succeed in
creer, to believe
deber, must, should
decidir, to decide to
dejar, to let, allow
desear, to desire to
determinar, to determine to
elegir, to choose to
esperar, to hope, expect to
evitar, to avoid
fingir, to pretend to
gustar, to be pleasing to
hacer, to do, to make
imaginarse, to imagine to
impedir, to prevent, to hinder
intentar, to try to, attempt to

jurar, to swear to
lograr, to succeed in
mandar, to order to
merecer, to deserve to
necesitar, to need to
negar, to deny
olvidar, to forget to
parecer, to appear, seem to
pensar, to intend to
permitir, to permit to
poder, to be able to
preferir, to prefer to
procurar, to try to
prohibir, to forbid to
prometer, to promise to
proponer, to propose to
querer, to wish to
reconocer, to recognize
recordar, to recall
resolver, to resolve to
saber, to know how to
sentir, to feel, to be sorry to
servirse, to be kind enough to
soler, to be used to
temer, to fear to

Notes. Verbs of perception by the senses—such as **oír,** to hear; **ver,** to see—are usually followed by an infinitive coming immediately after them.

> *e.g.,* **Veo jugar a los niños,** I see the children playing.
> **Oigo cantar a las muchachas,** I hear the girls singing.

Note the impersonal use of **gustar,** to be pleasing.

> **Me gusta leer novelas,** I like reading novels (*i.e.,* it is pleasing to me to read novels).

2. The following verbs take the preposition **a** before a verb:

(*a*) Verbs of motion: **ir,** to go; **venir,** to come; **correr,** to run; **subir,** to go up; **bajar,** to go down; **entrar,** to enter; **acercarse,** to approach; **apresurarse,** to hasten; etc.

> *e.g.,* **Vd. vino a verme,** you came to see me.

(*b*) Verbs of teaching (**enseñar,** to teach; etc.) and learning (**aprender,** to learn; etc.).

> *e.g.,* **Aprendo a hablar español,** I am learning to speak Spanish.

(*c*) Verbs of beginning (**empezar,** to begin; etc.) and continuing (**continuar,** to continue; etc.), except **seguir.**

> *e.g.,* **Los niños empiezan a leer bien,** the children are beginning to read well.

Note. **Seguir** in the sense of 'to continue' is followed by the Present Participle in Spanish.

> *e.g.,* **Siguió hablando,** he went on talking.

Continuar can also have this construction.

> *e.g.,* **Continúan escribiendo,** they go on writing.

(*d*) In addition to the above, the following are some of the commonest verbs taking **a** with an infinitive:

abandonarse a, to give oneself up to

acostumbrarse a, to get used to

animar a, to encourage to, to urge to

aplicarse a, to apply oneself to

aspirar a, to aspire to

atreverse a, to dare to

autorizar a, to authorize to

aventurarse a, to venture to

ayudar a, to help to

comprometerse a, to undertake to

condenar a, to condemn to

conspirar a, to conspire to

contribuir a, to contribute to

convidar a, to invite to

decidirse a, to decide to

dedicarse a, to devote oneself to

detenerse a, to stop to

disponerse a, to get ready to

enviar a, to send to

exponerse a, to expose oneself to

forzar a, to force to

incitar a, to incite to

inducir a, to induce to

invitar a, to invite to

limitarse a, to limit oneself to

llegar a, to come to, to succeed in

negarse a, to refuse to

obligar a, to oblige to

oponerse a, to object to

pararse a, to stop to

persuadir a, to persuade to

prepararse a, to prepare to

quedarse a, to remain to

reducir a, to reduce to

renunciar a, to renounce

resignarse a, to resign oneself to

resistirse a, to resist

resolverse a, to make up one's mind to

tornar a, to . . . again

volver a, to . . . again

3. The following are some of the verbs which take **de** before an infinitive:

acabar de, to have just

acordarse de, to remember

acusar de, to accuse of

alegrarse de, to be glad to

arrepentirse de, to repent of

avergonzarse de, to be ashamed of

cansarse de, to be tired of

cesar de, to cease to

cuidar de, to take care to

dejar de, to leave off, cease to

no dejar de, not to fail to

descuidar de, to neglect

desesperarse de, to despair of

desistir de, to desist from

detenerse de, to stop from

dispensar de, to excuse from

disuadir de, to dissuade from

encargar de, to entrust with

encargarse de, to undertake to

excusar de, to excuse from

guardarse de, to take care not to

haber de, to have to

hartarse de, to grow tired of

incomodarse de, to be annoyed at

indignarse de, to be indignant at

jactarse de, to boast of

maravillarse de, to wonder at

olvidar(se) de, to forget to

no poder menos de, not to be able to help

privarse de, to be deprived of

quejarse de, to complain of

sospechar de, to suspect of

terminar de, to finish

tratar de, to try to

tratarse de, to be a question of

The following are some of the verbs which take other prepositions before an Infinitive:

complacerse en, to take pleasure in
consentir en, to consent to
consistir en, to consist of
convenir en, to agree to
deleitarse en, to take a delight in
divertirse en, to amuse oneself
dudar en, to hesitate to
empeñarse en, to insist on
entretenerse en, to amuse oneself in

esforzarse por, to strive to
tener éxito en, to succeed in
no tener éxito en, to fail in
hacer bien (mal) en, to do well (badly) in
insistir en, to insist on
ocuparse en, to busy oneself
pensar en, to think of
persistir en, to persist in
quedar (se) en, to agree to
tardar en, to be long in
vacilar en, to hesitate to

acabar por, to finish by
comenzar, empezar, por, to begin by

estar por, to be still to be done
luchar por, to fight to
suspirar por, to sigh to

contar con, to count on
estar para, to be about to
soñar con, to dream of

servir para, to serve to, be used for

Exercises

1. We hope to enjoy ourselves on the beach. 2. He started by pretending to be ill. 3. They refused to help us. 4. She is accustomed to listen to the wireless every morning. 5. I can't draw or paint, can you? 6. He succeeded in preventing the accident. 7. I like to see kittens playing. 8. Have you ever heard my sister screaming? 9. I can't teach you singing without a piano. 10. She went up to see her mother who was in bed. 11. Do you remember trying to do my homework? 12. I intend to give up studying after supper. 13. They are going to help us solve the mystery. 14. The judge forced him to confess. 15. We shall stop to have lunch somewhere. 16. Nobody invited him to be present. 17. He stated again

that he had made a mistake. 18. When will he leave off praising himself? 19. They promised to stop complaining. 20. Sometimes I dream of flying in an aeroplane. 21. They had just stopped talking when the door opened. 22. I am getting tired of scolding him. 23. I am getting ready to receive our guest. 24. We never dare go and see him after nine o'clock. 25. You prefer to choose your own present, don't you?

The Use of Prepositions after Verbs with a Following Noun

(a) Here is a list of some commonly used verbs which take a preposition before a noun or pronoun:

abusar de, to abuse, misuse
acordarse de, to remember
asustarse de, to be frightened
burlarse de, to make fun of
cambiar de, to change
carecer de, to lack
darse cuenta de, to realize
desconfiar de, to mistrust
disfrutar de, to enjoy
dudar de, to doubt

enterarse de, to enquire about
gozar de, to enjoy
informarse de, to be informed about
olvidar(se) de, to forget
pasar de, to exceed
salir de, to leave
servirse de, to use
tirar de, to pull, drag

acercarse a, to approach
aproximarse a, to approach
asemejarse a, to resemble
asistir a, to attend, be present at
dar a, to overlook
faltar a, not to fulfil, to break (word or promise)

fiarse a, to trust
llegar a, to reach (place)
oponerse a, to oppose
parecerse a, to resemble
renunciar a, to renounce
resistir a, to resist

penetrar en, to penetrate
reparar en, to notice
entrar en, to enter

fijarse en, to notice
influir en, to influence

casarse con, to marry

reñir con, to quarrel with

(*b*) Some Spanish verbs take a direct object, whereas the English verb takes a preposition:

agradecer, to be grateful for
aguantar, to put up with
aprovechar, to take advantage of, to profit from
buscar, to look for
cuidar, to look after
escuchar, to listen to
esperar, to wait for

mirar, to look at
pedir, to ask for
recordar, to remind of
regalar, to make a present of
reprochar, to reproach with
señalar, to point to
sentir, to be sorry about
soportar, to put up with

(*c*) Some Spanish verbs which are followed by a different preposition from the one in English:

alimentarse de (or **con**), to feed on
asombrarse de, to wonder at
compadecerse de, to be sorry for
depender de, to depend on
maravillarse de, to wonder at

reírse de, to laugh at, make fun of
triunfar de, to triumph over
vengarse de, to take revenge for
vivir de (or **con**), to live on

consentir en, to consent to
consistir en, to consist of
convenir en, to agree to

destacarse en (or **sobre**), to stand out against
pensar en, to think of

contar con, to rely on

soñar con, to dream of

arrimarse a, to lean against
asomarse a (or **por**), to lean out of

jugar a, to play (a game)
oler a, to smell of
saber a, to taste of, smack of

felicitar por, to congratulate on

interesarse por, to be interested in

(*d*) Some Spanish verbs whose meaning differs according to the prepositions which follow them:

acordarse con, to agree with (persons); **acordarse de,** to remember.

contar, to count, to relate; contar con, to count on, to rely on.

convenir a, to suit; convenir con, to agree with.

entender, to understand; entender de, to know all about something.

preguntar, to ask; preguntar por, to ask for.

saber, to know; saber de, to know about.

(e) The following Spanish verbs take a with persons to render 'from' (or 'of').

arrancar, }
arrebatar, } to snatch
comprar, to buy
esconder, to hide
ocultar, to conceal

pedir, to ask for
quitar, to take away from
robar, to rob, steal
tomar, to take

e.g., Me robó el dinero a mí, he stole the money from me.

Exercises

1. The soldiers approached the town during the darkness.
2. I am enjoying the view. Isn't it wonderful? 3. Are you looking for your small brother? 4. Don't wait for me after eight o'clock! 5. Those girls are always laughing at me. 6. I don't like walking in the country when it is windy. 7. Isn't Rosita like her mother? 8. I remember clearly the whole matter. 9. I often listen to the Third programme. I like it. 10. My wife and I are giving up all luxury. 11. The customer enquired about the price of wines. 12. A thief stole a lot of money from my father. 13. I am relying on your friend to help us. 14. He noticed Juanito leaning out of a window. 15. They all consented to the proposal. 16. My uncle is a judge of wines. 17. The police entered the house by the bedroom window. 18. Will you please pay for the goods when they arrive? 19. I marvel at your audacity in the matter. 20. My cousin is marrying her employer tomorrow.

14. SOME NOTES ON CERTAIN VERBS

ACABAR, 'to finish.' **ACABAR DE,** 'to have just . . . .'

> *e.g.,* **Acabo de terminarlo,** I have just finished it.

Note that 'to finish' + verb is **terminar de.**

> *e.g.,* **Terminé de escribir la carta,** I finished writing the letter.

ANDAR and **IR.** Both verbs mean 'to go,' but **andar** only can be used to refer to mechanical things.

> *e.g.,* **Este gramófono no anda,** this gramophone doesn't work.
> **Iremos allí en bicicleta,** we shall go there on our bicycles.

N.B. **Ir andando,** to walk, go on foot.

CABER means literally 'to be contained in,' but can be rendered in a variety of ways in English.

> *e.g.,* **Aquí no caben todas estas cosas,** all these things won't go in here, *or* there isn't room for all these things in here.
> **No cabe,** it doesn't fit.

N.B. **No cabe duda,** there is no doubt; **no cabe más,** that is the limit.

CONOCER and **SABER.** Saber means to know a thing by means of one's reason, or through having learnt it. It also renders 'can,' etc., in the sense of 'to know how' (to do something). **Conocer** means 'to know' in the sense of 'to be acquainted with,' 'to know' a person or place.

> *e.g.,* **Sé que Vd. no tiene razón,** I know you are wrong.
> ¿ **Conoce Vd. a mi primo?** Do you know my cousin?
> **Él no sabe montar a caballo,** he doesn't know how to (*i.e.,* he can't) ride a horse.

DAR, 'to give,' occurs in many idiomatic expressions.

> *e.g.*, **estar dando las dos,** to strike two.
> **dar los buenos días,** to wish good morning.
> **dar a,** to look on to.
> **dar un paseo,** to go for a walk.
> **dar con,** to come across, to meet.

DEBER, 'to owe,' also 'must,' 'ought,' etc.; **deber de** plus Infinitive expresses probability.

> *e.g.*, **Vd. debe de estar cansado,** you must be tired.
> **Deben de tener sed,** they are probably thirsty, they must be thirsty.

N.B. The Conditional tense of **deber** means 'ought.'

> *e.g.*, **Vd. debería volver inmediatamente,** you ought to return at once.

HABER is mainly used as an auxiliary verb to form Compound tenses with the Past Participles of verbs.

N.B. **hay,** there is, there are; **había,** there was, there were; **hubo,** there was, there were; **habrá,** there will be; **habría,** there would be; **ha habido,** there has been, there have been.

> **He aquí,** here is, behold.
> **Hay que,** it is necessary to.
> **¿Qué hay?** What is the matter?
> **Hay muchas cosas que hacer,** there are many things to be done.
> **haber de,** am to, is to, are to, etc.; must. (This verb is often equivalent to a future.)

> > *e.g.*, **Le prometo que he de rehusarlo,** I promise you I shall refuse it.
> > **Estoy seguro de que ha de gustarte,** I am certain it will please you.

HACER. Note the following idiomatic uses:

> **hacer falta,** to need, want, to be necessary.

e.g., **Me hace falta una nueva corbata,** I need a new tie.
hacerse, to become, 'get.'
e.g., **Se hace oscuro,** it is getting dark.

Hace largo rato, a long while ago; **hacer construir una casa,** to have a house built; **hacer el favor de,** please . . . (with Infinitive) (*e.g.*, ¡ **Haga el favor de sentarse!** Please sit down!); **hacer una pregunta,** to ask a question; **hacer lo posible,** to do one's best.

PARECER used impersonally means 'think.'

e.g., **Me parece que se ha equivocado,** it is my opinion (*i.e.*, it appears to me) that he has made a mistake.
¿ **Qué le parece?** What do you think?
¿ **Cómo le parece este nuevo sombrero?** What do you think of this new hat?
Me parece que es demasiado grande, I think it is too big.

N.B. **Parecerse a,** to be like (*e.g.*, **El hijo se parece a su padre,** the son is like his father).

PEDIR, PREGUNTAR, and **ROGAR** all mean 'to ask.' **Preguntar,** to ask something; **pedir,** to ask for something; **rogar,** to ask somebody to do something: (**rogar** plus Subjunctive, with the **que** often omitted.)

e.g., **Le pedí dinero,** I asked him for money.
Le pregunté cómo se llamaba, I asked him what his name was.
Le rogué (que) me ayudase, I asked him to help me.

PODER, 'to be able,' 'can,' 'may,' etc., denotes physical ability, **SABER** ability in the sense of 'to know how to.'

e.g., **No puedo jugar al tenis porque me he dislocado el pie,** I can't play tennis because I have dislocated my foot.

Note. ¿**Se puede?** Is it possible?; **no poder (por) menos de,** not to be able to help . . . .

> *e.g.,* ¿**Se puede pasar?** Can I come in?
>> **No pude (por) menos de hacerlo,** I couldn't help doing it.

PONERSE, 'to put (or place) oneself,' 'to become' (with Adjectives), 'to set,' 'to begin,' 'to put on.'

> *e.g.,* **Me puse de pie,** I stood up.
>> **El sol se pone temprano en el invierno,** the sun sets early in winter.
>> **Ella se puso a llorar,** she began to cry.
>> **Se paró y se puso pálido,** he stopped and turned pale.
>> **Se puso los zapatos,** he put on his shoes.

SER DE means 'to belong to,' 'to become of,' 'to be from,' etc.

> *e.g.,* **Este cuarto es de Pedro,** this room is Peter's.
>> ¿**Qué ha sido de ellos?** What has become of them?
>> **Son de Londres,** they are from London.

SERVIR, 'to serve,' has a number of idiomatic uses.

> *e.g.,* **Sírvase Vd.** renders 'please' particularly when speaking to inferiors.
>> **servir de,** to serve as.
>> **servirse de,** to use, make use of.
>> ¿**Para qué sirve eso?** What is the good (use) of that?
>> **No sirve para nada,** it is good for nothing.

SOLER (with Infinitive), 'to be wont to,' 'to be used to,' 'to be in the habit of.' This verb is only used in the Present and Imperfect tenses.

> *e.g.,* **Suele dar un paseo todas las mañanas,** he is used to going for a walk every morning.
>> **Solía levantarse a las seis,** he was in the habit of getting up at six, *or* he usually got up at six.

TENER translates 'to have' in the sense of 'to possess,' 'to hold.'

N.B. **tener calor,** to be hot; **tener frío,** to be cold (both these expressions refer to persons only); **tener hambre,** to be hungry; **tener sed,** to be thirsty; **tener razón,** to be right; **tener miedo,** to be afraid; **tener sueño,** to be sleepy. **tener la bondad de,** to be good enough to; **tener ganas de,** to want to.

> *e.g.,* ¡ **Tenga la bondad de hablar más despacio!** Please speak more slowly!

> **tener que,** to have to, must (stronger than **haber de**).

> *e.g.,* **Tengo que verle en seguida,** I must see him at once.

> ¿ **Qué tiene Vd.?** What is the matter with you?

VALER, 'to be worth.'

> *e.g.,* ¿ **Cuánto vale?** How much is it?

> **No vale la pena,** it isn't worth while.

> **Más vale reír que llorar,** it is better to laugh than to cry.

N.B. **valerse de,** to avail oneself of, make use of.

VOLVER A plus Infinitive translates 'again,' 'back,' 'once more.'

> *e.g.,* **Volvió a reírse,** he laughed again.

Exercises

1. There has been a crisis in Portugal, hasn't there? 2. It is necessary to work harder. 3. The Queen is to pass this way to-morrow. 4. He is in the habit of going for a walk on Sundays. 5. She was very cold and hungry, so she went to bed. 6. "Are you sleepy? No, but I am very tired." 7. We must send that letter to-night. 8. I couldn't help looking at his tie. 9. Do you know that little church on the corner? 10. Mary can't play the piano but she can sing. 11. It wasn't worth while waiting for them. 12. He didn't ask me for advice. 13. I should like to ask whether your sister is married.

14. He has become very diligent. 15. I am having a new house built. 16. I wish my watch would go. 17. There is no doubt that his conduct has improved. 18. I think he is worthy of a good post. 19. "You can't help doing silly things, can you?" 20. This box won't hold all the apples. 21. "Many thanks," the old man said again. 22. The bedroom in which I sleep looks on to the street. 23. I have just sent him the book. I ought to have sent it sooner. 24. "May I come in? I want to talk to you." 25. "Please sit down," my employer said to me as I entered the room.

APPENDIX

(N.B. No vocabulary is provided for this section.)

*Questions set in Spanish at the School Certificate
Examinations (now the Ordinary Level of the
General Certificate of Education)*

I. DICTATION

1.   *A Morning Visit*

Yo he llegado a media mañana / a este pueblecillo / sosegado
y claro. / El sol iluminaba la ancha plaza; / unas sombras
azules, frescas, / caían en un ángulo / de los aleros de las
casas / y bañaban las puertas. / Yo me he detenido un
instante, / gozando del silencio profundo, / y luego he llamado /
en la casa del gran hombre. / La puerta estaba entreabierta, /
no era indiscreción el entrar. / El zaguán se hallaba desierto; /
sobre una mesa / he visto un candelero / con la vela a medio
consumir, / un vaso vacío, / y un rimero / de periódicos de la
provincia / con las fajas intactas. / Un profundo silencio /
reina en toda la casa; / los muebles están llenos de polvo.

(*Welsh Joint Education Committee*, 1950)

2.   *Consequences*

Vi con perfecta claridad / lo que iba a suceder. / La
muerte de aquel hombre / divulgada en seguida / por la
ciudad; / la policía / echándome mano; / la consternación /
de mi yerno, / los desmayos / de mi hija, / los gritos de mi
nietecita; / luego a la cárcel, / el proceso / arrastrándose
perezosamente / al través de los meses / y acaso de los años; /
la dificultad de probar / que había sido / en defensa propia; /
la acusación del fiscal / llamándome asesino, / como siempre
acaece / en estos casos; / la defensa de mi abogado / alegando /
mis honrados antecedentes; / luego la sentencia / de la Sala /
absolviéndome quizá, / quizá condenándome / al presidio.

(*Central Welsh Board*, 1949)

3. *A Knight's Dress*

El traje de paz / era éste: / primero se ponían la camisa, / después las calzas de paño / cubriendo toda la pierna, / y los zapatos, / que solían ir adornados / con labores. / Inmediatamente sobre la camisa / se ponían el brial, / túnica hecha / por lo común / de una tela de seda / entretejida con oro. / Llegaba hasta los pies / e iba hendido / delante y detrás / para poder cabalgar / cómodamente, / dejando caer / cada mitad de su falda / por uno y otro lado / del caballo. / Encima se ponía la piel, / abrigo más corto / que el brial, / con manga ancha / o perdida, / hecho de armiño / o de piel de conejo / o cordero, / y forrado al exterior / con seda. / Sobre la piel / se ponía el manto, / anudado o prendido / en el hombro derecho. /

(Oxford and Cambridge Schools Examination Board,
December 1950)

4. *The End of a Journey*

Era completamente / de día, / y por la ventanilla / del coche, / que había abierto / de par en par / el señor gordo, / entraban a la vez / el sol rojizo / y el aire fresco / de la mañana. / El juez, que, / por lo que podía / colegirse, / no veía la hora / de dejar / tan poco agradable reunión, / apenas se convenció / de que habíamos llegado, / se terció la capa / al hombro / y saltó al andén / con una agilidad / que nadie / hubiera sospechado / en sus años / y su gordura. / Yo tomé / el pequeño saco / que era todo mi equipaje, / y después de saludar / a mis compañeros, / salí del vagón / buscando a un chico / que llevase / aquel bulto / y me condujese / a una fonda cualquiera.

(Oxford and Cambridge Schools Examination Board,
July 1950)

5.

Al llegar a la fonda / me encontré / con la cuenta del doctor. / Sus experiencias, / tratamiento, / alimentación y dictamen / estaban valuados / en ocho mil pesos. / Las visitas, / consulta y dictamen / de sus colegas, / lo mismo de

los / que habían votado en pro, / que en contra, / que de los
que se callaron, / importaba en suma, / apareciendo en esta
cuestión / perfectamente unánimes, / veinte mil pesos. / ¡Me
había descuidado / en confesar / que era millonario! / Le
pagué religiosamente, / y me encontré peor / que antes de la
consulta, / con mi estado más abatido, / con mi existencia
anormal / sin remedio alguno, / y con mi bolsillo / algo más
exhausto. / Tomé pasaje en un buque / para España, /
convencido / de que el pobre curandero Juan / sabía más /
que todos estos doctores juntos. /

Cuando puse el pie / en el puerto, / me rodearon dos
agentes / y me condujeron a la cárcel. /

Un compañero de viaje, / al cual presté / durante la
travesía / algún dinero, / me había delatado / al capitán del
buque. /

(University of London, December 1950)

II. TRANSLATION FROM SPANISH

1.   *Street Scene*

La mujer, resignada, aprobaba todo lo que decía su marido.
Cuando descansó un rato, se levantó nuevamente.

— Y yo — dijo — que no he tenido tiempo de preparar la cena.

— Déjalo — repuso él —. No tengo ninguna gana. Nos
acostaremos sin cenar.

— No, saldré a buscar algo.

— Iremos los dos si quieres.

— ¿Y el niño?

— Volveremos en seguida. No se despertará.

La mujer marchó a la cocina a lavarse las manos, pero la
fuente[1] no corría.

— Estamos bien. Hay que ir por agua.

Ella se echó un mantón sobre los hombros y cogió una
botella; él ocultó otra de barro debajo de la capa y salieron sin
hacer el menor ruido. La noche de abril era fría y desapacible.

Al pasar junto al Teatro Real vieron montones de hombres
que dormían acurrucados[2] en el suelo.

---

[1] water-tap.   [2] huddled up.

Por la calle de Arenal pasaban los coches con un sonar grave y majestuoso por el pavimento de madera.

Llenaron las botellas en una fuente de la Plaza de Isabel, y con esa complacencia que se tiene para las impresiones dolorosas, al pasar se detuvieron otra vez un momento delante de los hombres dormidos en montón.

(*University of Cambridge Local Examinations Syndicate,*
November 1949)

2.   *Besieged by the Sheriff*

William de Cloudsley entró en la ciudad de Carlisle siendo ya noche oscura. Llegó a su casa y llamó a la puerta calladamente. Su esposa Alicia abrió sorprendida y miedosa de los hombres del sheriff que vigilaban siempre. Los niños miraban con asombro a su padre. Toda la casa se llenó de alegría aquella noche. . . .

William oyó pasos de gente armada. Rápidamente subió con su esposa y sus hijos a una habitación del piso alto. Por una estrecha ventana vio a los soldados que sitiaban la casa. La mañana se iba abriendo clara y llena de voces.

El cazador William no sintió miedo. Había traído un buen puñado de flechas[1] y estaba dispuesto a resistir. Apercibió al juez y al sheriff, sus dos enemigos. Apuntó con su arco. El arco se curvó fuertemente. Silbó la flecha y fue a romperse contra el pecho del juez, protegido por la cota de mallas.[2]

— Ríndete, William — gritaron desde fuera.

La valerosa Alicia respondió briosamente:

— Mi marido no se rinde. No es un cobarde como vosotros.
. . .

El sheriff, lleno de rabia, mandó prender fuego a la casa sin compasión para la mujer y los niños.

PUEBLOS Y LEYENDAS
(*University of Cambridge Local Examinations Syndicate,*
November 1950)

3.   *An Old Street in Toledo*

Hay en Toledo une calle estrecha, torcida y oscura, que guarda tan fielmente la huella de las cien generaciones que en

[1] arrows.   [2] coat of mail.

ella han habitado, que habla con tanta elocuencia a los ojos del artista, y le revela tantos secretos puntos de afinidad entre las ideas y las costumbres de cada siglo, con la forma y el carácter especial impreso en sus obras más insignificantes, que yo cerraría sus entradas con una barrera y pondría sobre la barrera un tarjetón con este letrero:

'En nombre de los poetas y de los artistas; en nombre de los que sueñan y de los que estudian, se prohibe a la civilización que toque a uno solo de estos ladrillos con su mano demoledora y prosaica.'

Da entrada a esta calle por uno de los extremos un arco macizo, que sostiene un pasadizo cubierto.

(*Oxford Local Examinations, December* 1950)

4.

Currín se quedó admirando su sello . . . y pensando en Finita. Era Currín un chico dulce de carácter, no muy travieso,[1] aficionado a los dramas tristes, a las novelas de aventuras extraordinarias, y a leer versos y aprendérselos de memoria. Siempre estaba pensando que le había de suceder algo raro y maravilloso; de noche soñaba mucho, y con cosas del otro mundo o con algo procedente de sus lecturas. Desde que coleccionaba sellos, soñaba también con viajes de circunnavegación y países desconocidos, a lo cual contribuía mucho el ser decidido admirador de Julio Verne. . . . Aquella noche realizó dormido una excursioncita breve . . . a Terranova, al país de los sellos hermosos. Mejor dicho, no era excursión, sino traslado instantáneo a otro mundo; y en una playa orlada[2] de monolitos de hielo, que alumbraba una aurora boreal, Finita y él se paseaban muy serios, cogidos del brazo. . . .

Al otro día, nuevo encuentro en la escalera. Currín llevaba duplicados de sellos para obsequiar a Finita. En cuanto la dama vio al galán, sonrió y se acercó con misterio. "Aquí te traigo esto," balbuceó[3] él.

(*University of London, June* 1949)

---

[1] mischievous.   [2] *orlar*, to border.   [3] *balbucear*, to stammer.

5.　　　　　　　*Effect of Holidays*

En mi vida ordinaria, trabajo todos los días. Pasar una hora tan sólo, de las destinadas al trabajo, charlando, es para mí inconcebible. Pues bien; en cuanto rompo con mi vida ordinaria y empiezo el veraneo,[1] soy otro hombre. La pereza me invade, se apodera de mí y me corta la actividad para todas aquellas cosas en que más activo soy desde el otoño a la primavera. No sé qué pasa en mi mente, pero el efecto es como si de pronto una nube envolviese todas las sensaciones del vivir ciudadano. De golpe pierde todo su interés lo que hasta entonces me ha interesado vivamente; no quiero pensar en ello, y me desagrada que me obliguen a dedicarle la menor atención. El correo me trae libros y cartas. Por movimiento instintivo rompo fajas[2] y abro sobres con curiosidad; mas apenas me entero de lo que cada cosa es, la dejo sobre la mesa, sin leerla, aunque el asunto me interese mucho de ordinario.

(*Welsh Joint Education Committee*, 1950)

6.　　　　　　　*El arpa*

Del salón en el ángulo obscuro,
De su dueño tal vez olvidada,
Silenciosa y cubierta de polvo
　　　Veíase el arpa.

¡Cuánta nota dormía en sus cuerdas,
Como el pájaro duerme en las ramas,
Esperando la mano de nieve
　　　Que sabe arrancarla!

¡Ay! pensé; cuántas veces el genio
Así duerme en el fondo del alma,
Y una voz, como Lázaro, espera
　　　Que le diga: "¡Levántate y anda!"

(*University of London, December* 1950)

[1] *veraneo*. summer holidays.　　[2] *fajas*, wrappings.

7.   *Trees*

El árbol es la mano de la tierra.
Son sus dedos las ramas retorcidas,
y, más que por el viento, estremecidas
por el dolor fatal que todo encierra.

Cual las del hombre en su incesante guerra,
las sarmentosas[1] manos florecidas
se debaten a Dios siempre extendidas,
mientras al suelo la raíz se aferra[2] . . . .

El árbol es la imagen del anhelo
desgarrador de cuanto aspira al cielo,
al placer, a la estrella y a la nube. . . .

Por eso, cuando el hacha cruel lo hiende
o lo devora el fuego que lo enciende,
su esencia, como el alma, al cielo sube.

                    (*Oxford Local Examinations, July* 1948)

III. COMPREHENSION TESTS

1. Read carefully the following passage, which is NOT to be translated:

La vuelta de Balboa (*Balboa's return*)

Todo el pueblo salió a recibirle. Los aplausos, los vivas, las demostraciones más exaltadas de la gratitud y de la admiración le siguieron desde el puerto hasta su casa, y todo parecía poco para honrarle. Domador[3] de los montes, pacificador del istmo y descubridor del mar Austral, trayendo consigo más de cuarenta mil pesos en oro, un sinnúmero de ropas de algodón y ochocientos Indios de servicio, poseedor en fin de todos los secretos de la tierra y lleno de esperanzas para lo futuro, era considerado por los colonos del Darién como un ser privilegiado del cielo y de la fortuna, y dándose el parabién[4] de tenerle por caudillo,[5] se creían invencibles y

[1] *sarmentosas*, twining.   [2] *se aferra*, embeds itself.
[3] *domar = vencer*.   [4] *darse el parabién = felicitarse*.   [5] *jefe*.

felices en su dirección y gobierno. Comparaban la constante prosperidad que había disfrutado la colonia, la perspectiva espléndida que tenía delante, el acierto[1] y felicidad de sus expediciones, con los infelices sucesos de Ojeda, de Nicuesa, y hasta del mismo Colón,[2] que no había podido asentar el pie con firmeza en el continente americano.

Answer the following questions in SPANISH. Each answer should be concise but should be a complete sentence, the form and tense of which should suit those of the question:

  (i) ¿Adónde salió el pueblo?
 (ii) ¿Cómo le recibió el pueblo a Balboa?
(iii) ¿De dónde había recién vuelto?
 (iv) ¿Qué descubrimientos había hecho?
  (v) ¿Por qué era considerado como un ser privilegiado?
 (vi) ¿Cómo sabe Vd. que les gustaba a los colonos tenerle por caudillo?
(vii) ¿Con qué comparaban los colonos su prosperidad?
(viii) ¿Por qué se creían invencibles?
 (ix) ¿Quién era Colón?
  (x) Explique qué diferencia había entre las expediciones de Balboa y las de Colón.

(University of Cambridge Local Examinations Syndicate, November 1949)

2. Read the following passage carefully and answer the questions set on it. The answers must be *entirely in English.* No credit will be given for anything written in Spanish.

— ¿Llamaba Vd., señorita?

— Si, Carlota. ¿Me haces el favor de decir a Jorge que en cuanto acabe su trabajo en el establo baje al despacho del notario para pedirle a D. Prudencio que venga esta tarde a discutir algunos asuntos sobre el testamentario? El médico dijo que informásemos al notario inmediatamente.

— Sí, señorita. Y ¿quiere Vd. que vaya a correr las cortinas de este lado de la casa? Las ventanas dan a la calle, y estaría mejor visto.

---

[1] *habilidad.* [2] Columbus.

— Sí, se me había olvidado. Ah, y cuando vengas con el café me traes mi medicina, el corazón no me ha andado muy bien hoy.

Carlota cerró la puerta sin ruido, y se retiró. Emilia se quedó sola.

Entonces por fin tenía tiempo de considerar. Ya se acabó todo, se dijo. Ya llegó el fin que había esperado y temido durante tanto tiempo, durante todos los veinte años que había pasado con su hermana viuda. Ya no podría llamar suya la casa tan simpática, grande y vieja; habría que venderla. Las habitaciones en donde había pasado los más felices años de su vida tendrían que desocuparse de todos aquellos muebles y recuerdos de Alicia. Todo pertenecía ahora a la familia de su difunto cuñado, y ella misma tendría que marcharse de la Casa de las Piedras, y vivir en alguna calle en donde la vida fuese más barata; en donde, según suponía, pasaría una vida triste, sin nada que hacer.

(a) What event had recently happened in the household?
(b) Why was D. Prudencio asked to call?
(c) What did Carlota suggest should be done, and why?
(d) Why did Emilia ask for medicine?
(e) Why would Emilia have to leave the house?
(f) Where did she expect to have to go?

(Oxford Local Examinations, December 1950)

IV. TRANSLATION INTO SPANISH

1.

Finita put one finger on her lips, as if to tell the boy to be silent. But he did not think that there was any harm in making her a present of his stamps and begged her to accept them. Finita remained, it appeared, rather sad; she had, undoubtedly, expected some other gift, and quickly approaching Currin, she said to him under her breath:

— And that . . . ?

— That?

— What you were telling me about, yesterday.

Currin sighed, looked down at his shoes and burst out suddenly:

— Oh that, that was nothing at all.

— Why do you say that it was nothing? cried Finita, furious. You seem to forget very quickly!

And the boy, holding the stamp even more tightly in his fingers and speaking close to the girl's ear, murmured gently:

— Yes, it was something. . . . I wanted to tell you that . . . that you are very pretty!

(*University of London, June* 1949)

2.

At about midday we arrived at a village called Moncloa. It consisted of a few miserable houses, a large ugly building which might have been a castle, and an inn, which we approached. A solitary tree raised its head above the outer wall and a dog lay sleeping outside the doorway. We entered the inn, tied up our horses, and, after ordering corn to be brought for them, we sat down before a large fire which burned in the middle of the principal room. A few minutes later our host and his wife also came and sat down beside us.

I looked at these two people carefully. They were both young; the man appeared to be about twenty-five years of age and his wife perhaps a little less. He was short and evidently of great strength; his face was handsome but was full of malice and deceit. His wife resembled him but had honest and gentle eyes. While they were talking together my companion drew closer to me and whispered in Italian. "They are evil people," he said, "and this is an evil house; it is a refuge of thieves and men have been murdered here if all tales be true."

(*Oxford and Cambridge Schools Examination Board,
July* 1950)

3.

(*a*) A month ago an American soldier came to see me. "Good-day, sir. Are you Mr James?" he asked. "Yes," I replied. "I am your cousin, Paul. My father, your father's brother, left England in 1904 and has been living in Washington for forty years. Before I left the United States, father told me to come and see you as soon as I had the opportunity."

My wife, who had arrived at that moment, said, "I am very glad to see you. I hope you will stay with us for a while."

(b) I have a daughter aged fifteen who goes to a school situated near the South Coast of England. The other day I received a letter telling me that she had had an accident. While she was playing in the field she fell down and broke her leg.

I told my wife the sad news and immediately we began to think of our poor daughter. "What shall we do?" I asked.

"Somebody must go and see her to-day," replied my wife, and, getting up, she filled a bag with fruit and books and set off for the station.

(*Northern Universities Joint Board, October* 1944)

4.

I had no time to lose, for it was now between ten and eleven in the morning. Fortunately I had plenty of food, for, on leaving the camp and the horses at the entrance to the valley, I had taken everything I was likely to want for four or five days. My servant had carried half, but had dropped it when he ran off and I found it when I ran after him. I had, therefore, his provisions as well as my own. So I took as many biscuits as I thought I could carry and also some tobacco, tea, and a few matches. I put all these inside my blankets, made these into a long roll,[1] tied the two ends together, and put the whole round my neck and over one shoulder. This is the easiest way of carrying them. Then I began to ascend the valley, crossing and recrossing the river several times without difficulty. At one o'clock I was at the foot of the last slope[2] leading up to the pass,[3] and I had reached the top before it was dark.

(*Welsh Joint Education Committee,* 1950)

[1] roll, *rollu.*   [2] slope, *cuesta.*   [3] pass, *puerto.*

5.

Two of my friends are very fond of walking in the mountains.
One day in May they went from Madrid to a place in the
Sierra de Guadarrama where they had not been since before
the civil war, in 1936. They had been climbing for two or
three hours along a rough path, with magnificent views in
almost every direction, when one of them fell and cut his
knee on a rock. He was washing the wound with water from
his water-bottle when he remembered that if he used it all
they would be very thirsty before they returned home.
Fortunately as they were having their lunch a man they knew
quite well happened to pass, and he gave them some of his
lemonade.

(Oxford Local Examinations, December 1949)

V. FREE COMPOSITION

1. Continue the story told in Section II (*Translation from
Spanish*), number 4, and Section IV (*Translation into Spanish*),
number 1. Use your imagination. (About 160 words.)

(University of London, July 1949)

2. Imagine you are a fireman. Describe the scenes at a
recent fire. (About 160 words.)

(University of London, December 1950)

3. Su madre de Vd. ha estado enferma algunos días, y Vd.
ha tenido que quedar en casa para cuidarla y para hacer todos
los trabajos de la casa. Describa lo que ha hecho durante
uno de estos días. (About 120 words.)

(Oxford Local Examinations, December 1949)

4. Write in Spanish about 130 words as suggested by the
outline below. Use the past tense except where dialogue, if
any, requires the use of some other. Irrelevant details should
be avoided:

Una mañana los padres de Pedro y María salen de visita
— ¿cómo se entretienen los chicos durante el día? — no han
vuelto los padres al anochecer — al fin llegan — ¿por qué
han tardado tanto?

(*Welsh Joint Education Committee*, 1950)

5. Write not less than 110 and not more than 130 words in
Spanish on the following subject, using the past tense except
where any dialogue you may use requires the present or the
future:

Una niña sueña que se ha vuelto invisible. Ella sale a la
calle donde tiene muchas aventuras divertidas. Luego se
despierta en la cama. Describa Vd. el sueño de la niña.

(*Northern Universities Joint Board, July* 1944)

SPANISH–ENGLISH VOCABULARY

la **abeja,** bee
abierto, open, cut
abrazar, to embrace
el **abrevadero,** drinking-place for animals
el **abrigo,** overcoat; shelter
abril, April
abrir, to open
la **abuela,** grandmother
el **abuelo,** grandfather
acabar, to finish, come to an end; — **de,** to have just . . . .
el **accidente,** accident; rough place
la **acción,** action
aceptar, to accept
acercar, to bring near; — **se a,** to approach
acobardado, scared
acomodar, to accommodate
acompañar, to accompany
acontecer, to happen
acosar, to harass
acostarse, to go to bed, to lie down
el **acto,** act; **en el —,** on the spot, in the act
acudir, to gather; to come in answer to a summons
adelantar(se), to advance, to put forward
adelante, forward
la **adelfa,** rose-bay
además, besides, moreover; **además de,** besides
adentro, in, within, inwards
admirar, to wonder at, to admire
adormecido, -a, asleep, drowsy

adquirir (ie), to acquire
adrede, specially, on purpose
la **aduana,** customs
advertir (ie, i), to warn, to inform
aéreo, -a, aerial
el **aeropuerto,** airport
afablemente, affably, amiably
afiebrado, -a, feverish
afuera, outside
las **afueras,** outskirts
los **ágapes,** feast
agarrarse a, to clutch, to cling
agitar, to wave
agolparse, to beat furiously
agradable, pleasant
agradecer, to thank
agregar, to add
el **agua** (*f.*), water
aguardar, to wait
el **agujero,** hole
aguzar, to sharpen
ahí, there
ahogarse, to be drowned
ahora, now
ahuyentar, to put to flight
el **aire,** air
ajeno, -a, alien, belonging to some one else
el **ala** (*f.*), wing
el **álamo,** poplar-tree
el **alba** (*f.*), dawn
el **albercón,** pool
alborotar, to stir up, to cause a riot
el **alcaide,** warden of a prison
el **alcalde,** mayor
la **alcoba,** bedroom
la **aldea,** village

aldeano, -a, rustic, of a village

alegrarse, to be glad

alegre, joyful, cheerful

la alegría, joy

los aleros, eaves

alertar, to alert

algo, something, anything

alguno, some

algunos, a few

el aliento, breath

el alma (f.), soul, heart, mind

el almacén, store

la almohada, pillow

alrededor, around

alterar, to disturb

alternativamente, alternately

alto, -a, high

¡ alto !, halt

el altozano, hill, mound

la altura, height

alumbrar, to light

alzar, to raise; —se, to rise

allá, there, thither, yonder; más —, further away

el ama (f.), housekeeper, mistress of the house

amablemente, amiably

amanecer (n. & v.), dawn

amansado, tamed, won over

amansar, to tame, to quieten

el ambiente, atmosphere

ambos, both

amén de, in addition to, besides

ameno, -a, pleasant, agreeable

amigo, -a, friend, friendly

la amistad, friendship

el amor, love

amoroso, -a, loving

el amparo, protection

amplio, -a, broad

amueblar, to furnish

anciano, -a, ancient, old; los ancianos, old men and women

ancho, -a, wide

¡ Anda ! go on !

andaluz, Andalusian

andar, to go, to walk

angosto, -a, narrow

la anguila, eel

animar, to encourage

el ánimo, mind, spirit

anochecer (n. & v.), nightfall

anonadar, to crush, to overwhelm

ante, before, in front of

la antena, lateen-yard

el antro, cave

el anuncio, notice, advertisement

añadir, to add

el año, year

apagar, to extinguish, to quieten

el aparato, machine

aparecer, to appear

la aparición, appearance

apartado, secluded, remote

apenas, scarcely

apiadarse de, to take pity on

apiñado, -a, thronging, close-packed

aplicar, to apply

apostado, -a, stationed

apoyado, -a, leaning

apreciable, esteemed, valued

apresurado, -a, hurried, hasty

apresurarse, to hurry

apretar, to press

aprisionar, to take prisoner, to seize

aproximarse, to approach

apuntar, to aim

aquel, -la, -los, -las, that, those, the former

aquí, here

el **arado,** plough
arañar, to scratch
el **árbol,** tree
arder, to burn
la **arena,** sand
argelino, from Algiers, Algerine
las **armas,** arms, weapons
armarse, to be organized, to take place
el **armatoste,** framework
arrancar, to snatch, to tear off
arreglar, to arrange, to settle, to put right
arriba, up; **hacia—,** upwards
el **arriero,** muleteer
arriesgar, to risk
arrodillarse, to kneel
arrojarse, to hurl oneself, to dash
la **arteria,** artery; thoroughfare
el **ascensor,** lift
asentar(ie), to set firmly, to establish, to settle in position
así, thus, so
así que, as soon as; so that
el **asiento,** seat
asir, to grip, to seize
asistir, to be present, to attend
el **asno,** ass, donkey
asomar, to appear
asombrarse, to be astonished
el **asombro,** amazement
el **aspa** (*f.*), blade of propeller
el **aspecto,** appearance
el **asunto,** matter, business
asustarse, to be frightened
atacar, to attack
atar, to tie
el **ataúd,** coffin

atento, -a, attentive, thoughtful
el **aterrizaje,** landing (see **tren**)
atinar (con), to hit the mark, to guess right
atisbar, to espy, to be on the watch
atormentar, to torture
atraer, to attract
atrás, ago, back, backwards
atravesar (ie), to cross, to traverse; **— por,** to pass through
el **aullido,** howl, howling
aun, even
aún, still, yet
aunque, although
el **auto,** car
el **autobús,** bus
el **autor,** author
autoritario, -a, authoritative
avanzar, to advance
avergonzado, -a, ashamed
el **averío,** poultry
el **avión,** aeroplane
¡ **ay !,** alas !
la **ayuda,** help, aid
ayudar, to help
la **azafata,** air-hostess
azorarse, to be terrified
azotar, to lash
azul, blue
el **azulejo,** tile

bailar, to dance
bajar, to descend, to get out
bajo (*adj.*), low; (*prep.*), underneath
la **bala,** bullet
balancear(se), to sway, to swing
el **balazo,** bullet-wound
balbucear, to stammer
el **balcón,** balcony
en balde, in vain
el **banco,** bench
la **bandada,** flock

la **bandera,** banner
el **bandido,** bandit, brigand
  bañar(se), to bathe
la **barca,** boat
el **barquero,** boatman
la **barra,** barrier, bar
el **barro,** clay, mud
el **barrote,** bar
  bastante, (*adj.*) enough, sufficient; (*adv.*) sufficiently, fairly, a good deal
  bastar, to be enough, to suffice
la **batalla,** battle
  batir, to bang
  beber, to drink
(el) **Belén,** Bethlehem; crib
la **berza,** cabbage
  besar, to kiss
la **bestia,** beast
  bíblico, -a, biblical
la **bicicleta,** bicycle
  bien, well; **no bien,** scarcely, no sooner
el **bigote,** moustache
  blanco, -a, white
  blando, -a, soft
el **blandón,** tall candle, torch
la **boca,** mouth
la **boda,** wedding
la **boina,** beret
la **bolsa,** shopping-bag; paper bag; purse
el **bolsillo,** pocket
la **borda,** gunwale
  bordar, to embroider
el **borde,** edge
 a **bordo de,** on board
el **bosque,** wood
el **bostezo,** yawn
el **boticario,** pharmacist
el **botón,** button; **— de arranque,** starter
la **bóveda,** vault, arched roof
  bravo, wild, fierce
el **brazo,** arm
  brillante, brilliant, shining

la **brillantez,** brilliancy
el **brío,** energy, vigour
la **brisa,** breeze
  brotar, to spout, to spurt
  bueno, good
el **buey,** ox
la **bufanda,** muffler
la **buhardilla,** attic
el **bullicio,** tumult, noise, shindy
el **buque,** ship
  burlón, joking, mocking
el **burro,** donkey
  buscar, to look for

  cabalgar, to ride
el **caballero,** gentleman
el **caballo,** horse
el **cabello,** hair
  caber, to be room for, to hold, to contain
la **cabeza,** head
la **cabezada,** nod; **dar —s,** to nod
  cabizbajo, -a, thoughtful, downcast
el **cabo,** corporal
  cada, each; **cada vez más,** more and more
la **cadena,** chain
  caer, to fall
la **caja, cajita,** box
  calado, -a, pulled down
el **calcetín,** sock
  calentador, -a, warming
el **calor,** heat
la **calzada,** roadway
  callar (se), to be silent
la **calle,** street
la **cama,** bed
  cambiar, to change
en **cambio,** in exchange, on the other hand
el **caminante,** wayfarer
  caminar, to go
el **camino,** road; **— de,** in the direction of

la **camisa,** shirt
la **camiseta,** sports-shirt
la **campana, campanilla,** bell
el **campanillazo,** ringing (of a bell)
el **campesino,** peasant
el **campo,** field; the country
  cansado, -a, tired; wearisome, boring
  cantar, to sing
la **cantarilla,** jug
la **caña,** cane, reed, splint
el **cañón,** cannon
la **capa,** cloak
el **capitán,** captain
la **cara,** face
el **carabinero,** customs officer
la **carátula,** grotesque mask
el **carbunclo,** carbuncle
la **carcajada,** guffaw, peal of laughter
la **cárcel,** prison
el **carcelero,** jailer
la **carga,** load, burden
  cargar, to load; — **con,** to pick up
la **carne,** meat; las **carnes,** flesh
la **carretera,** road
la **carta,** letter
la **cartita,** note
el **carruaje,** carriage, vehicle
la **casa,** house; firm
el **cascabel,** bell
el **casco,** hoof
el **caserón,** big house
  casi, almost
la **casilla,** hut, cottage
el **caso,** case; **no hacer —,** to pay no attention
el **castaño,** chestnut-tree
  castigar, to punish
el **castigo,** punishment
  cata, catad, look at, behold
el **caudal,** capital, fortune
  causar, to cause

la **caverna,** cave
  cavilar, to muse, to meditate, to turn over in one's mind
la **caza,** hunting, shooting
el **cazador,** hunter
  cazar, to hunt
  ceder, to yield; — **el paso,** to give way
la **ceja,** eyebrow
  celebrar, to celebrate
la **cena,** supper
  cenar, to have supper
  ceniciento, -a, ashen, grey
el **centenar,** a hundred
la **cera,** wax
  cerca de, near
  cercado, -a, fenced in, enclosed
  cercano, -a, near
la **cerda,** sow; **ganado de —,** herd of swine
el **cereal,** cornland
el **cerebro,** brain
la **cerradura,** lock
  cerrar (ie), to shut
  cesar, to cease
la **cesta, el cesto,** basket
el **ciclista,** cyclist
el **ciclo,** cycle, series
el **cielo,** sky, heaven
  cierto, -a, certain
la **cincha,** girth
  cincuenta, fifty
el **cine,** cinema
la **cinta,** ribbon
  circular, to circulate
el **círculo,** circle
  circundar, to surround
la **circunstancia,** circumstance
el **cirio,** candle
la **cita,** appointment, rendezvous
la **ciudad,** city
la **claridad,** clearness, brightness
la **clase,** class, kind

clavar, to nail; — los pies
en el suelo, to root to the
ground
el coche, coach, carriage, car
el cochero, driver, cabby
el cocido, dish of boiled meat
and vegetables
la cocina, kitchen
el codo, elbow
coger, to take hold of
la cola, tail, queue
el colegio, college
colgar (ue), to hang
colmar, to fill (to over-
flowing)
el colmillo, fang
el colmo, height, climax
colocar, to place
el colorín, bright colour
colosal, colossal, huge
el collarón, collar
el comandante, major
la comarca, district, region
el combatiente, combatant
el comedor, dining-room
el comensal, fellow-diner,
table-companion
comenzar (ie), to begin
comer, to eat, to dine
el comercio, business, shop
cometer, to commit
la comida, dinner, food
el comienzo, beginning
cominero, -a, effeminate
como, as, as if, how,
like
la cómoda, chest of drawers
la comodidad, comfort, convenience
el compañero, companion
componer, to compose
comprender, to understand,
to realise
común, common
la comunidad, community
con, with
concentrar, to concentrate

condenado, condemned, confounded
conducir, to lead
el conductor, driver
confesar (ie), to confess
confiar, to trust
la congestión,   congestion;
hora de — máxima, rush-
hour
congresarse, to gather together
conocer, to know, to be acquainted with
conseguir (i), to succeed in
obtaining, doing
el consejo, advice
la consideración, consideration
por consiguiente, in consequence, therefore
consistir en, to consist of
constante, constant
construir, to build
consultar, consult
contar (ue), to count;   to
relate, to tell
contener, to contain
contento, -a, satisfied
contestar, to answer
el continente, countenance
contra, against
el contrapunto, counterpoint
contrario, -a, contrary
el contrario, contrary; por el
—, on the contrary
el convencimiento, conviction
la conveniencia, suitability
conveniente, suitable, appropriate
convertir (ie, i), to convert
convidar, to invite
el corazón, heart
la corbata, tie
el cordel, cord
la cornisa, cornice, ledge
la corola, head of a flower
el corral, yard, farmyard
el corredor, corridor

el **correo**, mail, post
correr, to run
cortar, to cut
cortés, polite
el **cortijo**, farm
corto, -a, short
la **cosa**, thing; **otra —**, something else
la **costa**, cost
el **costal**, sack
costar (ue), to cost
la **costumbre**, custom
creer, to believe, to think
el **crepúsculo**, twilight
criado, -a, servant
la **criatura**, child
el **cristal**, glass, window
crujir, to creak
cruzar, to cross
cual, which, like
cualquier, cualquiera, any, some
cuán, how
cuando, when
cuanto, how much; **— antes**, as soon as possible
cuantos, how many; all those who
cuarenta, forty
el **cuarto**, room; copper
el **cuatrimotor**, four-engined plane
cubierto, see **cubrir**
el **cubo**, pail
cubrir, to cover
el **cuello**, neck
el **cuenco**, earthenware bowl
el **cuento**, tale
la **cuerda**, rope
el **cuerno**, horn
el **cuero**, leather
la **cuesta**, slope, hillside
la **cueva**, cave
la **cumbre**, mountain-top
el **cumplimiento**, fulfilment
cumplir, to attain; **cumplir con**, to fulfil, to carry out

la **cuneta**, ditch
la **cuña**, wedge, wedge formation
el **cura**, priest
cuyo, -a, -os, -as, whose

la **chica**, girl, lass
la **chicuela**, little girl
el **chorro**, jet
la **choza**, cottage

dar, to give
deber, to owe, must
el **deber**, duty
débil, weak
debajo de, underneath
decaer, to drop
decente, fitting, decent
decidirse a, to make up one's mind to
decir, to say
el **declive**, slope
defenderse, to defend oneself
dejar, to leave, to let, to miss; **— de**, to leave off, to stop doing something
delante, in front (of), before
delatar, to betray, to reveal
deleitar, to delight
deleitoso, -a, delightful
delicioso, -a, delightful, delicious
delirante, delirious
demás, rest; **los —**, the others
el **demonio**, devil
dentro de, inside
el **departamento**, compartment
el **depósito**, store
derecho, -a, right
derribar, to knock down, to overthrow
derrocado, -a, flung down
desafiar, to defy, to challenge

desarrollarse, to develop, to unfold

desbordar, to overflow

descabellar, to toss in disorder, to rumple

descalzo, -a, barefoot

descansar, to rest

el descanso, rest

descender (ie), to descend

descompuesto, -a, upset

desconfiado, -a, mistrustful

la desconfianza, mistrust

desconfiar, to mistrust

describir, to describe

desde, from, since

el desenlace, outcome

desencantar, to disillusion

desear, to desire

el deseo, desire

desesperado, -a, desperate

desfilar, to file past, to move in file

desgranar, to scatter

deslumbrar, to dazzle

desmayarse, to faint, to swoon, to droop

desnudo, -a, naked, bare

desolado, -a, desolate

el desorden, disorder

despacio, slowly

despejado, -a, clear

la despedida, farewell

la despensa, pantry

despertarse (ie), to wake up

desprevenido, -a, unprepared

después (de), after, next, later, since

destacar (se), to stand out

la destreza, skill

la desventaja, disadvantage

desviarse, to swerve

detenerse, to stop

devolver, to give back

el día, day; de — claro, (in) broad daylight

el diablo, devil

diciembre, December

dicho, see decir; — y hecho, no sooner said than done

difícil, difficult

diestro, -a, right (hand)

la dificultad, difficulty

dignarse, to deign, condescend

la dignidad, dignity

dilatado, -a, wide

la diligencia, stage-coach

el dinero, money

Dios, God

dirigir, to direct; —se a, to make for, to go forward, to address oneself to

discreto, -a, discreet

disminuir, to diminish

disparar, to fire

disponer, to dispose

distinguir, to distinguish

distraído, -a, absent-minded

distribuir, to distribute

diverso, -a, different

divertir (ie, i), to amuse; -se, to enjoy oneself

doblado, -a, bent

doce, twelve

el dolor, pain, grief

dominar, to dominate, to look down on

donde, where

dorado, -a, gilded, golden (in colour)

dorar, to gild

dormir (ue, u), sleep

dormitar, to doze

el dormitorio, bedroom

dos, two

la duda, doubt

dudar, to doubt

el duelo, duel

dulce, soft, sweet, gentle

durante, during

durar, to last

la dureza, hardness, sternness

el duro, dollar

duro, -a, hard; bleak

ebrio, -a, drunk
echar, to throw; **— a,** to start
la **educación,** education
la **educanda,** pupil (at a convent)
el **ejercicio,** exercise
elegir (i), to choose
elevarse, to rise
ello, it
embarazoso, -a, embarrassing
la **embarcación,** boat, vessel
sin **embargo,** nevertheless, all the same, however
embutir, to insert, to stuff
emigrar, to emigrate
empavesar, to deck with bunting
empezar (ie), to begin
el **empleado,** clerk, employee
emprender, to undertake
la **emulación,** emulation, rivalry
encaminarse (hacia), to go towards, to make for
encandecido, incandescent
el **encapuchado,** hooded man
encargarse de, to take charge of
encender (ie), to light
encerrar (ie), to shut up, to confine
el **encintado,** kerb
encomendado, -a, entrusted
encontrar (ue), to meet, to find; **—se,** to find oneself, to be
encorvarse, to bend down
el **enemigo,** enemy
enérgico, -a, energetic
el **energúmeno,** idiot
enfermo, -a, ill
enfilar, to go along (a street)

enfrente, opposite
engañar, to deceive; **—se,** to be mistaken
enguantado, gloved
el **enmascarado,** masked man
la **ensalada,** salad
enseñar, to show, to point to
enterar, to inform
enterarse (de), to inquire, to learn, to find out (about)
entonces, then, in that case
la **entrada,** entrance
entrar, to enter
entre, between
entregar, to hand over
entumecido, -a, numb, stiff
enviar, to send
la **envidia,** envy
envolver, to envelop, to cover
equilibrar, to balance
equivocarse, to be mistaken
erguir (i, ye), to erect
erizarse, to bristle, to stand on end
la **escalerilla,** ladder
escaparse, to escape
el **escaparate,** shop-window
el **escarabajo,** beetle
escaso, -a, rare, few, scarce
la **escopeta,** gun
la **escolta,** escort
el **escribano,** notary, scrivener
el **escritor,** writer
escuchar, to listen
ese, -a, -os, -as, that, those; **a eso de,** about
esforzarse (ue), to strive, to attempt
el **esfuerzo,** effort
esgrimir, to fence
esmerado, polished
esmerarse, to do one's best, to make great efforts
el **espacio,** space
espacioso, -a, spacious

la **espada**, sword
la **espalda**, back
espantoso, -a, terrifying
esparcir, to scatter, to spread
el **espectáculo**, sight, spectacle
el **espejo**, mirror
la **esperanza**, hope
esperar, to hope, to wait for
espesarse, to get thicker
espeso, -a, thick
el **espinazo**, spine, back
espinoso, -a, thorny, prickly
el **esplendor**, splendour
la **esposa**, wife
el **esposo**, husband; **los esposos**, married couple
la **espuma**, foam
el **esquilón**, cow- or sheep-bell
la **esquina**, corner
la **estación**, station; season
el **estaño**, tin
estar, to be
este, -a, -os, -as, this, these, the latter
la **estera**, mat
estirarse, to stretch oneself
esto (*pron. neut.*), this
estrecharse, to squeeze together
la **estrella**, star
el **estudio**, studio
evangélico, evangelical, biblical
evitar, to avoid
el **examen**, examination
exceder, to exceed
exclamar, to exclaim
excitar, to excite
experimentar, to experience, to feel
explicar, to explain
exponer, to expound, to explain
el **expreso**, express
extenderse (ie), to spread
extrañarse, to be surprised

extraño, -a, strange
el **extremo**, end

la **fachada**, façade, front
la **falda**, skirt, hillside
faltar, to.be missing
el **faro**, headlight
el **farolillo**, little lantern
fatigarse, to tire oneself out
fatigoso, -a, weary, toiling
la **faz**, face
la **fecha**, date
feliz, happy
el **festón**, festoon, garland
el **feudo**, domain
fiarse (en), to trust
la **fiesta**, holiday, festival
la **figura**, figure
figurarse, to imagine
fijarse (en), to notice, observe
la **fila**, file, line
el **fin**, end
la **firma**, signature
firme, firm
la **fisonomía**, face
flaco, -a, thin
la **flor**, flower; **a — de**, on a level with
florido, flowering
la **fonda**, inn
el **fondo**, background, bottom, far end
la **fortuna**, fortune
el **fósforo**, match
fragante, fragrant
Fray, Brother
frenar, to brake
la **frente**, forehead
fresco, -a, cool
el **fresco**, coolness
el **fresquecito**, draught
frío, cold
frondoso, -a, leafy
la **frontera**, frontier
el **fruto**, fruit, profit; **sin —** to no purpose

el **fuego**, fire; **hacer** —, to fire
el **fuego fatuo**, will o' the wisp
la **fuente**, tureen; fountain, pool, well
fuera de, outside, apart from; — **de sí**, beside himself
fuerte, strong
la **fuerza**, strength, force
fúlgido, -a, gleaming, flashing
el **fulgor**, bright glow
el **fusil**, rifle

las **gafas**, spectacles
la **galera**, galley
el **gallo**, cock
el **ganado**, flock, herd
ganar, to gain, to reach
el **ganso**, goose
garantizar, guarantee
el **gato**, cat
la **gaviota**, seagull
generalmente, usually, generally
la **gente**, people
el **gesto**, expression, face; **torcer el gesto**, to grimace
gigantesco, -a, gigantic, huge
el **golpe**, blow; **golpecito**, tap
golpear, to beat, strike
gordo, -a, fat, stout
el **gorrión**, sparrow
la **gota**, drop
gozar de, to enjoy
el **gozo**, joy, enjoyment
las **gracias**, thanks
la **grada**, step
gran, grande, great, big, large
la **grandeza**, greatness
grandioso, -a, grandiose
grato, -a, pleasant, pleasing, acceptable
grave, serious
gritar, to shout

el **grito**, cry, shout
el **gruñido**, growl
gruñón, grumbling
el **grupo**, group
guardar, to guard, to look after
la **guerra**, war
guiar, to guide
guijarroso, -a, stony
el **guiñapo**, rag
guisar, to stew, to cook
gustar, to please; **me gusta**, I like
el **gusto**, taste, pleasure

La **Habana**, Havana
haber, to have; — **de**, to have to, to be going to
la **habitación**, room
hablar, to speak, to talk
hacendoso, -a, busy
hacer, to make, to do
hacia, towards
la **hacienda**, job, work
hallar, to find; —**se**, to be found
harto, (*adj.*) replete, sated; (*adv.*), sufficiently
hasta, as far as, until; — **que**, until
el **haz**, bundle
la **hebilla**, buckle
hecho, see **hacer**
el **hedor**, stink, stench
la **hélice**, propeller
la **herida**, wound
herir (ie, i), to wound
la **hermana**, sister, nun
hermoso, -a, beautiful
la **herradura**, horse-shoe; **camino de** —, bridle-track
la **hierba**, grass
el **hierro**, iron
hilar, to spin
hincado, -a, kneeling
hinchar, to swell
hirsuto, -a, hairy

hizo, see **hacer**
el **hogar**, hearth, home
hogareño, -a, homely, family
la **hoja**, leaf
el **hombre**, man; ¡**hombre**! why! good heavens! (exclamation of surprise)
el **hombrecillo**, little man
el **hombro**, shoulder
hondo, -a, deep
el **honor**, honour
honrado, -a, honest, honourable
la **hora**, hour, time
el **horizonte**, horizon
hosco, -a, gloomy, bleak
hoy, to-day
el **huerto**, garden, orchard
el **hueso**, bone
el **huésped**, guest; **casa de huéspedes**, boardinghouse
huir, to flee
el **humo**, smoke
hundir, to sink, to plunge
hundirse, to sink
husmear, to sniff

la **iglesia**, church
igual, equal, like
ileso, -a, unhurt
iluminar, to illuminate
el **iluso**, dupe, one dazzled by a false idea
el **imperio**, rule, authority
imponer, impose
de **improviso**, suddenly, unexpectedly
el **impulso**, impulse
incierto, -a, uncertain
inclinarse, to bow, to bend down
incoloro, -a, colourless
el **inconveniente**, objection, inconvenience
la **indagación**, investigation

indeciso, -a, undecided
el **individuo**, individual
el **infierno**, hell, inferno
inglés, -a, -es, -as, English
ininterrumpido, -a, unbroken
la **injuria**, insult
las **inmediaciones** (*f.pl.*), neighbouring parts, district
inmóvil, motionless
inquieto, -a, anxious, uneasy
insaciable, insatiable
inseguro, -a, unsure
insoportable, unbearable
inspeccionar, to inspect, to examine
el **instante**, instant, moment
interesar, to interest
interrumpir, interrupt
íntimo, -a, intimate
intrépido, fearless
el **invierno**, winter
ir, to go
la **isleta**, islet
izquierdo, -a, left

el **jabalí**, wild boar
jadear, to pant
japonés, -a, Japanese
el **jardín**, garden
la **jarra**, vase
la **jaula**, cage
el **jefe**, chief; — **del tren**, guard
el **jergón**, straw mattress
el **jinete**, horseman
la **jornada**, journey
joven (*m. & f.*), young man or woman
la **joyería**, jeweller's shop
jugoso, -a, full of sap
junto, -a, close, next, nearby
juntos, -as, together
la **justicia**, justice, law
juzgar, to judge

la labor, toil, farming; bestia de —, draught-animal
labrado, -a, ploughed
el lado, side
ladrar, to bark
la lagartija, lizard
lanar, having to do with wool
la lancha (pesquera), fishing-boat
lánguido, -a, languid, lazy
lanzarse, to dash
el lápiz, pencil
largo, -a, long
lastimar to hurt, to damage,
la lata, tin; (slang) bore, nuisance
el látigo, whip-lash
latir, to yelp; to beat (heart)
lavar, to wash
la lección, lesson
la leche, milk
lechera, milch
el lecho, bed
la legua, league (= 4 km)
lejos, far; a lo —, in the distance
la lengua, tongue, language
lento, -a, slow
la leña, firewood
levantar, to lift; —se, to get up
la libertad, freedom, liberty
libertar, to set free
libre, free
la librería, book-shop
el lienzo, cloth (flag), canvas
el límite, limit, boundary
limpiar, to clean
listo, -a, ready
lívido, -a, livid·
lo cual, which
lo que, that which, what
el lobo, wolf
lóbrego, -a, dark, gloomy

loco, -a, mad
lograr, to succeed in
la loma, ridge
la lona, canvas
la longitud, length
la lontananza, distance
el loro, parrot
la losa, flagstone, stone slab
lozano, -a, luxuriant
luchar, to struggle
luego, then, next
el lugar, place, village
el lujo, luxury
la lumbre, flame, fire
la luna, moon
lustroso, -a, shiny
la luz, light

la llama, flame
llamar, to call, to knock; llamarse, to be called
llegar, to arrive
lleno, -a, full
la llegada, arrival
llenar, to fill
llevar, to carry, to bear, to wear, to take
llorar, to weep
llover (ue), to rain
la llovizna, drizzle
la lluvia, rain

la madera, wood
la madre, mother
la madrugada, early morning
madrugador, -a, early rising
madrugar, to get up early
magnífico, -a, splendid, magnificent
majestuoso, -a, majestic
maldecir, to curse
la maleta, suit-case, valise
malhumorado, -a, ill-tempered, gloomy
malo, -a, bad, ill
la malva real, hollyhock
el malvado, wicked man

el mancebo, youth
mandar, to order, to send
manejar, to handle
el manillar, handlebars
la mano, hand
un manotazo, buffet, blow with the hand
manso, -a, tame, quiet
la manta, blanket
el manzano, apple-tree
la mañana, morning, to-morrow
el, la mar, sea
la marca, make, brand
marcar, to mark
la marcha, march, journey, start
marchar, to go, to walk
marcial, martial, military
el marido, husband
la marina, shore
el marinero, sailor
marino, -a, of the sea
la mariposa, butterfly
más, more
la mata, shrub
matar, to kill
el matorral, thicket
el mayoral, driver
el mayordomo, steward, bailiff
la mayoría, majority
el mecánico, mechanic, engineer
la media, stocking
mediado, -a, halfway through
la medianoche, midnight
el médico, doctor
la medida, measure; a — que, in proportion as
el medio, middle, half
el mediodía, noon
mejor, better, best; a lo mejor, perhaps, probably
menester: ser —, to be necessary
menesteroso, -a, needy

menor, smaller, smallest, younger, youngest
menos, less; a — que, unless
menudo, -a, fine, minute; a —, often
el mercado, market
el mercancías, goods-train
el mercenario, hired soldier
merecer (se), to deserve
la merienda, picnic lunch
el mérito, merit
la mesa, table
meter, to put; —se en, to get in
el Metro, Underground
mi, my
mí, me
el miedo, fear; tener —, to be afraid
mientras, whilst; — tanto, meanwhile
mil, thousand
mimar, to spoil
la mimbrera, osier
mirar, to look; mirarse, to look at each other
la misa, mass
mismo, same, very, self
místico, -a, mystic
la mitad, half; a — de la corriente, midstream
la moda, fashion
la modista, dressmaker
el modo, kind, manner; a — de, as it were, a sort of
mojarse, to get wet; mojado hasta los huesos, wet through
la mole, mass, bulk
molestar, to worry, to bother, to be a nuisance
el molino, mill
el momento, moment
la moneda, coin
montar(se en), to ride, to mount

el **monte**, mountain, wood
la **montaña**, mountain
el **moño**, coil of hair
la **morcilla**, black pudding
mortecino, -a, dying
mostrar (ue), to show
el **motivo**, reason, motive
el **motor**, engine, motor
mover (ue), to move
la **moza**, girl
el **mozo**, porter
la **muchacha**, girl
el **muchacho**, boy
mucho, much; — s, many
los **muebles**, furniture
la **mueca**, grimace
muerto, -a, dead
mugriento, -a, greasy, grimy
la **mujer**, woman, wife
a **mujeriegas**, side-saddle
la **multitud**, crowd
el **mundo**, world; **todo el —**, everybody
murciano, -a, Murcian, from Murcia
el **muro**, wall
el **muslo**, thigh
mutuo, mutual
muy (*adv.*), very

nacer, to be born
nada, nothing
nadar, to swim
el **naranjal**, orange grove
la **nariz**, nose, nostril
la **nave**, ship
el **navegante**, navigator
navegar, to sail
la **Navidad**, Christmas
necesitar, to need
negro, -a, black
el **neumático**, tyre
la **nevada**, snowstorm
nevado, -a, covered with snow
ni, neither, nor, not even

la **niñería**, childishness
niño, -a, child
el **nivel**, level; **paso a —**, level-crossing
no bien, scarcely, no sooner
la **noche**, night
la **Nochebuena**, Christmas Eve
notar, to notice
las **noticias**, news
el **novio**, la **novia**, lover, sweetheart
nublado, -a, cloudy
el **nudo, nudito**, knot
nueve, nine; **las nueve**, nine o'clock
nuevo, -a, new
el **número**, number
nunca, never

obedecer, obey
el **objeto**, object
obligar, to oblige, to force
la **obscuridad**, darkness
el **obsequio**, present
obstante, no, nevertheless, however, notwithstanding
obstinado, -a, obstinate
a **ocasión**, opportunity
ocioso, -a, leisured
ocultar, to hide
ocurrir, to occur
la **oficiala**, workwoman
la **oficina**, office
el **oficio**, trade, profession
ofrecer, to offer
el **oído**, ear, hearing
oír, to hear
la **ojeada**, glance
el **ojo**, eye
el **ojo de la cerradura**, key-hole
la **ola**, wave
oler (hue), to smell
el **olivo**, olive-tree
el **olor**, smell, scent
la **onda**, wave, water

ondular, to wave, to float

opinar, to express an opinion

oprimir, to oppress, to overwhelm

ordenar, to order

ordinariamente, ordinarily, usually

la orgía, orgy

la orilla, bank, edge

orondo, -a, pompous

la osa, she-bear

el oso, bear

oscuro (obscuro), -a, dark; a oscuras, in the dark

otro, -a, other, another

la oveja, sheep (ewe)

el pabellón, flag

el padrino, godfather; second in a duel

pagar, to pay

el pago, payment

el paisaje, landscape, scenery

la paja, straw

el pájaro, bird

la palabra, word

pálido, -a, pale

la palmera, palm tree

la paloma, dove, pigeon

la palpitación, rippling

el pan, bread

los pantalones, trousers

el pañuelo, handkerchief; — de cintura, sash

el paquete, parcel, package

el par, pair, couple; de par en par, wide (open)

para, for

para que, in order that

¿para qué? why, with what purpose?

el parabrisas, windscreen

la parada, stop

parado, -a, still, quiet

parar, to stop

parecer, to appear; al —, apparently; — se a, to resemble, be like

el parentesco, relationship, kinship

los parientes, relatives

la parte, part; de todas partes, from all directions; en todas —, everywhere; por otra —, on the other hand

partir, to depart

el pasaje, passage

el pasajero, passenger

pasar, to pass, to happen; — de, to exceed

pasear (se), to go for a walk, to stroll

el paseo, walk, stroll

el pasillo, corridor

el paso, step; crossing, passage; a buen —, at a good pace

la pata, leg or foot of an animal

la paz, peace

la peana pedestal

el pecho, breast, chest

pedir, to ask for

la pedrezuela, pebble

la peletería, furrier's shop

peligroso, -a, dangerous

pellizcar, to pinch

pendiente, steep

el pendiente, ear-ring

la pendiente, slope, hill

penetrar, to penetrate, to enter

la penitencia, penance

el pensamiento, thought

pensar (ie), to think

el penúltimo, last but one

peor, worse, worst

pequeño, -a, small; — ito, tiny

perder (ie), to lose

las pérdidas, losses

el perdón, pardon, forgiveness

perezoso, -a, lazy

la perfidia, treachery, perfidy

el período, period

permanecer, to remain

el permiso, permission, leave

pero, but

el perro, dog

el personaje, personage, figure

pertenecer, to belong

perturbarse, to be worried

el pescado, fish (when caught)

el pescador, fisherman

el pescante, box, driver's seat

pescar, to fish

pese a, in spite of

el pez, fish (alive)

picado, -a, de viruelas, pock-marked

picar, to dive, to peck

el pico, beak; point, corner, peak

el pie, foot

la piel, skin

la piedra, stone

la pierna, leg

el pilar, basin, pool

el pinchazo, puncture

el pino, pine

pintar, to paint

la pinza, clip

pisar, to tread, to stamp

el piso, floor, storey

la pista de aterrizaje, runway, landing-strip

la pistola, pistol

el pito, whistle

la placa, plate

planear, to glide

el plátano, plane-tree

plateado, -a, silvery

la plática, conversation

el plato, dish, course

la playa, beach

la plazoleta, courtyard, little square

la población, population

poblar (ue), to inhabit, to populate

pobre, poor

poco, -a, little; pl. few; por —, nearly

el poder, power

poder, can, to be able

el poder, power

poderoso, -a, powerful

la pólvora, gunpowder

polvoriento, -a, dusty

pomposo, -a, pompous, magnificent

ponderar, to praise exaggeratedly

poner, to place, to put, to put on; —se en camino, to start out; ponerse, to become, to turn

la popa, poop, stern

por, by, for; — qué, why

porque, because

la portezuela, door of a car or carriage

el portón, big door

posarse, to alight, to land

posible, possible

postrero, -a, behind, last

el poyo, bench

la pradera, meadow

el prado, meadow

el precio, price

precipitadamente, hurriedly

preciso, precise; es preciso, it is necessary

preferir (ie, i), to prefer

la pregunta, question

preguntar, to ask

prender, to take, to catch

el presbiterio, chancel

presentir, to forecast, to feel beforehand, to foresee, to have a foreboding

prestar, to lend

presuroso, -a, hurriedly

la pretensión, pretension, claim

previsor, -a, with foresight

primer, primero, -a, first, earlier

el **principio,** beginning

la **prisa,** haste, hurry, speed; **darse —,** to hurry

la **prisión,** prison

la **proa,** prow, bows

probar, to try, to test, to prove

procurar, to procure, to try

profundo, -a, profound, deep

la **prole,** offspring

prolongado, -a, lengthy

prolongar, to prolong, to lengthen

pronto, soon, ready, quickly; **de —,** suddenly; **al —,** at first

pronunciar, to pronounce

prometedor, -a, promising

propicio, -a, favourable, propitious

proponer, to propose

provocar, to provoke, to call forth

próximo, -a, near, next

el **público,** public, people

el **pueblo,** village; **el pueblecito,** small village, hamlet

la **puerta,** door, gate

pues, well, then

la **punta,** point, tip

la **puntería,** aim

el **punto,** point; **— de mira,** point of aim; **al —,** at once

puntual, exact

el **puro,** cigar

que, that, which

quedar, to remain

quejarse, to complain

querer (ie), to wish, to love, to want; **querer decir,** to mean

querido, -a, dear

quien, who

quienquiera, whoever

quinto, fifth

quitar, to take away, to take off

el **rabo,** tail

el **radiotelegrafista,** wireless operator

la **ráfaga,** squall, gust of wind

la **raíz,** root

la **rama,** branch

el **ramaje,** foliage

el **ramo,** bouquet

el **ranchito,** little hut

raro, -a, strange, unusual

el **rascacielos,** skyscraper

el **rato,** period of time; **un buen —,** a good while

la **raya,** stripe

rayar, to dawn, to appear

el **rayo,** lightning, ray

el **rebaño,** flock

rebelde, rebellious

receloso, -a, suspicious

recibir, to receive

recio, -a, strong

un **recodo,** sharp turn

recoger, to gather, to pick up

recogido, -a, caught up

recomendado, recommended

recomendar, to recommend

reconocer, to recognize, to examine

recorrer, to examine, to make a tour of inspection, to go from end to end

recrear, to recreate

el **recreo,** recreation, "break"

la **recua,** string of pack-mules

rechazar, to refuse, to repulse

la **región,** region

registrar, to examine, to search

regresar, to return
reír, to laugh
el reloj, clock
la relojería, watchmaker's shop
reluciente, shining
relucir, to gleam, to shine
el rellano, landing
rematado, -a, ended, terminated
el remiendo, patch
el remilgo, fuss, affectation
el remo, oar
reparar (en), to notice
de repente, suddenly
repetir (i), to repeat
repleto, -a, full
replicar, to reply
reponer, to reply
el reposo, repose; con —, easily, calmly
repugnante, repulsive, repugnant
resistir (se), to resist
resonar, resound
la respiración, breathing
el resplandor, glow
responder, to answer, to respond
restallar, to crack
resuelto, -a, determined
resultar, to result, to turn out to be
resucitar, to revive
retenido, -a, detained
retirarse, to retire, to withdraw
el retorno, return; de —, back
retrasar, to delay
el retraso, delay
el retrato, portrait
revelar, to reveal
reventar, to burst
al revés, reversed
revolver, to turn over, to upset; revolverse, to twist, to writhe, to turn round

la revuelta, winding, sharp turn, bend
rezongar, to growl
la ribera, bank
rico, -a, rich
el rigor, rigour
el río, river
la riña, scolding
el risco, crag
risueño, smiling
rítmico, rhythmic, rhythmically
rizar el rizo, to loop the loop
el roble, oak
la roca, rock
la rociada, shower
rociar, to sprinkle, to wash down
el rocín, horse, nag
rodear, to surround
la rodilla, knee
rogar (ue), to ask (some one to do something)
rojizo, -a, reddish
rojo, -a, red
el romero, rosemary
romper, to break
roncar, to snore
la ropa, clothes
el rostro, face
roto, -a, broken
la rueda, wheel
el ruido, noise, sound
el rumor, roar, murmur, confused noise
runrunear, to hum, to purr
rutilante, gleaming, shining

saber, to know
el sable, sabre, cutlass
sabroso, fragrant, rich-smelling
sacar, to take out, to serve
el sacerdote, priest
el saco, bag
la sacristía, vestry

la **sala**, drawing-room, sitting-room

salgas, see **salir**

la **salida**, exit

salir, to go out

saltar, to jump

el **salto**, jump

saltón, protruding

saludar, to greet

salvaje, wild

la **sangre**, blood

santiguarse, to cross one-self

satisfecho, satisfied

saturar, to saturate

la **sazón**, time

seas, see **ser**

seco, -a, dry, sharp

la **sed**, thirst; **tener —**, to be thirsty

el **segador**, reaper

en **seguida**, at once

seguir (i), to follow, to go on, to continue

segundo, -a, second

seguro, -a, sure

según, according to

la **selva**, forest

semejante, such, similar

la **semilla**, seed

el **sendero**, path

el **seno**, cavity, compartment

sentarse (ie), to sit down

el **sentido**, sense, meaning

sentir (ie, i), to feel, to regret, to be sorry

la **señal**, signal

el **señor**, gentleman, sir

la **señora**, lady

señorial, lordly, of a manor or castle

señoril, noble

separar, to separate

ser, to be

la **serenidad**, serenity, calm

el **sereno**, watchman

sereno, -a, calm, serene

serio, -a, serious

el **servidor**, servant

servir (i), to serve; **— a**, to be used for; **— de**, to be used as; **— se de**, to use

si, if

sí, yes; himself, herself, yourself, etc.

siempre, always

la **sien**, temple

siendo, see **ser**

sietemesino, -a, puny, weak-minded

significar, to mean, to signify

silbar, to whistle

la **silla**, chair

sin, without

el **sinnúmero**, infinite number

sino, but, except

el **sitio**, place, spot, room

sobrar, to be more than enough

sobre, on, over, about, above

la **sobremesa**, sitting around the table talking after a meal

sobresaltado, astounded

sobrevivir, to survive

socarrón, ironical

el **sol**, sun

soler (ue), to be accustomed to, used to

solo, only, alone, single

sólo (*adv.*), only

la **sombra**, shade, shadow

sombrear, to shade

el **sombrero**, hat

sonar (ue), to sound

sonreír (i), to smile

soñar (ue), to dream

la **sopa**, soup

de **sopetón**, point-blank

el **soportal**, arch

sordamente, softly, in a low tone

sórdido, squalid, sordid

sospechar, to suspect
sostener, to sustain, to support
su, his, her, their, your
suavemente, smoothly
subir, to climb, go up
suceder, to happen
la suciedad, dirtiness, filth
sucio, -a, dirty
sudar, to sweat
el sudario, shroud
el sudor, sweat
sudoroso, -a, sweating
el suelo, ground, floor, soil
la suerte, luck; fashion; de todas — s, in any case
sujetar, to hold in place
sumir, to descend into, to go under
suplicar, to beg
suponer, to suppose
por supuesto, of course
el sur, south
surgir, to spring up, to appear
suspender, to suspend
suspenso, -a, in suspense
suspirar, to sigh
el susto, fright, fear
sutil, subtle

la tabla, plank
tal, such, such a
el taller, studio, workshop
el tallo, stalk
también, also
tampoco, neither, not ... either
tan, so, such
tanto, -a, so much, (pl.) so many; en —, while
la taquilla, box-office
tardar en, to be a long time, to delay
la tarde, afternoon or evening (until dark)
la tarea, task

el tejado, roof
temblar (ie), to tremble
temer, to fear
la temeridad, rashness, temerity
temible, to be feared
templado, -a, temperate
temprano, early
tender (ie), to hold out, to stretch; —se, to lie down; — la vista, to turn one's gaze
el tendero, shop-keeper
tener, to have; — que, to have to; tenerse, to hold fast, to stop
tenso, tense, intent
la tentación, temptation
tercero, -a, third
terminar, to end
la tertulia, social gathering
el testigo, witness
tibio, -a, warm
el tiempo, time; weather
a tientas, groping their way
la tierra, earth, land
tieso, -a, stiff, strong
las tinieblas, darkness
el tío, uncle, (as title) Old
el tipo, type, nature
tirar, to shoot, to fire; to throw
el tiritón, shudder, shiver
el tiro, shot
titubear, to hesitate
tocar, to touch; to fall to one's lot; to ring
todavía, still
el toro, bull
todo, -a, -os, -as, all, every
tomar, to take
el tomate, tomato
torcer (ue), to twist
el torno, turn; en — de, around
la torre, tower
trabajar, to work

el **trabajo**, work
el **trabuco**, blunderbuss
traer, to bring, to wear
tragar, to swallow
tragón, greedy
la **tranquilidad**, tranquility
tranquilizar, to calm
tranquilo, -a, calm
el **transeúnte**, passer-by
el **trapo**, rag
tras (de), after
traspasar, to transcend
el **traspaso**, agony
trasponer, to cross
tratar, to treat; **tratar de**, to try, to be about; — **se**, to be on friendly terms with; **tratarse de**, to be about, to be a question of
travieso, -a, mischievous
el **tren**, train; — **de aterrizaje**, undercarriage
trepar, to climb
el **trecho**, stretch, space; **de** — **en** —, here and there, every so far, so often
tres, three
¡**tric**! scratch!
el **trigal**, wheatfield
el **trigo**, wheat
los **tripulantes**, members of a ship's crew
triste, sad
el **tronco**, trunk
el **tropel**, rush, band, throng
tropezar (ie) en, to bump into; — **con**, to bump into, to trip over
la **trucha**, trout
el **tufo**, stench
tumbarse, to lie down

último, -a, last
el **umbral**, threshold
umbrío, -a, shady
único, -a, only, sole

unir, to unite
la **usanza**, usage; **a** — **de**, in the manner of
usar, to use
el **uso**, custom, use
las **uvas**, grapes

la **vaca**, cow
las **vacaciones**, holidays
la **vacilación**, hesitation
vacío, -a, empty
vagar, to wander
la **valla**, hedge, fence
en vano, in vain
la **vara**, yard (2.78 feet)
¡**vaya**! Come now!
veinte, twenty
la **vela**, sail
la **velocidad**, speed
velozmente, swiftly
vencer, to vanquish, to overcome
vender, to sell
venir, to come
la **ventaja**, advantage
la **ventana**, window; **la ventanilla**, window of a train or carriage
ver, to see; **tener algo que** — **con**, to have something to do with
de veras, in earnest, really
la **verdad**, truth; ¿**no es verdad?**, ¿**verdad?**, isn't it?, isn't he?, etc.
verdadero, -a, true
verde, green
el **verdor**, verdure, greenery
verificarse, to take place
la **verruga**, wart
vestir (i), to dress, to wear
la **vez**, time; **en** — **de**, instead of; **de** — **en cuando**, from time to time
la **vía**, way, railway track
el **viajante**, traveller, *especially* commercial traveller

el **viaje**, journey
el **viajero**, traveller
la **vid**, vine
la **vida**, life
la **vidriera**, window
el **vidrio**, glass, window-pane
viejo, -a, old
el **viento**, wind
vigilar, to watch over
el **villancico**, carol
villano, -a, base, mean
el **vino**, wine
la **viruela**, smallpox
la **vista**, sight, view
¡ **viva** !, long live . . . !, hurrah for . . . !
vívido de, alive with
la **vivienda**, dwelling
vivir, to live
el **volante**, steering-wheel
volar, to fly

volver, to return; — **se**, to turn round; — **a**, to do something again
vomitar, to vomit
la **voz**, voice
el **vuelo**, flight
la **vuelta**, return; **de** —, back
vuestra merced, your honour (origin of **Vd.**)

ya, already, now; — **no**, no longer; — **que**, since
yacer, to lie
yermo, -a, deserted, barren
la **yunta**, yoke of oxen

el **zagal**, shepherd, driver's assistant (of a stage-coach)
el **zapato**, shoe
el **zarzal**, bramble
el **zumbido**, hum

ENGLISH–SPANISH VOCABULARY

able, capaz; **to be —,** poder

about (*time*), a eso de, al punto de; **to be — to,** estar para, ir a; (*concerning*) de, sobre

to **accept,** aceptar

accident, el accidente

according to, según

to **accustom,** acostumbrar

accustomed: to be accustomed to, soler (ue)

to **ache,** doler (ue)

to **act,** actuar

action, la acción

actress, la actriz

to **admit,** admitir, confesar

ado: without more ado, sin más ni más

to **advance,** avanzar

advantage, la ventaja; **to take — of,** aprovechar

advice, el consejo

to **advise,** aconsejar

aerodrome, el aeródromo

aeroplane, el avión, el aeroplano

affection, el cariño

afraid: to be afraid, temer, tener miedo

after, después de; después que

afternoon, la tarde

afterwards, después

again, volver a + *verb*, otra vez

against, contra

ago, hace, hacía

to **agree,** estar de acuerdo, convenir

ahead of, delante de

to **ail,** doler (ue); **what ails you?,** ¿qué tiene Vd.?**

air, el aire

air-hostess, la azafata

airport, el aeropuerto

alike, parecido, igual

all, todo, -a; **— over,** por todo

almost, casi

alone, solo, -a; (*adv.*) sólo, únicamente

along, por, a lo largo de

alive, vivo, -a

already, ya

although, aunque

always, siempre

America, América, los Estados Unidos

among, entre

to **amuse,** divertir (ie, i)

amusing, divertido, -a

angle, el ángulo

angry, enfadado, -a, enojado, -a; **to grow —,** enojarse, enfadarse

animal, el animal

announce, anunciar

another, otro, -a

any, alguno, -a, cualquier

anyone, cualquiera, alguien

anything, cualquier cosa, algo

to **appear,** parecer, aparecer

apple, la manzana; **-tree,** el manzano

approach, acercarse a, llegarse a

approval, la aprobación

apricot, el albaricoque; **-tree,** el albaricoquero

arm, el brazo; **—s,** las armas

to **arm,** armar(se)

armchair, el sillón, la butaca

armed, armado, -a
army, el ejército
around, alrededor (de)
to **arrive,** llegar
as, como; tan . . . como; **as much —, as many —,** tanto(s) . . . como
to **ascertain,** enterarse de
ashamed, avergonzado, -a
to **ask,** preguntar; **— for,** pedir (i); **— to do something,** rogar (ue) + *Subj.*
asleep, adormecido, -a; **to fall —,** dormirse
ass, el asno
assistance, la ayuda
assistant, el ayudante; (*driver*) el zagal
astounded, asombrado, -a, aterrado, -a
authority, la autoridad
autumn, el otoño
to **attack,** atacar, acometer, embestir (i)
audacity, la temeridad
august, agosto (*m.*)
aunt, la tía
author, el autor
awake, despierto, -a
to **awake,** despertar(se) (ie)
away, a, fuera

bad, malo, -a
badly, mal, (*hurt*) gravemente
bad-tempered, malhumorado, -a
bailiff, el mayordomo
bag, el saco; **shopping —,** la bolsa; **hand —,** el bolso
band, la banda, el tropel
bank, el banco; (*river*) la orilla, la ribera
banquet, el banquete
bar, el barrote
bare, desnudo, -a; **-headed,** descubierta la cabeza

barefoot, descalzo, -a
to **bark,** ladrar
basket, el cesto
basque, el vasco; (*adj.*) vascongado, -a; (*lang.*) el vascuence
to **bathe,** bañarse
battle, la batalla
Bay of Biscay, el Golfo de Vizcaya
beach, la playa
bean, el haba (*f.*); **broad —,** la habichuela; **haricot —,** la judía
bear, el oso, la osa
to **bear,** soportar, aguantar
to **beat,** golpear, pegar, batir; **— down,** derribar; (*conquer*) vencer; (*heart*) latir
beautiful, hermoso, -a, bello, -a
to **become,** hacerse
bed, la cama; **to go to —,** acostarse (ue)
bedroom, el dormitorio, la alcoba
bee, la abeja
before, (*time*) antes; antes de, antes (de) que; (*place*) delante de; por delante
beggar, el mendigo
to **begin,** empezar (ie), iniciar, principiar, comenzar (ie)
behind, detrás (de)
to **believe,** creer
bell, la campana, campanilla, el timbre
to **belong,** pertenecer a
beneath, debajo (de)
bench, el banco, el poyo
bend, el recodo
beret, la boina
besides, además
best, mejor
bicycle, la bicicleta
big, grande, gran
to **bind,** atar, ligar

birth, el nacimiento
birthday, el (día de) cumpleaños
to bite, morder (ue)
bitter, amargo, -a
black, negro, -a
blackboard, la pizarra
blame, la culpa
to blame, culpar
blanket, la manta
blind, ciego, -a
blood, la sangre
bloom, la flor; to be in —,
florecer
blow, el golpe
to blow, soplar; tocar
blue, azul
blunderbuss, el trabuco
to blush, ruborizarse
board, la tabla; on —, a
bordo
to boast, jactarse de
boat, la barca, el barco
boatman, el barquero
body, el cuerpo
bolt, el cerrojo
book, el libro; -shop, la
librería
to borrow, pedir (i) prestado
both, ambos, -as, los (las)
dos
bottle, la botella
bottom, el fondo
to bow, inclinar(se)
box, la caja; (coach) el
pescante
boy, el muchacho, el mozo,
el niño
brake, el freno
to brake, frenar; — hard,
frenar en seco
to brandish, blandir
to break, romper
breakfast, el desayuno; to
have —, desayunarse
breathing-space, el huelgo
bridge, el puente

bright, brillante, encendido
(por)
to bring, traer
broken, roto, -a
brother, el hermano
brown, marrón, castaño, -a;
pardo, -a
bugle, la bocina
building, el edificio
bullet, la bala
bullfighter, el torero
bunting: dressed in —, em-
pavesado, -a
burglar, el ladrón
bus, el autobús
but, pero, sino
butter, la mantequilla
butterfly, la mariposa
button, el botón
to buy, comprar
by, por, cerca de
bystanders, los circunstantes

café, el café
cake, la torta
calf, el ternero
to call, llamar
called: to be called, llamarse
calm, tranquilo, -a
can, poder
Canada, el Canadá
candle, la vela, el cirio
capital, el caudal; la capital
captain, el capitán
to capture, capturar
car, el coche, el auto
card, la tarjeta, la postal;
(playing card) el naipe
cardboard, el cartón
care, el cuidado, el esmero
careful, cuidadoso, -a, esmerado, -a
cargo, el cargamento
cargo-boat, la barca de carga
carnation, el clavel
carol, el villancico
carpenter, el carpintero

carriage, el carruaje, el coche
carrot, la zanahoria
to **carry,** llevar
cart, la carreta
cartridge, el cartucho
carving, la escultura
case, el caso
to **catch,** atrapar, coger
caterpillar, la oruga
cathedral, la catedral
cautiously, cautelosamente
cave, la caverna, la cueva
centre, el centro
century, el siglo
ceremony, la ceremonia
certain, cierto, -a, seguro, -a
to **challenge,** desafiar
chance, la ocasión, la casu-
alidad, la suerte
to **change,** cambiar
chapter, el capítulo
charming, encantador, -a
chat, la charla, la plática
to **chatter,** charlar
to **check,** contener
cheerful, alegre
cherry, la cereza; **-tree,** el
cerezo
child, niño, -a
chimney, la chimenea
chocolate, el chocolate
choir, el coro, el presbiterio
choose, escoger
crib, el Belén
Christ, el Cristo
Christmas, la Navidad; —
Eve, la Nochebuena
church, la iglesia
cigar, el puro
cigarette, el cigarrillo, el
pitillo
cinema, el cine
to **claim,** pretender
class, la clase
clay, el barro
clear, claro, -a
to **clear,** aclararse, clarear

clerk, el empleado, el depen-
diente
clever, hábil
cliff, el acantilado
to **climb,** trepar, subir
to **cling,** agarrarse (a)
clock, el reloj
close, cerca
to **close,** cerrar (ie)
clothes, la ropa, los vestidos
club, el casino, el círculo, el
club
clumsy, tosco, -a, sin arte,
torpe
coarse, grosero, -a; — **word,**
la palabrota
coast, la costa; **-line,** el
litoral
coat, el sobretodo, el abrigo
coffee, el café
coffee-pot, la cafetera
coin, la moneda
cold, frío, -a; **to be —,** tener
frío (*persons*); hacer frío
(*weather*)
to **collect,** coger; colegir (i)
college, el colegio
to **comb,** peinar
to **come,** venir; — **in,** entrar,
pasar, llegar; — **back,**
volver (ue); — **up,** acudir,
acercarse, llegarse; — **for-**
ward, adelantarse; — **a-**
cross, tropezar con; — **on**
(*of light*), encenderse; —
out, salir; — **closer,** acercarse; **come on !,** ¡vamos !
comfortable, confortable, có-
modo, a gusto
committee, la comisión
companion, el compañero, la
compañera
company, la compañía
compartment, el departamento
competitor, el competidor
to **complain,** quejarse (de)

concert, el concierto
to conclude, concluir
conduct, la conducta
to confess, confesar (ie)
to consent, consentir (ie, i) (en)
consequence, la consecuen-
   cia; in —, por consiguiente
considerable, considerable
to consist, consistir en
to consult, consultar
to contain, contener
to continue, continuar (pres.
   continúo), seguir (i)
contrary, contrario, -a; on
   the —, al contrario, por
   el contrario
cool, fresco, -a
copy, el ejemplar
cordially, cordialmente
corner, el rincón; (street) la
   esquina
corporal, el cabo
correct, correcto, -a
to correct, corregir (i)
corridor, el corredor, el pasillo
cost, la costa; at the — of,
   a costa de, a fuerza de
to cost, costar (ue)
cottage, la choza, la casita
cotton, el algodón
country, el país; (not town)
   el campo
couple, la pareja, los esposos,
   el matrimonio; a couple
   of, un par de
courage, el valor
of course, por supuesto, desde
   luego, naturalmente, claro
courtyard, la plazoleta
cousin, primo, -a
to cover, cubrir
covered, cubierto, -a
to crack, (hacer) estallar
to crackle, chisporrotear
crag, el risco, la peña

crash, el estrépito, el choque
crew, la tripulación
crisis, la crisis
criminal, el reo
to cross, atravesar (ie), cruzar
to crouch, acurrucarse
crowd, la multitud, el tropel
crowded, lleno, -a
cry, el grito
to cry, gritar; llorar
cudgel, el garrote
cup, la taza
curtain, la cortina
customer, el parroquiano, el
   cliente
customs-house, la aduana
customs-man, el carabinero
to cut, cortar

daddy, papá, papaíto
danger, el peligro
dangerous, peligroso, -a
to dare, atrever (se) a
dark, oscuro, -a; negro, -a;
   moreno, -a
darkness, la obscuridad, las
   tinieblas
to dash, arrojarse, precipitarse
daughter, la hija
dawn, el alba, el amanecer
to dawn, amanecer, rayar el día
day, el día; — before yesterday, anteayer; — after
   to-morrow, pasado mañana
daybreak, el amanecer
daylight, la luz (del día)
dead, muerto, -a
deaf, sordo, -a
dearly, muchísimo
death, la muerte
to decay, decaer, pudrirse;
   (teeth) cariarse, dañarse
to decide, decidir
deck, la cubierta
deep, hondo, -a
definite, definitivo, -a

deliberately, de intento
delicious, delicioso, -a
delighted, encantado, -a
dentist, el dentista
to deny, negar (ie)
department store, el almacén
to describe, describir
description, la descripción
deserted, desierto, -a
desolate, desolado, -a
to destroy, destruir
to devote, dedicarse
to die, morir (ue, u)
different, diferente
difficult, difícil
difficulty, la dificultad
to dig, azadonar, cavar
diligent, diligente
dinner, la comida (midday);
  la cena (evening)
direct, directo, -a
to direct, dirigir
dirty, sucio, -a
to disappear, desaparecer
discussion, la discusión
to dismount, apearse
distance, la distancia; in the
  —, a lo lejos
distinction, la distinción
to distinguish, distinguir
ditch, la cuneta
to do, hacer
doctor, el médico, el doctor
dog, el perro
dollar, el duro, el peso
donkey, el burro, el asno
door, la puerta; (train or car)
  la portezuela
doorway, el portal
doubt, la duda; there is no
  —, no cabe duda
to doubt, dudar
downstairs, abajo; to go —,
  bajar
dozen, la docena
dragon-fly, la libélula
to draw, dibujar

drawing-room, la sala
dream, el sueño
to dream (of), soñar (con)
dress, el traje
to dress, vestirse
to drink, beber
driver, el mayoral (coach), el
  conductor, el chófer, el
  cochero
to drop, soltar (ue), dejar caer
to drown, ahogar(se)
duck, el pato
during, durante
duel, el duelo
duty, el deber

each, cada
ear-ring, el pendiente
early, temprano, -a; to be
  up —, madrugar
to eat, comer
edge, el borde, la orilla, el
  límite
to educate, educar
to efface, borrar
effort, el esfuerzo
either, o; not —, tampoco
eel, la anguila
else, otro, -a
to embarrass, desconcertar (ie)
embers, el rescoldo
emerald, la esmeralda
employer, el amo
empty, vacío, -a, desierto, -a
enchanting, encantador, -a
end, el fin, el cabo, el extremo; at, in the —, al fin
enemy, el enemigo
engine, (railway) la loco-
  motora; (car, aero) el
  motor
England, Inglaterra (f.)
English, inglés, inglesa
to enjoy, gozar, divertirse (ie, i)
enormous, enorme
enough, bastante (when adj.,
  takes s in plural)

to **enter,** entrar (en)
entire, entero, -a
entrance, la entrada
envelope, el sobre
to **envy,** envidiar
episode, el episodio
erect, erguido, -a
to **escape,** escaparse
escort, la escolta
especially, especialmente
estate, la finca
to **esteem,** estimar, apreciar
even, hasta, mismo; **not —,**
ni, ni . . . siquiera
evening, la tarde (*until dark*),
la noche (*after dark*)
eventually, al fin, después de
un rato
ever, jamás
every, todo, -a; **every day,**
todos los días
everybody, todo el mundo
everyday, diario, -a, cotidi-
ano, -a
everything, todo
everywhere, en todas partes
exactly, exactamente
except, sino, a excepción de
exercise, el ejercicio
exercise-book, el cuaderno
to **exclaim,** exclamar
exit, la salida
to **expect,** esperar
to **explain,** explicar
exploit, la hazaña
to **express,** expresar
extraordinary, extraordinar-
io, -a
eye, el ojo

face, la cara, el rostro, el
semblante
to **face,** dar cara a, dar a
fact, el hecho
to **fall,** caer, decaer; (*evening*)
atardecer
false, falso, -a

familiar, conocido, -a, familiar
famous, célebre
far, lejos; **as — as,** hasta
farm, el cortijo
farm-servant, el labriego
fast, rápido; (*asleep*) profundamente
fat, gordo, -a, grueso, -a
father, el padre
fault, la culpa
fear, el temor, el miedo
to **fear,** temer, tener miedo
to **feed,** dar de comer a
to **feel,** sentir (ie, i)
feeling, el sentimiento, la
impresión
fellow, el hombre, el mozo
to **fetch,** ir a buscar
fever, la fiebre
few, pocos, -as; **a —,** algunos, -as, unos pocos
fiancé, -e, el novio, la novia
fierce, feroz; (*fight*) encarni-
zado, -a
to **fight,** luchar, pelear
figure, la figurita
to **fill,** llenar
finally, finalmente, al fin;
use acabar por + *infin.*
to **find,** hallar, encontrar (ue);
— out, descubrir, enterarse
fine, hermoso, -a, magnífico,
-a; **to be —** (*weather*),
hacer buen tiempo, hacer
bueno
to **finish,** acabar, terminar; **—
off,** rematar
fire, el fuego, la lumbre; los
tiros (*collective fire of an
enemy*)
to **fire,** disparar, hacer fuego
firewood, la leña
first, primero, -a
fish, el pez; (*when caught*) el
pescado

to **fish**, pescar
fisherman, el pescador
fishing, pescar
fixedly, fijamente
flashing, encendido, -a
flat, el piso
to **flatten**, aplastar(se)
to **flow**, correr, deslizarse
flower, la flor; — **bed**, el macizo; — **pot**, la maceta
to **fly**, volar (ue)
foal, el potro
to **follow**, seguir (i)
fond of, aficionado a
food, la comida
foot, el pie
football, el football, el fútbol
footstep, el paso
for, para, por
to **forbid**, prohibir
force, la fuerza
to **force**, forzar (ue)
forehead, la frente
fore-paws, los brazos
foreign, extranjero, -a
forest, la selva
to **forget**, olvidar(se de)
formerly, antiguamente
former, aquél, -la, -los, -las
fortnight, quince días
fortunately, afortunadamente
fortune, la fortuna
fowls, los pollos
frame, el marco
France, Francia (*f.*)
to **freeze**, helar (ie)
French, (el) francés
Frenchman, el francés
Friday, el viernes
friend, el amigo, la amiga
frightened, asustado, -a; **to be —**, tener miedo, asustarse
from, de, desde
frontier, la frontera
to **frown**, fruncir el entrecejo

fruit, la fruta; **-tree**, el frutal
fuel, el combustible
full, lleno, -a
fun: to make — of, reírse (i) de, burlarse de
furious, furioso, -a
furrier's shop, la peletería

galley, la galera
game, el juego; el deporte (*sport*)
gamekeeper, el guardabosque
garage, el garaje (*or* garage)
garden, el jardín, el huerto
gate, la puerta, la barrera
to **gather**, coger
gay, alegre
to **gaze**, mirar, contemplar
gear: to change —, cambiar de marcha
general, general; (*noun*) el general
German, el alemán
Germany, Alemania (*f.*)
to **get**, obtener, tener, recibir; — **out**, sacar; — **down**, descender; — **up**, levantarse; — **on**, montar, subir; — **off**, descender
ghost, el duende
to **give**, dar; — **up**, renunciar
girl, la muchacha, la moza, la niña
glad, contento, -a
to **glance**, dar una ojeada a
glass, el vidrio; el vaso
to **glimpse**, columbrar, vislumbrar
glove, el guante
to **go**, ir, andar; — **down**, bajar; — **in**, entrar; — **out**, salir; — **up**, subir; — **on**, seguir (i); — **back**, volver (ue)
God, Dios (*m.*)
gold, el oro; (*adj.*) de oro

good, bueno, -a; (*noun*) el bien

good-bye, adios, hasta luego, hasta la vista; to say —, despedirse

goods, los géneros

to gossip, charlar, chismear

grammar, la gramática

grammar-school, el instituto

gramophone, el gramófono

grandmother, la abuela

grandparents, los abuelos

grapes, las uvas

grateful, agradecido, -a

grating, la reja

great, grande, gran

green, verde

to greet, saludar

grey, gris, agrisado, -a

ground, la tierra, el suelo

group, el grupo

to grow, cultivar; crecer; hacerse, ponerse

guard, el jefe del tren

to guess, adivinar

guest, el huésped, el convidado

guide, el guía

gun, el cañón (*large*); la escopeta (*shotgun*)

gun-dog, el perro de caza

gunwale, la borda

gutter, la gotera

hair, el pelo; dark hair, pelo negro, moreno

half, medio, -a; (*noun*) la mitad

hall, la sala, el vestíbulo

to halt, hacer alto; halt! ¡alto!

hand, la mano

handsome, hermoso, -a, guapo, -a

to hang, colgar (ue)

to happen, suceder, acontecer

happy, dichoso, -a, contento, -a, feliz

hard, duro, -a, recio, -a; (*work*) mucho

hardly, apenas, no bien

to harness, atalajar

harvest, la cosecha

hat, el sombrero

haughtily, con altivez

Havana, la Habana

to have, tener; (*auxiliary*) haber; to have to, tener que; (*tea, etc.*) tomar

hay, el heno

head, la cabeza

headmaster, el director

health, la salud

to hear, oír

heart, el corazón

hearth, el hogar

heat, el calor

to heat, calentar (ie)

heath, el páramo

heave, el tirón

heavy, pesado, -a

hedge, el seto

help, la ayuda

to help, ayudar; I can't help, no puedo menos de

hen, la gallina; hens, los pollos

Henry, Enrique

her, su, suyo, -a; hers, el suyo, la suya, etc.

here, aquí, acá

to hesitate, vacilar

to hide, esconder

high, alto, -a

highwayman, el bandido

hill, la colina

to hinder, impedir

hind-legs, las patas traseras

his, su, suyo, -a, el suyo, la suya, etc.

to hit, golpear, pegar

hoarse, ronco, -a

to hoist, izar

holiday, la fiesta, las vacaciones

hollyhock, la malva real
home, el hogar, la casa; (*adv.*) a casa; **at —,** en casa
homework, el deber
honey, la miel
honour, el honor, la honra
to **hope,** esperar
horse, el caballo
hospital, el hospital
hot, caliente; **to be —,** tener calor (*persons*), hacer calor (*weather*)
hotel, el hotel
hour, la hora
house, la casa
how, como, lo; **— much,** cuanto, -a
however, sin embargo, con todo, pero, por
to **howl,** aullar
howling, el aullido
huge, inmenso, -a
hulking (*use -ón suffix with noun*)
hundred, ciento, cien; (*noun*) un centenar
hungry, hambriento, -a; **to be —,** tener hambre
húrriedly, de prisa
hurry, la prisa
to **hurry,** darse prisa, apresurarse
to **hurt,** herir (ie, i)
husband, el marido
hymn, el himno

idea, la idea
idol, el ídolo
ignorant, necio, -a, ignorante
ill, enfermo, -a
illness, la enfermedad
illustrated, ilustrado, -a
to **imagine,** imaginar(se), figurar(se)
immediately, inmediatamente, en seguida

impolite, descortés
important, importante; **to be —,** importar
impossible, imposible
to **improve,** mejorar (se)
to **improvise,** improvisar
impudent, impudente, impertinente
Indian, indio, -a
influence, el ascendiente
to **inform,** enterar (de), informar
iniquitous, inicuo, -a
to **injure,** herir (ie, i)
inn, la fonda
inn-keeper, el tabernero
inside, dentro de
inspection, la inspección
instead of, en vez de, en lugar de
instruction, la instrucción
intelligent, inteligente
to **intend,** pensar (ie), proyectar, tener la intención de
intention, la intención
interesting, interesante
interminable, interminable, ininterrumpido, -a
to **introduce,** presentar
to **investigate,** investigar, averiguar
to **invite,** invitar, convidar
iron, el hierro; (*adj.*) de hierro
islet, la isleta
island, la isla
it, ello, lo, la, él, ella

jail, la cárcel
jailer, el carcelero
jar, el jarro
jeweller's shop, la joyería
Johnny, Juanito
to **join,** unirse, juntarse
joke, la chanza, el chiste
to **joke,** chancear
Joseph, José

journey, el viaje
to journey, viajar
joy, el gozo
judge, el juez, el conocedor
jug, el jarro
to jump, saltar
just, justo, -a, exactamente, sólo, sencillamente; **to have —,** acabar de; **— as,** al punto que

to keep, guardar, conservar
kick, el puntapié
to kill, matar
kilometre, el kilómetro
kind, bueno, -a, bondadoso, -a
kind, la clase
kindness, la bondad
king, el rey
kitchen, la cocina
kitten, el gatito
knife, el cuchillo
knock, el golpe
to knock, llamar, golpear
knocking, golpes
to know, saber, conocer

laden, cargado, -a
lady, la dama, la señora
lake, el lago
lamb, el cordero
lamp, la lámpara, el candil
lamp-post, el farol
landscape, el paisaje
language, la lengua, el idioma
last, último, -a, pasado, -a; **— night,** anoche; **at —,** al fin
late, (*adv.*) tarde; (*adj.*) tardío, -a
lateen, latino, -a
lately, recientemente
later, después, más tarde
latter, éste, -a, -os, -as
to laugh, reír; **— at,** reírse de
law, la ley

lawn, el césped, el cuadro de hierba
lawyer, el abogado
lazy, perezoso, -a
to lead, conducir
leader, el jefe
to lean, apoyarse; **— out,** asomar(se) por
to learn, aprender
least, el menor, menos; **at —,** por lo menos, al menos
to leave, dejar, salir de, partir; **— off,** dejar de
left, izquierdo, -a; **to the —,** a la izquierda
left: **to be —,** quedar
to lend, prestar
less, menor (*adj.*); menos (*adv.*)
lettuce, la lechuga
lie, la mentira
to lie, yacer; **— down,** acostarse (ue)
to lie (**tell a lie**), mentir (ie, i)
life, la vida
light, la luz
light (*weight*), ligero, -a
to light, encender
like, como, parecido (-a) a; **to be like,** parecerse a
to like, *say 'it pleases me' for 'I like it,'* using gustar, *'to please'*
to line, linear
to linger, tardar (en volver), demorarse, entretenerse
to listen, escuchar
letter, la carta
little, pequeño, -a; poco; **a little,** un poco
to live, vivir
load, el fardo, la carga
to load, cargar
London, Londres
long, largo, -a
long (time), mucho tiempo

to **look,** mirar; — **for,** buscar; (*seem*) parecer; — **on to,** dar a; **to — up at,** levantar la cabeza hacia

loose, suelto, -a; **to let —,** soltar (ue)

to **lose,** perder (ie)

lot, lots, mucho, -a

loud, alto, -a, fuerte

Louis, Luis

to **love,** querer, amar (*persons and pets*); gustar a (*things*)

to **lower,** bajar

lucky: to be —, tener suerte

luggage, el equipaje

lunch, el almuerzo, la merienda; **to have —,** almorzar (ue), merendar (ie)

luxurious, lujoso, -a

luxury, el lujo

machine, la máquina, el aparato

mad, loco, -a

madam, señora

magistrate, el juez

mail, el correo

main, principal, mayor

to **maintain,** mantener

magic, la magia

maid, la criada

major, el comandante

majority, la mayoría

to **make,** hacer; — **for,** dirigirse a

male, el macho

man, el hombre

to **manage,** conseguir (i)

manager, el director

many, muchos, -as

mare, la yegua

market, el mercado

to **marry,** casarse (con)

marsh, el pantano

marvel, la maravilla

to **marvel,** maravillarse, admirar(se)

Mary, María

mask, la máscara

mast, el palo, el mástil

master, el maestro, el profesor; el amo; (*owner*) el dueño

matter, el asunto; **What is the — with you?,** ¿Qué tiene Vd.?, ¿Qué le pasa?

to **matter,** importar

may, poder

me, me; mí

to **mean,** querer decir

means, los medios

meanwhile, mientras tanto, entretanto

meat, la carne

Mediterranean, el (mar) mediterráneo

meek, humilde

to **meet,** encontrar (ue); (*make acquaintance of*) conocer

meeting, la reunión

melon, el melón

member, el miembro

memory, el recuerdo, la memoria

merely, meramente, sólo

message, el mensaje, el recado

metre, el metro

middle, el medio; **in the – of,** en medio de

mile, la milla

milk, la leche

to **milk,** ordeñar

mill, el molino

miller, el molinero

million, el millón

mind, la mente; **to make up one's —,** decidirse

mind !, ¡cuidado!

mine, (el) mío, (la) mía

miniature, en miniatura

minute, el minuto

mirror, el espejo

mischievous, travieso, -a

to **miss,** perder (ie)

mistake, la equivocación, la falta
mistaken: to be —, equivocarse
misty: to be —, hacer (haber) neblina
moment, el momento
money, el dinero
monotonous, monótono, -a
monument, el monumento
moon, la luna
moor, el moro
more, más
moreover, además
morning, la mañana
mother, la madre
motionless, inmóvil
motor-cycle, la motocicleta, la moto
mountain, la montaña
to move, mover (ue), marchar, estar en marcha
much, mucho, -a; (adv.) mucho
mud, el lodo
mudguard, el guardabarro
muffler, la bufanda
mule, la mula
murmur(ing), el murmullo
museum, el museo
music, la música
must, deber (de), tener que
myself, yo mismo; me
mystery, el misterio

name, el nombre
narrow, estrecho, -a
native, natal, nativo, -a
natural, natural
near, cerca de; próximo, -a
nearly, casi, cerca de
necessary, necessario, -a; to be —, ser preciso, ser menester (impersonal), hacer falta
to need, necesitar
neighbour, el (la) vecino (-a)

neither, ni, tampoco
never, nunca, jamás
nevertheless, sin embargo, no obstante
new, nuevo, -a
news, las noticias
next, (adj.) próximo, -a, siguiente; (adv.) luego, en seguida
nice, simpático, -a, ameno, -a, agradable
nickname, el apodo
night, la noche; last —, anoche
nightfall, el anochecer
nightmare, la pesadilla
no, no
no, ninguno, -a, ningún
nobody, nadie
noise, el ruido
nor, ni, tampoco
north, el norte; (adj.) del norte
nothing, nada
to notice, reparar (en), notar, fijarse en
now, ahora

oak-tree, el roble
to obey, obedecer (a)
to oblige, obligar
to obtain, obtener
obvious, evidente
occupation, la ocupación
to occupy, ocupar
to offer, ofrecer
office, la oficina, el despacho
often, a menudo, muchas veces
oil, el aceite
old, viejo, -a
older, mayor, de más edad
on, en, sobre, encima de
once, una vez; at —, pronto, en seguida, a la vez; all at —, de repente, de pronto
onion, la cebolla

only, solo, -a, único, -a; (*adv.*) sólo, no . . . más que

open, abierto, -a

to **open,** abrir

opening, la boca

opera, la ópera

opinion, la opinión, el parecer

opportunity, la ocasión, la oportunidad

opposite, enfrente; frente a

orange, la naranja; **-tree,** el naranjo; — **blossom,** el azahar

orchard, el huerto

order, el orden; **in — to,** para; **in — that,** para que

to **order,** mandar, ordenar

other, otro, -a

our, nuestro, -a

outer, exterior

outside, fuera (de), afuera; delante de

over, sobre, encima de; — **there,** allá

owner, el dueño

overcoat, el sobretodo

to **overcome,** vencer

own, propio, -a

to **own,** admitir, confesar, darse por; poseer, tener

ox, el buey

pace, el paso

to **pace,** medir (i) a pasos

packed, colmado, -a, atestado, -a

page, la página

pain, el dolor

to **paint,** pintar

pair, el par, la pareja

pale, pálido, -a

paper, el papel

parcel, el paquete

parents, los padres

parish priest, el cura, el párroco

part, la parte; (*theatre*) el papel

to **part,** partir, separarse

party, la tertulia, la reunión

to **pass,** pasar

passage, el corredor, el pasillo, el pasaje

passenger, el viajero, el pasajero

path, el sendero

patience, la paciencia

patient, paciente; (*noun*) el paciente

to **pay,** pagar

peach, el melocotón; **-tree,** el melocotonero

peak, el pico, la peña, la cumbre

pear, la pera; **-tree,** el peral

pebble, el guijarro

pen, la pluma

pencil, el lápiz

penitent, el penitente

penknife, el cortaplumas, la navaja

people, la gente

perfume, el perfume

perhaps, acaso, quizá(s), a lo mejor

peril, el peligro

periodical, el periódico

to **perish,** perecer

perished (*with cold*), aterido, -a

person, la persona

Peter, Pedro

photograph, la fotografía

piano, el piano

to **pick,** coger, escoger; — **up,** recoger

picture, el cuadro; **pictures,** el cine

piece, un pedazo

pier, el muelle

pig, el cerdo

pine-tree, el pino

pipe, la pipa

pirate, el pirata
pistol, la pistola
pity, la lástima
place, el sitio, el lugar
to place, poner
platform, el andén
platinum, el platino
play, (*theatre*) la comedia
to play, jugar (ue); (*a game*) jugar a; (*music*) tocar; to — a part, desempeñar un papel
pleasant, agradable
please, por favor, sírvase, haga el favor de, tenga la bondad de . . .
to please, placer, gustar
pleased, contento, -a
pleasure, el placer, el gusto
plough, el arado
to plough, labrar
plum, la ciruela; -tree, el ciruelo
pocket, el bolsillo
poem, el poema, la poesía
point, el punto, la punta; on the — of, a punto de
to point, señalar (del dedo)
policeman, el policía
polite, cortés
poop, la popa
poor, pobre
poplar, el álamo
porcelain, la porcelana
port, el puerto
porter, el mozo
portrait, el retrato
portuguese, portugués, -a
position, la posición
post, el puesto; el correo
to post, echar al correo
post-office, la casa de correos
potato, la patata
pothole, la hondonada
pound, la libra
powder, el polvo; gun- —, la pólvora

to practise, ejercer
to praise, alabar, celebrar
to prefer, preferir (ie, i)
to prepare, preparar
presence, la presencia
present, el regalo, el obsequio
to present, regalar
present: to be — at, asistir a, presenciar
to press, apretar
pretty, bonito, -a, guapo, -a
to prevent, impedir (i)
price, el precio
principal, principal
to print, imprimir
private, particular, personal
prize, el premio
probable, probable
procession, la procesión, la cadena
profit, el provecho, el beneficio
to profit, aprovechar, sacar provecho de
programme, el programa
progress, el progreso, la marcha
proposal, la proposición
protest, la protesta
to protest, protestar
proud, orgulloso, -a
prow, la proa
to punish, castigar
pupil, alumno, -a
to push, empujar
to put, poner, meter; — out, apagar

quarrel, la riña
to quarrel, reñir, disputar
quarter, el cuarto, el barrio
quickly, rápidamente
quiet, silencioso, -a, tranquilo, -a

rabbit, el conejo
race, la carrera, la corrida

rack, la red
rag, el harapo, el trapo
rage, la rabia, la furia
rain, la lluvia
to rain, llover (ue)
raincoat, el impermeable
to raise, levantar, alzar
rate: at any rate, de todos modos
rather, bastante, un poco
ray, el rayo
to reach, alcanzar, llegar a
reactionary, reaccionario, -a
to read, leer
ready, listo, -a; to get —, disponerse a, preparar (se) a
real, verdadero, -a
to realise, darse cuenta (de)
really, verdaderamente
to rear (up), incorporarse
reason, la razón
to receive, recibir
recent, reciente, recién
to recognise, reconocer
recommendation, la recomendación
to recover, recobrar (la salud)
recovery, la convalecencia
red, rojo, -a; (wine) tinto, -a
reed, la caña; bed of reeds, el carrizal
to refuse, negarse (ie) a
regatta, la regata
regiment, el regimiento
region, la región
regret, el sentimiento
to regret, sentir (ie, i), arrepentirse (ie, i)
to relate, referir (ie, i); contar (ue)
relation, el, la pariente
to rely, contar (ue) con, fiarse de
to remain, quedar(se), permanecer
remark, la observación

to remark, observar
to remember, acordarse (ue) de, recordar (ue)
remote, apartado, -a
to repeat, repetir (i)
to repent, arrepentirse (ie, i)
to reply, contestar, responder
report, el estampido, la memoria
to report, referir (ie, i)
to represent, representar
reproduction, la representación
republic, la república
to resemble, asemejarse a, parecerse a
resigned, resignado, -a; to become —, resignarse
respect, el respeto
to respect, respetar, acatar
respectful, respetuoso, -a
rest, el descanso
the rest, los (las) demás, el resto
to rest, descansar; apoyar
result, el resultado
to retreat, retroceder
to return, volver (ue), regresar; (give back) devolver (ue)
in return, en cambio
to reveal, revelar
review, la revista
rice, el arroz
rich, rico, -a
to ride, cabalgar, montar
rifle, el fusil
right, derecho, -a
right: to be —, tener razón
ring, el círculo, la sortija
to ring, sonar (ue), hacer sonar; llamar (a la puerta)
ripe, maduro, -a
to rise, levantarse, alzarse
risk, el riesgo
to risk, arriesgarse
rivalry, la rivalidad, la emulación

river, el río
road, el camino, la carretera
roadway, la calzada
roar, el bramido; (*engines*) el zumbido
to roar, bramar, rugir; retumbar
rogue, el bribón, el, la canalla (*very strong*)
room, la habitación; el sitio; no room for, no caber
root, la raíz
rope, la cuerda
rose, la rosa
round, redondo, -a
round (*prep. & adv.*), alrededor (de), en torno (de)
row, la fila
ruby, el rubí
to ruin, arruinar, perder (ie)
to run, correr; — into, tropezar con, dar con; — down, atropellar; — away, huir, escapar
runway, la pista de aterrizaje
rush hour, hora de congestión máxima
to rush, arrojarse
Russia, la Rusia
Russian, ruso, -a; (*noun*) el ruso

sack, el costal, el saco
sad, triste
saddlebags, las alforjas
safe, seguro, -a, salvo, -a
sail, la vela
to sail, navegar
sailor, el marinero
saint, el santo; Santo, San
salad, la ensalada
to salute, saludar
same, mismo, -a
sand, la arena
sardine, la sardina
satisfaction, la satisfacción
satisfied, satisfecho

to satisfy, satisfacer
Saturday, el sábado
to save, salvar; (*money*) ahorrar
to say, decir
scene, el escenario
scholar, alumno, -a
school, la escuela
schoolmaster, el profesor, el maestro de escuela
schoolmistress, la maestra, la profesora
scimitar, la cimitarra, el alfanje
to scold, reñir (i), reprender
to scream, gritar
sea, el (la) mar
seaside, el borde del mar
seat, el asiento, la silla, el sitio
second, segundo, -a; (*duel*) el padrino
to see, ver
to seize, asir, agarrar
to send, enviar (*pres.* envío); — away, despedir
to separate, separar
to set, (*sun*) ponerse; — out, partir, ponerse en marcha
several, varios, -as
shade, la sombra
shadow, la sombra
sharp, agudo, puntiagudo; (*time*) en punto
shed, el cobertizo, el tinglado
sheep, la oveja
to shine, brillar
ship, el buque, el barco
shoe, el zapato
shooting, la caza
shop, la tienda
to shop, ir de tiendas
shop-assistant, el vendedor
shop-window, el escaparate
shopkeeper, el tendero
short, corto, -a, breve
shoulder, el hombro
to shout, gritar
to show, mostrar (ue), enseñar

shower, la lluvia
shroud, el sudario
to shrug one's shoulders, enco-
   gerse de hombros
shut, cerrado, -a
to shut, cerrar (ie)
shyness, la timidez
side, el lado
sigh, el suspiro
to sigh, suspirar
silence, el silencio
silk, la seda
silly, tonto, -a
silver, la plata; (*adj.*) de
   plata; — **paper**, el papel
   de estaño
simple, sencillo, -a, puro, -a
since, después de; después
   que, ya que, pues
to sing, cantar
sister, la hermana
to sit (down), sentarse (ie); (*be
   sitting*) estar sentado, -a
to skid, patinar
skill, la destreza
skipper, el patrón
to sleep, dormir (ue, u)
sleepy, soñoliento, -a, adormecido, -a; **to be —**, tener
   sueño
slow, lento, -a; **-ly**, lentamente, despacio
to slow down, aflojar el paso
small, pequeño, -a
to smell, oler (hue)
smile, la sonrisa
to smile, sonreír
smoke, el humo
to smoke, fumar; (*fire*) echar
   humo
smuggler, el contrabandista
snow, la nieve
to snow, nevar (ie)
snow-covered, nevado, -a
so, así, lo, de modo que, tan;
   — **that**, de modo que,
   para que

soaked to the skin, calado
   hasta los huesos
soft, dulce; (*voice*) bajo, -a
soldier, el soldado
to solve, aclarar
some, unos, -as, algunos, -as
somebody, someone, alguien
something, algo
sometimes, algunas veces, a
   veces
somewhat, algo, un poco
somewhere, en alguna parte
son, el hijo
song, la canción
sonny, chico
soon, pronto; **as — as**, tan
   pronto como, luego que,
   en cuanto
sooner, más bien, más pronto; **no — said than done**,
   dicho y hecho; **no —**, no
   bien
sorry: **to be —**, sentir (ie, i)
sound, el son
to sound, sonar (ue), tocar
south, el sur; — **American**,
   sudamericano, -a
south-west, el sudoeste
Soviet, soviético, -a
space, el espacio
Spain, España (*f.*)
Spaniard, Spanish, español, -a
spare wheel, la rueda de re-
   puesta
to spare, perdonar, salvar
speak, hablar; (*truth*) decir
spectacle, el espectáculo
speed, la velocidad; **at full
   —**, a toda prisa
spend, (*time*) pasar; (*money*)
   gastar
spite: **in — of**, a pesar de
spot, el sitio
to spot, fijarse en
to spout, chorrear
to spread, extenderse (ie), pro-
   pagar

spring, la primavera
square, la plaza; (adj.) cuadrado, -a
stable, la cuadra
stage-coach, la diligencia
stairs, la escalera, la escalerilla
to stammer, balbucear
stamp, el sello
to stamp, sellar; pisar
to stand, levantarse, estar de pie; (bear) aguantar; — aside, apartarse; — on end, erizarse
to stare, clavar la vista en, fijar los ojos, la vista
to start, ponerse en marcha; (train) arrancar; — back, emprender el camino de regreso
startled, sobresaltado, -a
state, el estado
to state, declarar, decir
station, la estación
statue, la estatua
to stay, quedar(se), parar(se)
to steal, hurtar, robar
steamer, el vapor
steep, empinado, -a
step, la grada, el peldaño, el paso
stick, el bastón, el pedazo
to stick fast, quedar atascado
still, todavía
to stir (up), avivar
stone, la piedra
stony, guijarroso, -a
stop, la parada
to stop, detenerse, pararse, cesar de
story, el cuento, la historia
strange, extraño, -a, desconocido, -a
street, la calle
strength, la fuerza
stretch, el trecho

to stretch, tender (ie), extender (se) (ie)
to strike, (time) dar las . . .
strip, la tira
stroke, el golpe
to stroke, acariciar
strong, fuerte, recio, -a
struggle, la lucha
stubborn, obstinado, -a, inflexible
study, el gabinete, el despacho
to study, estudiar
to stumble, tropezar
stupid, estúpido, -a
to succeed, conseguir, lograr, tener éxito
success, el buen éxito, el triunfo
such, tal, semejante; así, tan
sudden, súbito, -a, repentino, -a
suddenly, de repente, de pronto, de improviso
sugar, el azúcar
to suggest, sugerir (ie, i)
suit, el traje (completo)
suitcase, la maleta
summer, el verano
sun, el sol
sure, seguro, -a
surprise, la sorpresa, el asombro
to surprise, sorprender(se), asombrar(se)
supper, la cena; to have —, cenar
to surround, rodear
suspicious, sospechoso, -a
to suspect, sospechar
sweat, el sudor
sweet, dulce
to swerve, desviarse
to swim, nadar
switch, el interruptor
sword, la espada

table, la mesa
tailor, el sastre
to take, tomar, llevar; (a journey) hacer; (photo) sacar; — place, verificarse; — out, sacar; — off, quitar
tale, el cuento
to talk, hablar
tall, alto, -a, grande
task, la tarea
tavern, la taberna
tavern-keeper, el tabernero
taxi, el taxi
tea, el té
to teach, enseñar, dar (una lección)
teacher, el profesor, la profesora
tear, la lágrima
telegram, el telegrama
to tell, decir, contar (ue)
temptation, la tentación
tendency, la tendencia
tennis, el tenis
to terrify, asustar, aterrar
terror, el terror; -stricken, espantado, -a
Thames, el Támesis
to thank, agradecer; dar las gracias; — you, gracias
that, ese, -a, -os, -as, eso; aquel, -la, -los, -las, aquello
theatre, el teatro
their, su
theirs, (el)suyo,(la)suya, etc.
them, los, las, les
then, luego, entonces, pues
there, allí, ahí, allá; — is, hay
thick, espeso, -a
thicket, la maleza, el matorral
thief, el ladrón
thing, la cosa
to think, creer, pensar (ie) en
third, tercero, -a, tercer

this, este, -a, -os, -as, esto
thousand, mil
to threaten, amenazar
threshold, el umbral
through, por, a través de
to throw, echar, lanzar, tirar
thunderstorm, la tormenta
Thursday, el jueves
ticket, el billete
ticket-collector, el revisor de billetes
tie, la corbata
to tie, atar
tightly, estrechamente
time, el tiempo; la vez; el rato; la hora
tin, la lata
tired, cansado, -a; to get —, cansarse; to be —, estar cansado
tiresome, cansado, -a, aburrido, -a
to-day, hoy
to-morrow, mañana (f.)
to-night, esta noche
toast, tostar(se)
tobacco, el tabaco
together, juntos, -as
too, demasiado; (also) también; — much, demasiado, -a
tooth, el diente
top, la cumbre, la cima
top-deck, la parte de arriba
to touch, tocar
tourist, el turista
tower, la torre
town, la ciudad
trace, la huella
traditional, tradicional
train, el tren
tram, el tranvía
to travel, viajar
traveller, el viajero
treason, la traición
tree, el árbol

tremendous, tremendo, -a, tremebundo, -a
to tremble, temblar (ie)
trembling, (*hand*) tembloroso, -a; (*voice*) temblón, -a
trench, la trinchera
triangular, triangular
tribe, la horda
trivet, las trébedes
trouble, la molestia, la pena
to trouble, molestar, perturbar
trout, la trucha
true, verdadero, -a
truth, la verdad
trunk, (*tree*) el tronco
to try, procurar, intentar, tratar de; probar (ue)
tube, el Metro
tunic, el túnico
tunny, el atún
turban, el turbante
turn, el turno
to turn, volver (ue), tornar; — round, volverse; — out, resultar
turnip, el nabo
Twelfth Night, el día de reyes
twilight, el crepúsculo
two-decker, de dos pisos
tyrant, el tirano

ugly, feo, -a
unable, incapaz de; to be —, no poder
uncle, el tío
to uncover, descubrir
to understand, comprender, entender (ie)
unhappy, desdichado, -a, desdichoso, -a
unfriendly, hostil, antipático
unharmed, ileso, -a
unhurt, ileso, -a
unknown, desconocido, -a
unpunished, sin castigar
to untie, desatar

until, hasta; hasta que
unwell, enfermo, -a, malo, -a
upstairs, arriba; to go —, subir (la escalera)
urchin, el rapaz, el pilluelo
us, nos, nosotros
to use, usar, emplear, servirse (i) de
used: to be — to, soler (ue)
useful, útil
useless, inútil
usual, usual, ordinario; as —, de costumbre, según su costumbre
usually, generalmente
to utter, dar, proferir (ie, i)

vacant, vacío, -a
vain, vanidoso, -a; in —, en vano, en balde
valuable, precioso, -a
vast, inmenso, -a
very, muy; (*with nouns*) mucho, mismo
vegetable, la hortaliza, la legumbre; — garden, el huerto
view, la vista, el panorama
village, el pueblo, la aldea
villager, el aldeano
violent, violento, -a
virtue, la virtud
visit, la visita
to visit, visitar
visitor, la visita
voice, la voz
voyage, el viaje

to wait, esperar, aguardar
to wake, despertar (ie)
walk, el paseo; to go for a —, pasear(se), dar un paseo
to walk, andar, marchar, ir a pie; — out, salir
wall, la pared, el muro
to wander, errar (ye)

to want, querer, necesitar
war, la guerra
warm, caliente, tibio, -a
to warm, calentar (ie)
to warn, avisar, advertir (ie, i)
warning, el aviso
to wash, lavar(se)
water, el agua (f.)
watch, el reloj
to watch, mirar, contemplar
watchman, el sereno, el vigi-
 lante
wave, la ola
to wave, agitar
way, el medio, la vía, el
 camino; in such a —
 that, de tal modo que;
 that —, por allí; go on
 one's —, seguir su camino
weapons, las armas
to wear, llevar, vestir, traer
weather, el tiempo
week, la semana
to weep, llorar
welcome, grato, -a
to welcome, dar la bienvenida,
 acoger
well, la fuente
well, bien; as —, también
west, el oeste
wet, mojado, -a; lluvioso,
 -a; húmedo, -a
what, ¿qué?; lo que
whatever, cualquier, cualquiera (que)
wheat, el trigo, — field, el
 trigal; — fields, las mieses,
 el sembrado
wheel, la rueda
when, cuando
whenever, cuandoquiera que
whether, si; — . . . or, sea
 . . . o sea . . .
which, que, el que, el cual;
 cuál
while, mientras; (noun) un
 rato

whip, el látigo
to whisper, cuchichear
whistle, el pito
to whistle, silbar
whitewashed, enjalbegado, -a
who, quien, que
whoever, quienquiera (que)
whole, entero, -a, todo, -a,
 completo, -a
whose, cuyo, -a, de quién
why, por qué
wide, ancho, -a
wife, la mujer, la esposa
wild, salvaje; — beast, la
 fiera
window, la ventana; (train
 or car) la ventanilla
wine, el vino
wireless, la radio
within, dentro de
without, sin; sin que
woman, la mujer
wonder, la admiración; to
 —, preguntarse
wonderful, maravilloso, -a
wood, la madera; el bosque;
 (firewood) la leña
wooden, de madera
word, la palabra
work, el trabajo
to work, trabajar
workman, el obrero
worm-eaten, carcomido, -a
to worry, molestar
worse, peor
worth: to be —, valer; to
 be — while, valer la
 pena
would that!, ¡ojalá!
wound, la herida
to wound, herir (ie, i)
wrapped, embozado, -a
wrinkled, arrugado, -a
to write, escribir
writing, la escritura
wrong: to be —, no tener
 razón, equivocarse

yard, el corral; (*length*) una vara

yawn, el bostezo

to yawn, bostezar

year, el año

yell, el grito

yelp, el gañido

yes, sí

yesterday, ayer

yet, aun, todavía, a la vez

yoke of oxen, la yunta

you, usted, ustedes, vosotros, os, tú, ti

young, joven; — man, woman, el, la joven, el chico, la chica

younger, menor, de menor edad

your, su, vuestro, -a, tu

yours, el tuyo, la tuya, etc.; el vuestro, el suyo, etc.